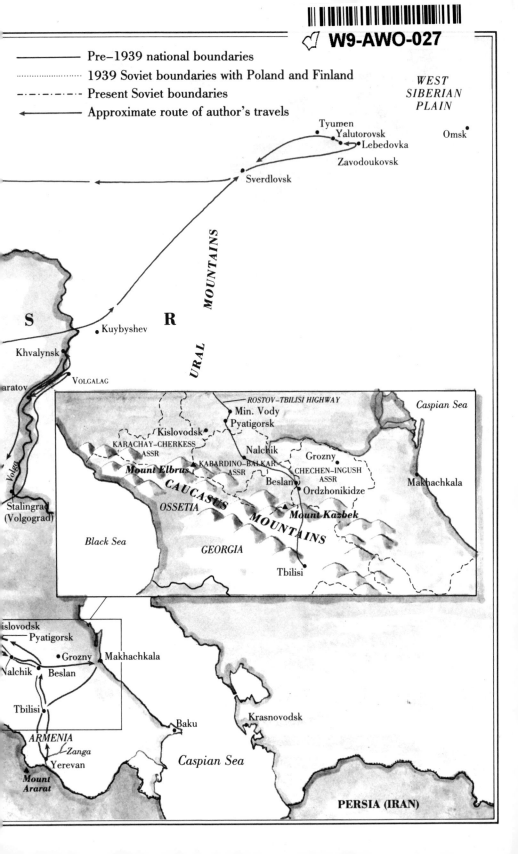

W9-AWO-027

──────── Pre–1939 national boundaries
············· 1939 Soviet boundaries with Poland and Finland
─·─·─·─·─ Present Soviet boundaries
◄──────── Approximate route of author's travels

WEST SIBERIAN PLAIN

Tyumen
Yalutorovsk
Lebedovka
Omsk
Zavodoukovsk

Sverdlovsk

URAL MOUNTAINS

S
R

Kuybyshev

Khvalynsk

VOLGALAG

aratov

Volga

Stalingrad
(Volgograd)

Black Sea

ROSTOV–TBILISI HIGHWAY
Min. Vody
Pyatigorsk
Kislovodsk
KARACHAY–CHERKESS ASSR
Nalchik
KABARDINO–BALKAR ASSR
Mount Elbrus
Grozny
CHECHEN–INGUSH ASSR
Beslan
Ordzhonikidze
Makhachkala
CAUCASUS
OSSETIA
Mount Kazbek
MOUNTAINS
GEORGIA
Tbilisi
Caspian Sea

islovodsk
Pyatigorsk
Grozny
Makhachkala
Nalchik
Beslan
Tbilisi
Baku
Krasnovodsk
ARMENIA
Zanga
Yerevan
Mount Ararat
Caspian Sea

PERSIA (IRAN)

Between Two Worlds

Other Books by K. S. Karol

Visa for Poland
Khrushchev and the West
China: The Other Communism
Guerrillas in Power: The Course of the Cuban Revolution
The Second Chinese Revolution

BETWEEN

TWO

WORLDS

The Life of a Young Pole
in Russia
1939—46

K.S.KAROL

Translated from the French
by Eamonn McArdle

A NEW REPUBLIC BOOK

HENRY HOLT AND COMPANY · NEW YORK

Library of Congress Cataloging in Publication Data
Karol, K. S.
Between two worlds.

Translation of: Solik.
"A New Republic book."
1. Karol, K. S. 2. World War, 1939–1945—
Personal narratives, Polish. 3. World War, 1939–1945—
Soviet Union. 4. Students—Soviet Union—Biography.
5. Students—Poland—Biography. 6. Soviet Union—
History—German occupation, 1941–1945. I. Title.
D811.5.K36813 1987 940.54'81'438 86–14254
ISBN 0-8050-0099-2

First American Edition

Designed by Jeffrey L. Ward
Printed in the United States of America
1 3 5 7 9 10 8 6 4 2

ISBN 0-8050-0099-2

Contents

Between Two Worlds

1

SOLIK

At the high school in Rostov-on-the-Don, I was nicknamed Solik, diminutive of the Russian word for salt, but I no longer recall why. That was, it is true, more than forty-five years ago, and it is useless to protest my good memory; it sometimes lets me down. As early as the school year of 1940–41, however, I knew that one day I would tell Solik's story. This conviction never faded in the seven years that I would spend in the Soviet Union in the Red Army, in prison, in a labor camp, then once again in Rostov, at the university and in a factory. Like a good reporter, I noted everything, but only in my head; it was not a propitious time to keep a journal, even in Polish—my native tongue—which theoretically would have protected it from indiscreet glances. I am going to do my best, nonetheless, in soliciting my memory, to recount, through Solik, this strange Soviet world that puzzles, intrigues, and disturbs so many people.

My school, in Rostov, is located on a street parallel to the River Don and parallel also to the city's longest and most famous avenue, which bears the name of Friedrich Engels but which everyone, even young people born after the 1917 Revolution, continues to call by its former name, the Sadovaya—meaning "Avenue of the Garden"—doubtless because of the tall trees that border its wide sidewalks. Since it was founded by the Soviet regime, my high school has no "former" name, but only a number—44. To get there, you have to go down at right angles from the Sadovaya in the direction of the Don; I remember it very well because of the glacial wind that blows in winter from the river toward the slopes, forcing us to walk backwards to protect our faces, especially our noses, which are very vulnerable to the cold, but also our eyes, because this wind carries, in addition to snow, a great deal of dust.

After this descent along an avenue that bears the name Voroshilov—but that used to be called Bolshoi Prospekt—you experience, as soon as you cross the school's threshold, a sensation of relief and well-being: my school is very well heated. Otherwise, to my sixteen-year-old Polish eyes, it is a very poor school. In my hometown of Lodz, in Poland, I attended an altogether more elegant high school, a private school equipped with laboratories, endowed with a large assembly hall, to say nothing of the gymnasium and sports fields. Still, during the long, cold winter of 1940–41, School No. 44 is a place that I like very much. Unfortunately, you stay there for only five hours, at most five and a half hours if you count the time spent in the cloakroom.

My school, like a factory, has three shifts: the first in the morning from eight to one; the second in the afternoon from two to seven; and the third in the evening, several times a week, when night classes are held for adults studying to be construction engineers. Our classrooms are in constant use and, for this reason, are energetically heated day and night, but are cleaned only at long intervals, which gives them a slightly rundown appearance. In my private high school in Lodz we walked on parquet floors, and in order not to dirty them, as soon as we arrived, we had to put on slippers of a prescribed style; like our distinctive made-to-measure uniforms, they symbolized our membership in a "superior" educational establishment. In Rostov there are neither slippers nor uniforms, and the cloakroom is a nondescript sort of room, without spaces allocated to different classes, without individual lockers for shoes or personal effects. There is no cloakroom attendant, and the students hang up their coats in any old way—less carefully, needless to say, than it was done by the paid personnel in my high school in Poland.

But for me, what matters most is attending, for the first time, a mixed high school with girls who are almost young women. It is even one of these girls, Vera—it is coming back to me bit by bit—who gives me my nickname. In Russian, Karol means "king" and, she declares, it is hardly decent to bear such a name in the land of Lenin, which has irrevocably broken with monarchy and everything connected with it. Henceforth, I shall be known as Solik. There are only two other girls that I remember from my class: Klava, a Cossack who, beautiful and smiling and even more timid than I, sits next to me; and Clarissa. Throughout the winter I nourish a secret passion for her without mentioning a word of it to my closest friends. Clarissa pays no attention to me, however. She isn't even interested by the prestige of my status as an exotic foreigner.

My position in Rostov is unique. I am the only student in this city to have lived abroad and to have been born in Poland. But this distinction is of dubious value. Because while a part of Poland is now possessed by the Soviets, having been annexed after the partition in 1939, until then it was a capitalist country, linked to the old imperial powers of France and Great Britain. Praising anything Polish is therefore out of the question. It is impossible to explain to my Rostov friends that I owe my good grades (later I will place first in my class) not to any particular diligence on my part, but to the baggage of learning that I brought with me, thanks to my bourgeois family and my "superior" school in Lodz. Nor is it the only secret that I cannot confide to them. I have another, more important and more dangerous.

Contrary to what I tell one and all—and contrary to what everyone believes—I did not come to Rostov direct from the Soviet-controlled zone of Poland. My path was altogether longer and more perilous. Before ending up in the capital of the Don, I passed through Western Siberia. I didn't go there as a tourist either. I was deported there, with more than a million other Poles, but, since I did not greatly appreciate the large forest that extends between Tyumen and Omsk, I decided to run away and succeeded in getting as far as Rostov, taking in Moscow en route. At School No. 44, nobody, I bet, can pride himself on such an exploit.

My new school friends are not great travelers. Kola, the most adventurous among them, has only taken the shuttle between Mye-chotka, his hometown, and Rostov. Misha says that he would like to see the world, but until now he has gone no farther than Nakhi-chevan, an area not too distant from the center of town. Even among our teachers, those who have been to Moscow, let alone to foreign countries, which exist for them only in the atlas, are the exception. I am tempted to boast about my travels, but my instinct for self-preservation obliges me to keep silent and to pretend hypocritically that I would like nothing better than to go to Moscow and see Red Square—when in fact I have already walked the length and breadth of it.

Nevertheless, I feel good at School No. 44, flattered on the one hand by my good grades, and my interest aroused on the other by the novelty of my precarious position and by the incessant discovery of the peculiarities of Soviet daily life. My secret, or secrets, do not weigh heavily on me; I live from day to day, forgetful of dangers already encountered and heedless of those that still lie in wait. Sometimes I feel guilty that I have no confidence in my friends. But do they tell me everything? Don't they too have their secrets, more redoubtable, perhaps, than mine?

Clarissa, for example. I met her at Matvei's home—Motya to his intimates—a young mathematics teacher at the university, whom a stroke of luck put in my way. His home, a handsome room with a balcony in a communal apartment, is always open, although Motya has a lot of work to do and although his wife, Tima, a student, is often studying for examinations. One day, in private, I ask Motya: "How is it that Clarissa is always so well dressed? She is more carefully made up than the other girls her age." I take care not to admit that I also find her very pretty; it would be embarrassing to admit such a feeling for a girl who pays no attention whatever to me, despite the exotic aura that surrounds me. But without giving myself away I can reasonably ask him about Clarissa, whose elegant appearance is so startling in a poor and relatively egalitarian country like the USSR. In Poland, a woman's elegance could be explained by her wealth, by her patronage of *haute couture*. Here, such explanations won't do. I add that I notice that Clarissa, without appearing obviously very sad by nature, talks very little and is reluctant to engage in conversation.

"She is an orphan like you," Motya replies laconically. Although alone in Rostov, I am not an orphan, having by no means lost hope of finding my parents, who stayed on in Lodz when the Germans occupied it. What is Clarissa's story? Is she, like me, only waiting to see her parents again, with whom for the moment she is unable to communicate? Is it this secret that weighs on her and renders her so silent? I do not know. All I know is that Motya, himself an orphan, has a lot of friends, for the most part mathematicians like himself, and that I enjoy a great deal of his Russian hospitality, even more than does Clarissa. What attracts me to his home is its studious atmosphere, its cleanliness, and the parquet floors—so welcome a change from the minuscule room I rent at the home of a militiaman, a decent sort, whose wife totally ignores him and is outrageously unfaithful to him. When he is away on duty she hardly bothers to conceal her lover's visits. Lost in their frolics, they forget that my little room doesn't even have a door, but only a curtain. I don't really have a place of my own, therefore, but simply a bed to sleep on. After the well-heated high school and a few hours spent at the Karl Marx Municipal Library, if I don't go to Misha's house, which is quite far, I turn up sooner or later at Motya's. No matter what the time, Tima ritually asks, "Have you eaten yet?" but, nine times out of ten, I decline to take advantage of her hospitality. I don't come to Motya's home to eat, but am drawn there out of a sense of affinity.

Motya reciprocates this sentiment by calling me *Solik Shukharnoi paren*—Solik, the funny kid. I make him laugh a lot, often unintentionally, by telling him my impressions of School No. 44, of the Karl Marx Library, of life in Rostov. He wants me to become a mathematician, assuring me, "It's the best career for you, believe me." I trust his judgment but feel no vocation whatever for science. To overcome my reservations, Motya sometimes brings me along to his own evening class. Its relaxed atmosphere pleases me enormously. Ignoring all of the usual academic formalities, it is rather more like a group of friends, a sort of working meeting between people of roughly the same age. Motya, although already well qualified (he is a Master of Mathematical Sciences and is a short step away from obtaining his doctorate), is only twenty-six years old and appears even younger. With his robust, athletic build he doesn't resemble at all the popular caricatures of mathematicians, figures with their heads in the clouds or chasing butterflies. I follow the technical conversation only with difficulty, but with Motya and his friends I feel more adult, a university student already. I also feel better protected.

Motya is not interested solely in mathematics. He loves poetry and particularly admires Alexander Blok. He knows Blok's poems by heart, and his talent in reciting them is really worthy of an actor. And he doesn't recite only "The Twelve" or "The Scythians," the standard sixth-form fare; "his" Blok is especially that of the *Nyeznakomka* ("The Unknown One"), dressed in splendid silk, at once beautiful and ephemeral, woman and mirage. To tell the truth, Motya's recitations would have wearied me eventually, had there not been in "his" Blok a very Western melody that struck a distinctive chord in me, recalling to me my past, my origins, my sense of belonging to "another world." I have only been a "Soviet citizen" for one year, after all. For me, "The Unknown One" is just an exotic lady—not yet a metaphor for the elusive soul of this strange country—on a par with Greta Garbo or Marlene Dietrich, both still fresh in my memory from the movies I saw in Lodz. Nevertheless, at the end of the school year I begin to think seriously about studying mathematics at the University of Rostov in order to become a real student of Motya's; I also vow to read Alexander Blok.

Some months later, I shall no longer be faced with a choice: The war will decide for us all. I was not to return to Rostov until April 1944, after having lost all contact with my friends. The town was disfigured: The cyclone of war had passed through it three times, sparing nothing, neither the Sadovaya nor the university nor the large tank-shaped theater in the center of town. Motya's house, however, had remained intact amid the ruins. Tima received me in their spacious room with the parquet floor and balcony, but there was no more Motya. An artillery officer, he was reported to have been killed at

Sevastopol in 1942. The news, fortunately, was unconfirmed because the army had still not sent any formal notification of his death. Much later I went back again to ask for any news of him. This time Tima didn't show me in: She seemed to have just gotten out of bed, and it was clear that, in the large room with the balcony, there was another man to whom she didn't care to introduce me.

As for Clarissa, she died of typhus in Rostov in 1942, during the German occupation. I shall never know, therefore, whether she really was an orphan, or for what reason she crossed our world with such an elegant aspect, almost in silence, as if on tiptoe.

It wasn't chance that brought me to Rostov-on-the-Don after I fled Western Siberia. It seemed to me that I already knew its streets, starting with the Sadovaya; they had been lovingly described to me by my family, who had lived for a long time on the banks of the Don before settling in Poland. Nostalgia for this past, which had been shattered by the Bolshevik Revolution, was kept alive by a tenacious linguistic loyalty: At home, in Lodz, I spoke only Russian; in school only Polish. I was proud of being bilingual, of knowing Pushkin and Lermontov, Chekhov and Tolstoy, not to mention Gorky and Mayakovsky. Thanks to them, in Rostov, as Solik I would astound my teachers by my knowledge of Russian and Soviet literature.

In Lodz I was careful not to flaunt these interests too much for fear of being taken for a *moskal,* or "Russky," the common pejorative name given to Russians. I felt myself to be Polish; I didn't set myself apart in any way from my school friends, and I took part in their games and amusements. But the feeling of belonging to another world, vaster than the confined framework of a single country, was sufficiently powerful to render me immune to the anti-Russian rhetoric of Poland under the colonels. In vain did my "superior" high school teachers praise to the skies the Polish Nobel Laureates Henryk Sienkiewicz and Władysław Reymont: I knew that Tolstoy and Dostoyevsky had been immeasurably greater.

Even though my parents were fervent atheists, they had decided to send me to a Catholic high school, contenting themselves with securing for me an exemption from all religious teaching. Every morning, however, I had to attend morning prayer, so as not to appear unduly privileged in arriving a quarter of an hour later than everyone else. Present but mute, I took part daily in a rite that for me was deprived of all meaning, under the distrustful eye of the priest, who sometimes made me recite the prayer, alleging that I was exempted only from the obligation to say "Amen." To make matters worse, the school was named after the Abbot Ignacy Skorupka, a "martyr priest" who perished, we were told, in 1920 on the Vistula front after having repulsed the "Bolshevik hordes" by making signs of the cross. Ceremonies were devoted to his glory each year, and I was expected to participate in them. "It's a good school and you should take advantage of it, without concerning yourself with these priests' tall tales," my mother would reply when I complained.

On this point—it was practically the only one—my father agreed with her. In other respects my parents weren't a very harmonious couple, either in terms of age—my father was twenty-five years older than my mother—or of cultural interests. My father must have been fifty years old when I was born in 1924. He had been a wealthy man in Rostov-on-the-Don, but in Lodz he was materially dependent on his young wife, a lawyer, an intellectual, and a socialist. On coming home from school, I would find this already elderly man boasting without any great conviction of his former riches and in fact thinking only of the imagined or real infidelities of his pretty and active spouse. Having witnessed these scenes, my sister Alicia, my elder by two years, and I had genuine difficulty in discerning what could have brought our parents together in Rostov. Money, perhaps? But our mother, in our eyes, was the most disinterested of persons, the least calculating kind of woman that one could imagine.

Solving this mystery would have required knowing our father during his heyday in Rostov. There, in this far-off town, he had furnished proof of talent as an entrepreneur, and had succeeded in leaving a province designated "open" to Jews, to become a banker and a property owner, and to receive a residence permit in Rostov—a town that was, in theory, "closed" to Jews—made out in the rank of Merchant of the First Guild, which, for a bourgeois in Czarist Russia, was the highest of social distinctions. Married, the father of three sons—my stepbrothers—he had fallen in love during the First World War with a young student—my mother. (She was in Rostov attending the University of Warsaw, which had been evacuated there.) The providential death of his first wife—though suicide was also mentioned—allowed him to remarry, with ostentation befitting his rank, and to organize a sumptuous honeymoon voyage that included a cohort of friends aboard a cruiser on the River Volga, then at Yalta. Only one of my stepbrothers, Eugene—a student by then—was allowed to join these almost legendary festivities. Boris and Alexander were too young, and so had to stay home under the strict supervision of their French governess. Out of jealousy, they gave the eldest brother the sobriquet *stchaslivchik*, or "lucky devil."

When the Revolution put the era of cruises on the Volga to an end, my stepbrother Genya—diminutive of Eugene—accompanied the family as far as Lodz in 1921. But he left soon afterward for London, where he found work in a large import-export company and became in the course of time a loyal subject of His Majesty, George VI. He came back to visit us only at holidays, for Christmas, sometimes at Easter, loaded with presents but hardly at all inclined—understandably—to become involved in my parents' domestic scenes, and still less inclined to talk with a youngster like myself about the origin of their marriage.

Papa had still possessed the means to send his other two sons to study abroad—Boris in France, Alexander in Austria—but his "sacrifices" were poorly rewarded. Having returned to Lodz at the height of the Depression of the 1930s, neither of them found a job worthy of their education and so never helped the family at all. At the University of Bordeaux, Boris had learned bridge and he became one of the pioneers of the game in Poland, which obliged him to lead a nocturnal life criticized all the more by the family in view of his uncertain income. With Alexander the situation was worse still. Having witnessed the lost battle of the Schutzbund in Vienna, he veered squarely toward the far left and declared himself a Communist. Even for my mother it was too much; as for Papa, he often baited Alexander with defiant taunts: "Help yourself to the fresh cream, go on. When your Bolshevik friends come, that will be an end of it, just as in Rostov." Young as I was, I became his sole defender within the family. For his part, he was delighted to take charge of my political education, beginning with Bukharin and Preobrajenski's *ABC of Communism.*

Sometimes on Sundays he brought me to the park where, as if by accident, we would always meet his friends and they would talk earnestly about "the fascist Pilsudski regime." I could hardly contribute to these discussions, but I learned a lot about these "useless men," peasants without land and the unemployed, forced into exile in the West to work at only the harshest and most menial jobs, about the poverty of the eastern provinces where, to economize, people were reduced to "cutting each matchstick in four," about the persecution of national minorities, about the Bereza-Kartuska concentration camp. About the anti-Semitism of the Catholic Church or of the so-called National Democracy (*Endecja*) they didn't have to tell me. Though I was never personally beaten up as a "dirty Yid," the whole moral climate of the time was poisoned by anti-Semitism, often leading to open violence. "You have a fine first name," one of my brother's comrades said to me one day, "just like Marx and Liebknecht." I blushed with pleasure.

I was twelve years and one month old when, in September 1936, Alexander was arrested somewhere in the eastern provinces, the "Polish Ukraine," for clandestine activities. My mother, with the help of her socialist lawyer friends, managed to get him out of prison but wouldn't forgive him for having "tarnished the family's good name." Alexander then made his home in Gdynia on the Baltic coast, married Zosia, a young worker, and showed his face at our home as rarely as Genya, only for the principal holidays. His presence always sparked impassioned political discussions, and even though they both represented the "left wing" of the family, it was always my mother, the social democrat, and my brother, the Communist, who confronted each other. My mother expressed herself better; it was, after all, her job and, good lawyer that she was, she knew how to expose, for example, all the lies of the Moscow Show Trials, which, in her view, had demonstrated the degeneration of socialism in the USSR.

Alexander replied only with defensive quips, as if he too remained unconvinced by the confessions of this same Bukharin, whom he had made me read as a ten-year-old. Nevertheless, he insisted that it was in the Soviet Union that "the future was being built," and not in our society, which was rotten to the marrow with injustice. Alone against everyone, he even went so far as to affirm that "we would have done better to stay in Rostov." I hadn't the courage to come to his aid; I knew little enough about Rostov, and my mother's accounts of the situation in Russia worried me.

Alexander regained stature in my eyes when he spoke about the Polish Socialist Party's ineffective opposition, which the regime tolerated merely in order to maintain a democratic façade, or when he evoked the Nazi monster that he had seen with his own eyes, "back home in Austria." He knew everything there was to know about the origin of Hitlerian barbarism: It was nothing but big capital's war machine against the workers' movement and against the USSR. In his view, "Stalin and his loyal comrades"—an expression engraved on my memory ever since—were alone in consistently fighting the Nazi threat and were the only ones capable of ridding the world of it. He predicted that, without the USSR, Poland would be the first to be submerged, because its French and British allies were playing a double game and pushing Hitler toward the east.

My mother didn't share this viewpoint, no more than did Genya, or Boris, the least politicized of my brothers, who had learned "back home in France" to trust in the Republic. However, in 1938, after Munich, events proved Alexander singularly right, at least in my view. At Easter in 1939, Genya arrived from Prague, where he had had business to settle; he had seen the Nazi monster at work. He had never brought us so many presents, almost as if he knew that it amounted to a final good-bye. He was so surprised to see me almost as tall as himself that he left me a suit he had had custom-made by

Herman Horovitz, the best tailor in Prague. Little did he imagine that, a few months later, his present would open for me the road to his native Rostov. Not that I had any hint myself of my future Siberian wanderings. Genya reported that Churchill's arrival in power was imminent and that he was resolved to cut short Hitler's career once and for all. Alexander smiled ironically and reminded us softly that he had been right all along: that without the help of the USSR it would be impossible to crush Hitler's Reich.

My mother was depressed; the participation of the Polish colonels' regime in the dismemberment of Czechoslovakia after the Munich Accords had sapped her morale. Her long-standing advocacy of a "class struggle without hatred"—the favorite theme of her epic debates with Alexander—gave way to more violent language against Warsaw's ruling class, now acting as Hitler's unwitting accomplice. But the alliance with Stalin's Russia appeared to her to be impracticable and dangerous; the "guarantee" that Britain had accorded Poland didn't reassure her; and she couldn't forgive the French for having brought down Léon Blum's government. In the end, in her view, only the awakening of the Polish people could be counted upon.

I took up the thread of my brother's argument, contesting even more radically the analysis made by my mother. Instead of reproaching me for my excessive tone or the provocative style of my arguments, my mother, who was normally excitable, became very sad and was on the verge of tears. A strange silence descended upon this last family reunion; to bring it to an end, my mother uttered only one sentence in a strangled voice: "You haven't understood anything at all; at this stage it is certain that no one will save us."

It was because of soccer, however, that shortly afterward my relations with my mother soured for good. I had succeeded, after a great deal of trouble, in getting accepted into the junior league of the Lodz Sports Club. Two afternoons a week I practiced diligently and with enthusiasm. My schoolwork was hardly affected by my extracurricular passion; in any case, I was already certain of a place in the upper sixth form as the spring term drew to a close. Nevertheless, the school authorities ordered me not to set foot in the sports club anymore. I felt that they were trying to prevent me from associating with ordinary young people (delinquents, no doubt, in their view), the better to keep me in the privileged ghetto of a well-behaved bourgeois elite. Perhaps they even worried that I might somehow tarnish their school's good reputation. My mother was asked to write a note assuring them that I wouldn't disobey this ban. She did so without batting an eyelash, insisting that because I was two years younger than my classmates, I had to avoid any conflict with the high school; otherwise, I might be prevented from sitting for the baccalaureat on the pretext that I was too young.

At the high school, I was lucky to receive sympathy and solidarity from my liberal-progressive drawing teacher, Stefan Wegner. He was not merely a teacher and a radical. As a gifted painter he was linked to the group of avant-garde artists around Władysław Strzeminski and his wife Katarzyna Kobro, and he seemed to be the incarnation of intelligence and kindness. His convictions about art had led him to a radical critique of society and to practical nonconformism in his life. At that time an invisible wall still separated the teaching staff from their pupils; teachers were not expected to entertain informal relations with those in their charge. Wegner nevertheless invited me to his home with two of his other "favorites," Jurek B. and Rysiek D., both sons of printers linked to the opposition—a fortuitous coincidence.

We often went with Wegner to Lodz's museum, and sometimes to Strzeminski's home, and not to become better acquainted with painting (in his view, the appreciation of art was a private affair), but rather to talk about the movement of antifascist intellectuals in the West and about the great international battle of "reason" against obscurantism and barbarism. Neither of them belonged to the Communist Party; Strzeminski was even a disabled veteran of the anti-Bolshevik war of 1920. But their political and cultural beliefs were close to those of my Communist brother Alexander. The enemy to be defeated was Nazism, and the USSR could only be an ally in this battle since it was threatened just as we were and belonged, in the final analysis, to the camp of the left.

I concluded that my mother's warnings against "Stalin and his loyal comrades" reflected in fact the anti-Bolshevik rancor of her husband, who had been ruined by the October Revolution, and that they were explicable in terms of the peculiar history of my family rather than by History with a capital *H*. But what really separated us, even if I hardly ever spoke about it, was the fact that my heart was beating more and more in unison with the USSR, because over there, I was convinced, there was surely more justice, and the future was not choked off as it was in Poland under the colonels' regime.

On September 1, 1939, my classmates and I were just finishing up a month in the countryside, in Wlodzimierzow on the Pilica, in a military training camp. It had been a boring time but, all things considered, almost like a holiday. The course was compulsory for baccalaureat candidates. We were due to return to Lodz that day, but it was also the day that the Germans chose to attack Poland—and to launch the Second World War. I remember that we were all indignant but certain of Poland's quick victory.

The camp's commander—a lieutenant—thought differently. He announced that the war would be a long one and that we would have a chance to fight when we reached eighteen or even twenty-one years of age. For now, however, he wanted some volunteers to protect public buildings, perhaps in Warsaw, thereby freeing a company of the regular army for duty on the front. Every one of us a patriot, we all took a step forward. I imagine that we resembled closely those schoolboys of the Kaiser's Germany, described so well by Erich Maria Remarque in *All Quiet on the Western Front*. Just as with them, patriotic ardor glazed over our eyes. For Jurek, Rysiek, and myself—Stefan Wegner's three protégés—enthusiasm consisted above all of antifascist élan. I also promised myself that in the Hour of Victory, after crushing the Germans, I would redirect my gun at the oppressor regime in Poland. But guarding public buildings would do until then; our army at the front had to have its rear guard well secured.

The only problem was that the front seemed to be everywhere, beginning with the road we took to Warsaw. In undisputed command

of the air, the Luftwaffe bombed everything that moved, at least in
western Poland. In the beginning, we were terrified. During the first
raid, Sergeant Major Bartczak, a stupid and cruel man, even ordered
a peasant woman to strangle her baby so that it would stop exposing
us to risk with its crying. Fortunately the brave woman refused.
Slowly we became used to the Luftwaffe; it had claimed no victims
among our little troop, which comprised a hundred "auxiliary soldiers" and ten or so regular soldiers who flanked us. The real problems were slow progress in marching and the palpable lowering of
morale, prompted by the fear that perhaps we weren't on the winning
side after all.

Where were *our* planes? Did Poland have any planes? Some of us
took comfort from pretending that our air force was active on the
front, unlike the Luftwaffe, which was being used against civilians,
including women and children. But this explanation, based on trust
in the moral superiority of our pilots, collapsed when, on September
5, we at last reached the suburbs of the capital. Muffled rumblings of
artillery fire convinced us that the front couldn't be very far away;
and, alas, there wasn't a Polish plane in sight. Worse still, nourished
by the myth of the combined might of France and Great Britain, we
half expected to see their squadrons flying above our country. Instead, they were conspicuous by their absence.

Things were bad--much worse than our most pessimistic fears.
The weary eyes of our camp commander betrayed fatigue and confusion; in Warsaw they hadn't any need of us, and it was too late to send
us back to Lodz, which was now occupied by the Germans. Our
leader recovered his verve only after meeting a group of officers
among whom was a major who agreed to speak to him, to help him, to
help us. I remember that after their conversation they separated on a
perky note: "See you again, after another miracle on the Vistula!" I
too was sure that the Polish Army still had the capacity to wage a
victorious battle on the outskirts of the capital. Hadn't my mother told
me that in the hour of danger our people were capable of surpassing
themselves, of revealing unsuspected reserves of heroism?

Nevertheless, our small troop was not supposed to contribute to this exploit. Our leader, after assembling our supplies and receiving his instructions, ordered us to march—singing!—in the direction of Lublin. In our song, even the trees were supposed to salute us, because it was "for our Poland" that we were going into combat.

In reality, neither man nor beast nor any other living thing paid us any honor, and we didn't have the opportunity to fire a single shot. The enemy always came from the air, and even when they flew very low, they were still beyond the range of our old Mausers. The spectacle of the war therefore rapidly became monotonous; day after day we saw the same scenes: civilians running to save themselves from air raids, convoys dispersing, trucks or carts on fire. The smell along the road was unchanging, too. It was the smell of dead horses that no one had bothered to bury and that stank to high heaven. We moved only at night and we learned to sleep while marching; smoking was forbidden out of fear that the glow of a cigarette could bring down on us the all-powerful Luftwaffe.

It was a marvelous month, that September of 1939: mild, sunny, worthy of the end of an Italian summer, and we weren't cold.

Two weeks after our departure from Warsaw, when we had already gone well beyond Lublin, our leader suddenly ordered us to make an about-face. We were going back toward the west, toward Chelm. What had happened? Had the miracle on the Vistula materialized? Were we finally going to protect the public buildings of Warsaw? In an army, orders are never explained—and the Polish Army was no exception to the rule. But along the roads, day or night, we were never alone; other soldiers and civilians were also on the march, and, thanks to the ubiquitous rumor mill called in some parts of the West the "Arab telephone" and in the USSR "Radio Yerevan," we learned that no miracle had taken place. We were heading west because the Russians were arriving from the east. And not to come to our aid, either, to fight "in a consistent manner against the Nazis" as my Communist brother's old formula had it! "Stalin and his loyal comrades" were coming quite simply to gobble up their share of Poland.

Rysiek, Jurek, and I were seized with consternation. If the Bolsheviks had become friends with the Nazis, then principles no longer mattered; there was no longer any hope for our poor Poland. On the other hand, why should we go to meet the Germans, who had attacked us first, rather than toward the Russians, who, as far as one could tell, were neither bombing nor destroying everything in their way? Should we talk to our leader about his decision? Such a step would certainly have yielded nothing and would have marked us as Communist sympathizers—which, in Poland, even at this moment of total disarray, could only lead to unfortunate results. What, then, if all three of us took off to try to join up with the Russians? But this solution didn't have much to recommend it, either. After much discussion, we decided that if there was a way out of the trap that enclosed us, it was still our commander who had some hope of finding it. So we followed him to the end, but we were bitterly disappointed at having been betrayed by all sides: by the Western powers, by the Russians, and by our own government, which had already bolted to Romania.

While still marching, I began to sleep more and more deeply. I began to dream as if I were in bed. One night I saw the sky fill with countless Soviet squadrons. They were coming to deliver us from the Nazis, and our commander thanked them, as a comrade-in-arms who knows how to appreciate fraternal bravery and help. Even Sergeant Major Bartczak, a vitriolic anti-Bolshevik who never missed an opportunity to curse the Reds, ignoring the fact that it was the Germans who had attacked us, embraced the Russian tank drivers as they rolled down the road in their powerful armored vehicles. Bartczak cried out, "We are all part of the same Slav family." Our Soviet liberators also had an enormous tank of fresh cream, which they were distributing generously, as if to show just how wrong my father had been to think that there wasn't any to be had under the Bolshevik regime.

"Are you crazy or what?" Jurek asked, pulling me toward a gully as some Luftwaffe planes roared over our heads. According to Jurek, I replied that they were Soviet squadrons, but I don't remember anything of this. Ever since this rudely interrupted dream of the great Russo-Polish antifascist reconciliation, however, I have talked in my sleep, and I even reply, apparently, to questions, just as if I were awake.

We marched around in circles for one week more. Warsaw surrendered on September 27, but we continued our march until October 5, when we found ourselves encircled, along with some detachments of the regular army, by the Germans, near the village of Krzywda (Injustice). The Wehrmacht, for its own amusement or to encourage us to lay down our arms more quickly, sprayed us copiously with bursts of machine-gun fire and bombarded us with grenades. I caught something in the eye almost without noticing it, and without feeling any pain. My right eye simply closed and I could no longer open it except with the help of my fingers, by forcing the eyelid. I didn't make a fuss about it, believing that it would pass, and I took part in all of the farewell ceremonies. A high-ranking Polish officer, a colonel or perhaps even a general, had been authorized by our German captors to make a speech to us in which he said that the war was not over, that the Polish Army, under the command of General Sikorski, fought on in France, and that our powerful Western allies were more than ever at our side. Our camp commander also came to say good-bye; the Germans were separating the officers from the NCOs and the rank-and-file troops.

We were taken to Demblin Fortress, on the Vistula. I would spend ten days there before being sent to a hospital in Radom. It wasn't a camp like the one I had seen in Jean Renoir's film *La Grande Illusion,* replete with barracks, beds, and even a theater. In Demblin we were shut up in a large depot full of racks for arms—emptied, obviously— and were allowed out only to line up, in the rain, in front of an improvised, open-air kitchen. At night we arranged bunks as best we could with boards torn from the partitions and placed on the racks because, without them, there wouldn't even have been enough space for everyone on the ground. Our bunks, however, had an unfortunate tendency to collapse, which often provoked a good deal of stumbling and swearing in the darkness. The Germans would arrive forthwith, hurling abuse and insults, the wealth and variety of which far exceeded anything I had learned at Skorupka High School. Blows

struck with rifle butts landed here and there on the heads of these
"*polnische Schweinerhunde*" but I was lucky enough to avoid them.

We waited for them to take a census of their prisoners, so that we
could explain our peculiar situation as student auxiliaries, but they
didn't seem to be in any hurry. Instead, we were subjected to another
sort of census altogether. One rainy morning, one of the Wehrmacht
loudmouths came into our depot, screaming, "*Alles was Jude ist,
aufstehen.*" ("Anyone who is Jewish, stand up.") "These savages only
know how to speak the most brutal German," remarked Jurek, who
was one-hundred-percent Aryan but who was still more afraid than I,
because he had a bronze tint and a flattish nose that had earned him
the nickname "golliwog" at the high school.

At St. Casimir Hospital in Radom, where I was finally sent to have
my eye attended to, the groans of the wounded seemed restful to my
ears after the screams of Demblin. The atmosphere of this hospital
was tense and a little surrealistic: The Germans had taken charge of
everything, from surgery to administration, but they had left the
religious at their posts. The nuns were excellent nurses and especially strong Polish patriots, conspirators even. The sister who looked
after me had a German-sounding first name, Kunegunda, but she
would rather have had her tongue torn out than pronounce a word in
that language. As with all the other religious, the occupiers had to
speak to her through an interpreter. The German military doctors
didn't believe in talking to the wounded. I only learned the details of
my operation from Sister Kunegunda. The usual procedure, she said,
was to remove a splinter of grenade shrapnel from the eye by means of
a magnet (it was such a fragment that had pierced my eye). In my
case, however, these Teutons, these butchers, had proceeded directly to enucleate my eye, without administering any general anes-
thesia, in order to maximize my suffering. Many years later I learned
that it was too late to save my eye at Radom. Perhaps an operation
could have been performed on the day the injury happened, but not
ten days later—the ten days that I spent in Demblin Fortress. At the
time I was convinced that I had been intentionally mutilated by the
barbarians of the German *Herrenvolk*.

Sister Kunegunda was very kind to me, perhaps in the hope of bringing me to religion, or more simply because of my relative youth. She sometimes brought me sweets and promised to contact my family with the help of another sister who happened to be traveling to Lodz. I wrote my parents a long letter, which ended by declaring my irrevocable decision to move to the provinces incorporated in the USSR, beyond the River Bug. Days passed, the snow fell on Radom, but no reply arrived from Lodz. Despair loomed. Did my parents remain silent as a way of expressing their disapproval? Or had they died during the awful bombing? Then one morning the doctor announced the arrival of *"eine Dame,"* my mother. This was one of the rare occasions in which he consented to say a few words to me, but it was obvious that he had eyes only for Mama, this young woman wearing a pretty hat with a veil, which hid her face from him and gave her eyes a mysterious look. After having complimented her on her command of German, he assured her very courteously that, thanks to prosthetic devices "made in Reich," one would hardly even notice that I had lost an eye. And, still pursuing this almost sociable conversation, he sent someone off to look for the "spare part"; while waiting for it he deplored aloud this useless war, stupidly provoked by England. Then, unexpectedly, he expressed surprise that a woman so young should have a son in the army. "He is only fifteen years old," my mother replied, whereupon the chivalrous German surgeon, who ought to have known it from my dossier, raised his arms in the air as if to say that, really, these Poles were even more bellicose than the English. He left us alone for a moment, then returned to announce to my mother that she could take me home, half hinting that he himself had issued the requisite authorization. In fact—though I found this out only later—all my comrades from the high school detachments had been released from Demblin at roughly the same time.

At the home of some friends of Sister Kunegunda in Radom, my mother gave me a suitcase with all my things carefully arranged, and directions on the best way to cross the Bug. Once we were alone together, my mother's nerves, which she had controlled admirably at the hospital in the presence of the Germans, began to fray, and showed the extent of her fatigue and despair. Her elbows resting on the table, she supported her head in her hands and said, "It is far worse in Lodz than anything you can imagine." She wasn't going to try to keep me at home; Lodz was doomed. I suggested she come with me to the USSR, despite her political apprehensions. But it was out of the question. My father, forced to wear the yellow star, had been completely shattered and was no longer able to travel. She refused to leave him in Lodz: a marriage is for life, even if it is no longer harmonious. My sister and her fiancé would help her, she added, as if to reassure me. She also gave me an envelope from Papa with twelve pounds sterling—which Genya had probably left him—and the Russian addresses of his two sisters, one of whom lived in Rostov, the other in Moscow. Later, when she accompanied me to the train station, my mother straightened up again, almost like at the hospital. She held back her tears, but whispered in my ear, "I'll not see you again, ever."

On November 30, 1939, at nightfall, I cross a vast, melancholy, white landscape under the direction of a guide, with about ten others. We are walking across the frozen River Bug. The bedsheets that serve as camouflage keep slipping from our shoulders; we stumble repeatedly as a deep layer of fresh snow hinders our steps. If a frontier patrol were to pass by, it would spot us without difficulty. Then the guide murmurs some directions to us and leaves to return to his village on the German side; we must find our Russian guide alone. We carry on in silence, for too long to be sure of going in the right direction. In the snow-laden mist of this moonless night we can't see the least light or the slightest sign of an inhabited place. "Siberia must be like this," I think, "the snow, the cold, and not a soul for a hundred miles around." Suddenly we hear voices. Someone is approaching, apparently without nervousness. Everything turns on whether he will cry "halt" or *stoi*, whether he is German or Russian. This waiting seems to last an eternity because the stranger, or strangers, are unable to clear a path in the snow. But gradually as they approach my apprehensions dissolve; these newcomers swear in unmistakable Russian.

The crossing of the Bug went better than I had feared. The Soviet frontier guards, in spite of their dreadful vocabulary—at least to my ears, which were accustomed to a more literary Russian—were not at all unfriendly. On the contrary, they brought us to a warm shelter, gave us tea, and, having discovered that I spoke Russian, positively warmed to me. They even found a truck for me that was leaving the next day for Lvov. Their manner of addressing me—*"Eh ty Russkiy"* ("You there, the Russian")—made me somewhat uncomfortable; Sister Kunegunda's last piece of advice still resounded in my ears: *"Badz Polakiem"* ("Be Polish"), with its unspoken implication: "Fight for Poland." Upon arriving in Lvov, I learned that November 30 was a fateful day for others as well. On that day the USSR had declared war—not against the Third Reich, but against poor little Finland. My hope that the USSR would break off its pact with Hitler and liberate Lodz, and that I would be reunited with my family, seemed increasingly forlorn.

Lvov was a far more beautiful town than Lodz, and in fact far more Polish.* In vain was it proclaimed the capital of the Western Socialist Ukraine, to no avail were its walls covered with posters in the Siberian language: Its predominantly Polish population remained more than ever attached to the prewar nationalist ideology. The Soviet attack against Finland and the reactions it provoked in the West only confirmed their conviction that the world was divided into two camps: on one side the Western democracies, pledged to defend small countries such as our own or Finland, and on the other side the totalitarian regimes, in whose front ranks were Hitler's Germany and Stalin's Russia.

I felt ill at ease with these categories. How was it possible to equate the USSR with the Third Reich, the one with its prestigious history, its aspirations, its struggle for the future, the other with its primitive obscurantism? My experience suggested that the nature of these totalitarian regimes was quite different. There was a world of difference,

---

* By turns Russian, Polish, Austrian (from 1772 to 1918), and once again Polish after the First World War, the town had been taken in 1939 by the Germans, who then ceded it to the Soviets on September 22. When I arrived, Lvov had been "Soviet" for only two months.

as I had seen for myself, between the behavior of the Wehrmacht soldiers in Demblin and those of the Red Army on the Bug. Besides, if my anti-Communist mother had advised me to go to Lvov rather than return to Lodz, she must have had good reasons for doing so, reasons that were at odds with the Manichaean vision of our compatriots in Lvov. But I had no other friends than they, having little contact with the Ukrainians and still less with the soldiers of the Red Army.

I managed to find a modest job in a chemistry laboratory where I washed test tubes, and even more modest lodgings (a kitchen commode on which I stretched out at night, my feet dangling in the air) at the home of a retired Polish lady who was poor but very obliging; if I remember correctly, she was an acquaintance of Sister Kunegunda. The snow that fell abundantly that year was also my ally; the authorities' decree that all citizens had to clean the streets resulted in notables and slackers hiring young people like me to substitute for them. The few rubles a day that I earned at this were not superfluous to my meager budget. For lack of time, however, I no longer studied anything or went to any public entertainments, or even read newspapers; besides, the *Ukraine Pravda,* with its unerring instinct for dogma and the dull, would have discouraged anyone from taking the slightest interest in politics.

Nevertheless, one day I decided to enroll in the Komsomol. My decision was prompted by an anti-Russian evening of doubtful taste at the home of one of my landlady's friends. Everyone there gloated over these shabbily dressed Russians and their ragged army, which had been held in check by Finland; when all was said and done, the Germans were far more serious and respectable. My landlady, by way of proof, related how the wives of Russian officers had bought up all the nightgowns from the shops in Lvov, thinking that they were buying evening dresses. "That's the way your Communist ladies put on the style to go to the opera." And the poor woman burst out laughing even though she herself hadn't a stitch to put on her back, and never frequented the theater. Feeling myself under an obligation, having no one there who shared my views, I hadn't the courage to preach solidarity among the dispossessed, or to argue against the "old ideas," but I felt that the time had come for me simply to go to the Communists and discover what they were really saying among themselves, outside of their official speeches, the stupidity of which doubtless derived from tactical considerations.

My expedition to the Komsomol was rewarded by a humiliating failure. I had written and learned by heart a text of adherence, a very nuanced piece that declared my support for the goals of the Komsomol, avoided thorny subjects such as the pact with Hitler and the war in Finland, and insisted instead on my desire to help build socialism and, in particular, to improve communication with the Polish minority in the Western Ukraine. I rehearsed my speech in front of a man of about forty who listened to me without the least interest and gratified me only with a sentence that left me stupefied: "Lenin's Komsomol is not a public house where anyone can enter whenever he wishes. To become part of the Komsomol you have to be chosen." He didn't condescend to note my name, persuaded that I would never be "chosen." (He was mistaken.)

Having thus established the superfluous character of my projected contribution to the "process of transition to socialism in the Western Ukraine," I remembered that I had the addresses of my two aunts in Rostov and in Moscow. What I really wanted was for them to invite me to join them in the "real Russia," but to want to travel around the Soviet Union on one's own was still a more reckless project than to want to join the Komsomol. We belonged to the same republic, administratively speaking, but not in terms of railway communications. My Rostov aunt didn't reply to my letter, while my aunt in Moscow declared herself delighted to learn that her brother had a grown boy like me, but requested that I not write to her too often, because the big bad dog in the courtyard of her apartment house frightened the postman. So there wasn't a great deal to be expected from this quarter, either. Nevertheless, seven months after my arrival in Lvov, I found myself in a convoy headed to that "real Russia" for which I had so often longed. But I hadn't joined it of my own free will, and it was to go a lot farther than I would have wished—as far as Western Siberia.

At the time, I knew of Western Siberia only from Polish films whose heroes were patriots deported by the Czars. I had the impression that it consisted of an interminable, snow-covered steppe swept by an Arctic wind, an open-air prison where the temperature was permanently forty degrees below zero. Animated by hatred of the Czarist regime, our Polish patriots generally succeeded in returning to their fiancées, played by the most beautiful actresses, after an escape on foot or by sleigh across the infernal Siberian peneplain. In Lvov, in any case, after the unhappy memory of the frozen Bug, I wouldn't have agreed to any expedition across the snow, not even if the patriotic fiancée who awaited my return had been Greta Garbo.

In fact, my stay in Siberia bore no resemblance at all to the scenarios of Polish films. I was swept up in what was without doubt the greatest police operation that Europe (outside the USSR) had ever seen, and possibly one of the most destructive: the massive deportation of more than a million and a half Poles to the East. Why, at a single stroke and at such great cost, were such a large number of people, of all ages and professions, banished to Siberia? Why these people in particular? To accomplish what task? Couldn't their skills have been used in a more rational manner? One day, when the Kremlin's archives are opened, perhaps we will find the answers to these questions. It would be interesting also to know how many of these deportees—and their children—went on to help found the People's Republic of Poland, and how many became leaders of the new state of Israel. For, thanks to a strange reversal, this terrible episode ultimately showed itself favorable to many of those who, at its outset, had been its victims.

In Lvov, people were disappearing. A selective but systematic repression struck at members of the former upper classes as well as left-wing militants: one of the first targets was the Communist poet Władysław Broniewski, who, in a poem that was to become famous, had evoked "the red flag flying over liberated Warsaw." Now, according to the Nazi-Soviet Pact, Poland ought not to exist ever again. If the Bolshevik regime bared its claws in this manner, it was because it found support nowhere. The Ukrainians and Byelorussians, mostly peasants, who were supposed to have supported socialism, wanted no part of Stalin's collectivization. Among the Polish population, the Polish Communist Party could perhaps have lent a helping hand, but Stalin had dissolved it in 1938. Its leaders and best party cadres were summoned to Moscow and murdered in the course of a Soviet St. Bartholomew's Day Massacre. There remained in Lvov only a small group of intellectuals around Wanda Wasilewska, who didn't enjoy sufficient influence to reassure a public that was either apprehensive or hostile. But the whole of Europe was living in a suspended frame of mind, as if in parentheses. The war was spreading and it seemed reasonable to think that the USSR, after its semi-victory over Finland in March 1940, would choose to act according to the old British motto, "When in doubt, do nothing."

Instead, Moscow decided to strike a major blow in what had formerly been eastern Poland. At the beginning of June 1940 these provinces, with their 15 million or more inhabitants, were suddenly cut off from the outside world; all means of transport and communication were blocked, toward the west and toward the east alike. A virtual state of siege had been proclaimed except that, in the daytime, nothing happened: it was only at night that the men in the blue peaked caps of the NKVD, the Soviet secret police, moved into action. In house after house, in cities such as Lvov but also in the towns and villages, they pulled people from their beds and forced them to show their Soviet passports.

What were they looking for? Did they have lists of those suspected of trying to organize an armed Polish resistance? Not at all, it seemed; they were apprehending all those who had no passports, to whom passports had been refused on the grounds that they were not originally from the region. For these people, no avenue of appeal was available; convoys to the east awaited them at the nearest railroad station.

Jews who had come from the German-occupied zone formed a clear majority of those apprehended. Persecuted by the Nazis and forced to flee, they had sought a safe refuge in the zone controlled by the

USSR. But there were also many Poles originally from the western provinces, who hadn't asked for a Soviet passport because they thought of themselves as "in transit," who were hoping to emigrate to other continents or to join up with General Sikorski's army in France. Yet others, of assorted origins and faiths, had sinned by negligence in underestimating the paranoid sensibilities of the Soviet administration. In my own case, I had no passport for the simple reason that I hadn't yet reached the minimum legal age—sixteen years—to have one issued to me.

My birth certificate and a bundle of documents from the Skorupka High School ought to have sufficed to throw light on my case, but the three men in blue peaked caps were not disposed to read them; what's more, it was possible that they didn't even know how to read the Latin alphabet. My landlady, outraged by their contempt for the written word, offered testimony in which she pretended to have been present at my birth. But charged with carrying out an exact order, uncompromisingly, the NKVD men remained coldly impassive. The choice was simple: passport or convoy. A neighbor who had passed the ordeal, being properly in possession of his passport, came to ask them, "What are you going to do with this youngster? Why are you insisting on throwing him overboard from society?" Although something of an intellectual, this neighbor spoke a very awkward Russian, and his phrase sounded as clumsy in that language as it does in English. It is for this reason, perhaps, that the question left an indelible impression and came back to me some years later, at a critical moment of my life in the USSR. In the panic of departure I didn't appreciate its inner meaning and thought simply that, once overboard, I would merely have to learn to swim. The trio from the NKVD reassured my friend: "He has nothing to worry about. He will be given a good job in our country, far from the frontier provinces."

The next three days were very difficult. It isn't easy to find oneself suddenly enclosed in a *tyeplushka,* with fifty or so strangers. The *tyeplushka* is a freight car fitted with rudimentary bunks (bare boards arranged on three tiers) and provided with an iron stove for heating and cooking. The name, which derives from the word *tyeplo* (warm, lukewarm), was familiar to me from my early childhood days: It was in a *tyeplushka* that my parents had left the USSR in 1921. Here I was in 1940, taking the same route once again but in the opposite direction, in similar conditions, moving away from Poland, lost among these strangers who made up a "representative sample" of the deportees.

The Jews, who were a majority in my *tyeplushka*, comprised very different groups: some were from very orthodox families, of the Hasidic persuasion; they huddled together, spoke very little with the others, and seemed almost oblivious to the outside world, except for the details of daily life; others were from less religious families or were nonbelievers who spoke better Polish and discussed their opinions openly. All Jewish political tendencies were represented, from left-wing Zionists to ultraconservatives. The sociological spread of the Catholics among us was more difficult to gauge because many preferred not to discuss either their religion or their past activities. Several of those aboard belonged to the liberal professions, but there was also a Renault foreman who had come to spend the month of August on vacation with his Polish relatives, and there was even a veteran of the International Brigade who had fought in Spain.

No one knew where we were being taken, but in theory, according to the initial rumors at any rate, we were going to disembark at Donbass, in the homeland of Alexei Stakhanov, the most productive miner in the history of coal mining. At the end of three days, just as we thought we were nearing our destination, a man in a blue peaked cap came to disabuse us and announced, at the same time, a "liberal reform": our *tyeplushka* would henceforward be opened and a delegate from each wagon would be permitted to make purchases during prolonged stops near stations.

In retrospect, the origin of this "liberalization" is not hard to understand: The Soviet authorities were well equipped to apprehend individuals found to be without the proper papers, but they were less prepared to transport them en masse over long distances. Thousands of enormous convoys carrying more than one and a half million people amounted to a wholly unaccustomed burden, which proved to be too much for the Soviet railway network, notoriously the Achilles' heel of the country's economy. To facilitate their uninterrupted passage it would have been necessary to bring all passenger and freight traffic to a halt, which clearly wasn't possible. Therefore, we were parked on secondary lines while awaiting the green light for a further phase of the journey, marked by a renewed halt of indeterminate duration. Our NKVD guards knew that at this pace the rations they had received for us wouldn't be sufficient for the journey. Fortunately, near each station there was a *kolkhoz* mini-market where a little bit of everything was on sale, even ready-cooked dishes. Not wanting to let us out of their sight, our guards hadn't said to their precious recruits, "Over there, all of you. Quickly!" Instead, we were allowed to elect delegates from among ourselves who would then go and do the collective shopping. Thus it was that in my capacity as the delegate of *tyeplushka* No. 27, I began to discover the "real Russia."

I was struck by the fact that the peasant women of the mini-markets much preferred barter to normal commerce in rubles. News of the passage of Poles had spread to all the stations, probably because of convoys that had preceded us. And the dealers, who seemed to know in advance what we had in our *tyeplushki*, presented their lists of requests in an imperative fashion. Everything was included— clothes, household goods, bedding—as though we were a mobile Woolworth's. "But I have rubles," I would say to one of them who had prepared a whole mountain of *piroshki*. "So have I," she replied, while urging me to find a better currency of exchange before her dish got cold and lost all its flavor.

This method of provisioning encouraged the emergence of a new social hierarchy within the wagon, favoring the richest families, or at least those who had managed to bring a lot of baggage with them. In my *tyeplushka*, for example, a shoe manufacturer from Lublin, at first self-effacing and a little ashamed of his social origins, began to play a dominant role. He and his family ate sumptuous meals, to which he did not hesitate to invite the guards. His children—three boys and four girls—were offered the best places for the night, and the other passengers, who, at the beginning, had been contemptuous of their poor upbringing, now found them "charming."

We crossed all of Central and Eastern Russia in this fashion. Then one day at the end of June in the early afternoon, our convoy came to a halt on a secondary line at Sverdlovsk, capital of the Urals. It was a stop like any other, it seemed; we had completed our purchases and eaten, and most of us had settled down for the night. It must have been quite late in the evening when I saw a truly big train go by marked Vladivostok-Moscow, the famous Trans-Siberian line. Then our convoy shook in its turn, slowly as usual, and took the same track, but toward the east; from this moment on it was no longer possible to doubt our destination—we were entering Western Siberia. We were about to become the new generation of Siberian deportees. It felt as though we ought to have been doing something, protesting before the worst came to pass. But the unofficial leader of the *tyeplushka* refused to hear me out, while the others slept on peaceably, as if they were still traveling between Lvov and Rovno. In front of the half-open door, alone and too excited to sleep, I waited to see the steppe appear and hear the Siberian wind. But to my surprise, the landscape became more and more wooded, and—surprise! surprise!—it was actually quite warm.

We had been brought to a place that, for want of a better term, is called a forest. In Poland the forest frightens no one: You go there to picnic, to gather mushrooms, to rest in the shade, without experiencing any fear. You no longer hear of people or even children who lose themselves in the forest. But can the enormous wooded expanse that stretches between Tyumen and Omsk, and that is three-quarters the size of France, be included in the category "forest"? Shouldn't there be another word that conveys the awesome character of this infinite space and the impossibility of escaping its labyrinth, of crossing it without losing oneself forever?

After a journey by truck and a long march on foot, we arrived exhausted in a clearing, where more secret police were waiting to receive us. "This place," said their chief, "is called Lebedovka. There is only one exit and it is closely guarded. So get used to the idea that you are here for good, and think only about organizing your life accordingly. We will teach you how to cut wood, which will make up the bulk of your activities. But all initiatives will be encouraged and there will be plenty of work for you to do. It will be paid at the full rate, according to the scales in operation in our socialist Fatherland, because you are not prisoners but *pereselentzy* [displaced persons]. You will have a good wage if you work hard, and productivity bonuses, in accordance with our principle, 'From each according to his abilities, to each according to his work.' With what you earn, you will be able to buy yourselves anything that will be of use to you in your life here, and even a cow."

No doubt he would have wanted to say more, to describe to us in detail this great Siberian destiny that had been decided for us, but his last sentence, interpreted as "A single cow is as much wealth as you can aspire to," provoked the sudden nervous collapse of those present. Collective lamentations rose up on all sides. The women cried, as did their children, and the men screamed, swore, or prayed, all in a jumble of different languages. The NKVD men appeared baffled by this outcry and didn't attempt to reestablish silence. Things quieted down by sunset, however, when a swarm of mosquitoes dispersed the assembly more effectively than any merely human threats. There is no answer to these insects, except to be hermetically sealed up in the barracks, even if it is still hot outside and the air indoors is unbreathable.

I spent the entire summer of 1940 at Lebedovka, and it was there that I got to know my first "real" Russian. We called him simply *mastyer*. He was a real expert on tree-felling, and he liked a job well done. In contrast to the other *mastyera*, he quickly realized that Russian is not a universal language and that, to make himself understood, he had to have his instructions translated into Polish. He chose me as interpreter, a position for which there was no official provision. He got around this obstacle by inventing a fictive function for me, very well paid by socialist standards, that created between us, in addition to a mutual liking, something like a link of complicity.

My *mastyer* was about thirty years old, perhaps more, but he didn't like to talk about himself or about those who, before us, had occupied the already ancient barracks of Lebedovka. Today I am inclined to believe that he was the son of a deportee or was a former deportee himself, who had been released some years before. But at the time, observing his reticence, I didn't ask him any questions. He, on the other hand, often questioned me about life in Poland and even wanted to learn Polish. He had me tell him a dozen times over the story of my departure from Lvov, and at the end of each of my retellings, he shook his head with compassion and astonishment and said, *"Nye poviezlo."* ("Really bad luck.")

When one of his colleagues set off on official business or for medical treatment in Zavodoukovsk, the nearest railway center, he invited me to sleep in the vacant bed in the *mastyera*'s barracks, which were more spacious and comfortable than ours.

Thus it was that the idea came to me of going legally to Zavodoukovsk myself, on a strictly one-way ticket, on the pretext of consulting a doctor to discover whether my (entirely imaginary) migraines were linked to the injury to my right eye of the previous year. This plan was good as far as the first stage—leaving the forest through the guarded route—but it left everything else to luck and to improvisation, and today it still appears to me to have been extremely reckless. Even as it stood, it could only be realized with the help of my *mastyer*, or at least by abusing his trust: Only he could ask permission from the NKVD to allow me to be examined by an eye specialist in Zavodoukovsk.

I hesitated seriously; it was my first Soviet attack of conscience. Despite my *mastyer*'s sympathy toward me, nothing indicated that he would accept the role of accomplice in an undertaking that might backfire on him if he was found guilty of an "administrative irregularity." I decided, therefore, to make him believe that I really was suffering from headaches, and he took the necessary steps without suspecting anything of my project. At the moment of my departure he suspected nothing. He offered to look after my suitcase for me, to save me the bother of carrying it for perhaps kilometers; it was certainly true that it might be some time before I found a truck on the allegedly passable track (it was passable only by Siberian standards). Nevertheless, I set out with my suitcase, abusing right to the end his trust and goodwill.

For once I was very lucky. On arrival in Zavodoukovsk I presented myself at the *Kolkhozniki* Center, the town's only hotel. My dormitory neighbor—a neat coincidence—was a railway worker. That very evening, without having seen an eye specialist (to whom in any case I would have had nothing to say), I proposed a swap to my neighbor: the suit that my brother Genya had left me, or the Omega watch that my parents had bought me for my fifteenth birthday, for a ticket to Moscow. The railway worker, who expressed interest in the exchange, went off to check things out with his friends but brought back a negative answer. It would only be possible to get on the Trans-Siberian if a passenger got off at Zavodoukovsk, which, alas, happened but once every two months or so, sometimes even more rarely. Impressed nevertheless by the Herman Horovitz suit from the best tailor in Prague, the railway man wasn't ready to give up so easily. (The Omega had less success, Western Siberia having still not entered the age of the watch.) "Come to Tyumen with me," he said. "After two or three days there, I'm sure I can fix you up with a train for Moscow." "I haven't got a permit to go there," I replied. "There is no inspection on this trip," he said, "and in Tyumen you can stay with me and have some of my wife's borscht." The invitation seemed irresistible.

The railway worker lived in an isolated wooden shed, not far from the Tyumen station. We arrived at night. No one saw us. My host and his wife set out for work early in the morning, leaving me alone. I listened to the radio and read their few books, among which, in the place of honor, was the *History of the CPSU (Bolsheviks)*. In the evenings the railwayman's wife did indeed prepare a good borscht and sometimes a stew, which she ladled out, pronouncing as she did so Stalin's famous phrase: "Life has become better, life has become gayer."

No news came about a ticket for Moscow; Trans-Siberian passengers apparently did not get off at Tyumen in large numbers, either. At last the railwayman found a solution: I would take the Novosibirsk-Leningrad train as far as Buy, and after a ten-hour wait, I could continue on to Moscow aboard a medium-range express that would have plenty of spare room. As proof of his goodwill he gave me, in addition to a ticket, some used clothes of an inimitably Soviet cut, which would assure me of a trip without incident.

On the Novosibirsk-Leningrad train an odd incident occurred. An important passenger who was due to get off the train at Sverdlovsk had his boots stolen. It was the middle of the night, and in the penumbra of the poorly lit carriages, there was a generalized shambles. The militia launched a thorough search, checking not only passports but also all the baggage. I could see no way out; panic prevented me from even thinking of any sort of ruse to extricate myself. I remained immobile on my bunk close to the ceiling, my head pressed against my suitcase, my eyes closed, mortified at the thought that I hadn't even succeeded in crossing the Western Siberian frontier. This momentary paralysis saved me. A woman passenger, convinced that in order to sleep through such a racket I must have had a few, said to the militia, "He is *podpivchyi* [less than drunk, barely tipsy], and since he hasn't budged since Tyumen, he certainly hasn't stolen the boots." Her argument was probably decisive. Sverdlovsk also was rapidly getting closer, and the militia had no time to lose if they were to find the culprit.

The Tyumen railwayman hadn't told me the whole truth about the train connection at Buy. Instead of telling me about the ten-hour wait I had to expect, he ought to have warned me that in order to board the other train, it would be necessary to have my ticket officially stamped, which meant showing a passport, just as at the time of the initial purchase. On learning this, I thought first of contacting a railway worker in Buy, but circumstances didn't lend themselves to a new bartering deal. I took my place in the line in front of the ticket window for Moscow-bound passengers, resigned and without any definite plan.

As the hours went by, the line grew longer and longer, becoming nearly a kilometer in length. Other trains also were pouring passengers bound for Moscow into the station. The ticket window remained closed; the regulations did not permit it to open until thirty minutes before the departure of the fast train for Moscow (which on that day was five hours late). During this long wait the passengers had time to organize themselves, to allocate numbers to themselves, and, obviously, to discuss their respective chances of having their tickets stamped and their passports checked.

Finding myself almost at the head of this interminable line of passengers already exhausted by earlier stages of their journey, I had received several offers: some wanted to buy my place in line (which didn't interest me at all), while others wanted me to show several tickets alongside my own, in order to speed things along. It was thanks to this that, when the ticket window finally opened, I had five passports and six tickets (it was my ticket, obviously, that accounted for the discrepancy). Pressed for time, the clerk didn't ask me for any explanation of this collective journey, and without counting either the passports or the tickets, he duly stamped them. I boarded the train quickly; the trip to Moscow went off without a hitch.

At Moscow a sort of tribunal composed of seven people, one of whom was a general in the Red Army, formally decided, after having examined my papers, that the secret police in Lvov had made an error. But the members of this improvised court did not have the power to make reparations for all the wrongs that had been committed—for the simple reason that they were my cousins, hastily assembled by my Aunt Lisa, immediately after my unexpected arrival in Moscow.

The idea that I had formed in Lvov of my septuagenarian Muscovite aunt proved to be completely wrong. I had imagined her small, stooped, and timid. In fact, she was tall, thin, ramrod straight, and not at all shy.

The ridiculous story of the wicked dog that prowled around her courtyard, which she had mentioned in her letter to me, must have been invented by some member of her family who wished to keep me at a safe distance, because my Aunt Lisa would willingly have taken me into her home. Only her daughter Maria continued to live with her, but she was hardly ever at home. Apart from companionship, she lacked for nothing. Her apartment at the bottom of the courtyard, in a building after the rustic Russian style—the ground floor in brick and the first floor in wood—was quite spacious: forty-odd square meters. Aunt Lisa certainly hadn't exaggerated the success of her seven sons. Only Soviet citizens who had really made it in life could give their mother such comfortable accommodations in the heart of Moscow, in the Arbat, a stone's throw from the subway.

To discuss the possibility of my moving in with her, she had summoned her sons to come and join her after work had finished for the day, at seven o'clock, as soon as dinner was over. The news that a Polish cousin who had escaped from Western Siberia had just arrived at the house gave an urgent character to her convocation; at the other end of the telephone line, strangled voices asked her not to prolong the conversation, and at seven o'clock sharp, her sons dutifully arrived. We waited in vain for Maria to show up. My first family reunion in Russia was about to begin.

It wasn't a particularly happy affair. Aunt Lisa, seated beside me, tried to plead my case, but my cousins, with the exception of Stepan, the general, were doubtful. They seemed to feel that sheltering me might put their own families in jeopardy. "Mama, I have a family too, and children of his age," was a frequent refrain. In order not to frighten her, they did not emphasize the great danger that I presented for her and her family, but the lugubrious tone of their voices and the tension in their faces suggested that a successful Soviet citizen could not permit himself to have parents abroad. Even less could he expect his relatives to harbor him—and above all, he shouldn't be from Western Siberia.

The meeting was a long one, and some of my cousins paced up and down to stretch their legs or to calm their nerves. Apart from Stepan's, I remember neither the names nor the faces of my cousins; it seems to me that I saw them only this once, on the evening of my arrival. Nevertheless, in the course of this single meeting they subjected me to a lengthy interrogation, as though they were taking part in a punctilious commission of inquiry that was obsessed with each detail of the story of my escape.

When I finished telling them how I had managed to make my way to Moscow, there was complete silence. My cousins, having satisfied their curiosity, seemed plunged into deep meditation. All of them were heavy smokers and they filled my aunt's dining room with a cloud of tobacco smoke so thick that you would have thought yourself inside a second-class railway carriage. My aunt, after having protested and even having threatened to forbid cigarettes, appeared resigned, although half-asphyxiated.

One of my cousins doubted my story: "To cover three-quarters of the Soviet Union without encountering an identity check appears to me to be improbable." Aunt Lisa flew to my aid, recalling a long journey that she had once made without being stopped either by the railway militia or by any other authority. "You have a short memory," my cousin replied, "for I was with you, and our passports were checked at least three times!" Aunt Lisa denied it; my cousin insisted. Finally, Stepan intervened.

At last, a cousin sitting at the end of the table took on the task of summarizing the essentials of the situation. From a legal point of view, my position was indefensible because I ought to have taken, while I was still in Siberia, the steps necessary to correct the mistake made in Lvov, and not to have fled like a thief in the night. On the other hand, even if I had pursued the proper channels and had been vindicated in Yalutorovsk or in Omsk, my chances of obtaining permission to live in Moscow would have been about zero—he made a figure O with two fingers to dispel any misunderstanding—because the capital fiercely defended itself against any influx from the provinces.

Another cousin was anxious lest, in the questionnaires that I might have filled out in Lvov or Siberia, I had mentioned the existence of my relations in Moscow. My reply in the negative—I had been asked nothing in Lvov, even when I was put aboard the *tyeplushka*—provoked a sigh of general relief; even the affable General Stepan seemed reassured.

Gradually, the idea of sending me back to Lvov emerged. The purchase of a rail ticket didn't pose an insurmountable obstacle—as it happened, they had much better contacts in the train stations in Moscow than did my railway worker in Tyumen—but since, as one of my cousins said, "Lvov counts as 'abroad,' " the police checks on this line were going to be altogether more rigorous than on the Novosibirsk-Leningrad train. According to Stepan, although he was probably joking, it would have been easier to send me to Istanbul than to the Western Ukraine.

As my opinion was not sought, I was slowly overtaken by somnolence—the previous night, spent in Buy station, I hadn't slept a wink—and so began to drift off. My mother sits near me, makes some remarks to me touching upon minor details of my life in Siberia, then turns toward the family tribunal and pleads in favor of the right of everyone to choose his own place of residence; she protests against a bureaucracy devoid of soul or reason. Suddenly she abandons her advocate's robe to dress up as on the First of May, with flowers in her hair. She recites a text of Lermontov against the police, followed by a line of Pushkin's exalting men of noble sentiments—those who, even in the darkest hour, know how to defend freedom. My mother is very beautiful with her impassioned air and her flowers, and her smile indicates to me that all this is hardly serious, that everything will work out.

Suddenly I was startled awake by a genuine screaming match. Having lost the thread of my cousins' discussion, I was unaware of the origin of these brusquely acerbic exchanges that filled the air. I had the impression that they were divided on the prudence of taking steps to help me in Moscow. According to Stepan and another cousin, probably supported by my Aunt Lisa, something had to be tried, even if only to have me sent back to Lvov. The others found this view "suicidal," arguing that it might compromise the family; they wished that I would undertake the journey at my own risk, confident that I would emerge unscathed since I had such good luck with trains. The argument had become quite heated.

"We must speak with Mishka," the general said forcefully. (I discovered later that he meant Mikhail Kalinin, the President of the Republic.)

"Why not with Stalin while you're at it?" the chief of the opposing faction burst out.

"Because I haven't access to him," Stepan retorted, "whereas you can invite Mishka to call at Mama's for tea with our Polish cousin."

Sorely tried by it all, Aunt Lisa said, "You have ended up by vexing me. All of you leave, right now." Incredible as it may seem, they obeyed her dutifully and immediately, without arranging a time for a further meeting. It was clear that a mother in Russia enjoyed more authority than one in Poland—more than mine, at any rate.

During the two weeks of September 1940 that I spent in Moscow, I learned to "do as the Soviets do"—thanks to my Aunt Lisa and her son, General Stepan Vladimirovich, who was an important engineer in the armaments industry. From them I learned to behave like everyone else in public places, to read the newspapers, to learn the pecking order of the members of the Politburo, and a thousand other things without which I would surely have had much less chance of getting accepted at School No. 44 in Rostov-on-the-Don, and of adapting myself to it, of finding friends there, of becoming Solik.

Try as I might, I don't really remember when or where Aunt Lisa sent me out for the first time to do some shopping for her. All I know is that she described the route to me with minute precision, that she explained to me, point by point, as if I were an overgrown child, the way I ought to behave toward the shop assistants.

On the other hand, I remember as though it were yesterday the morning that Aunt Lisa said to me, "It's a fine day, let's go and see the *kolkhoz* exhibition." We took the subway and she explained to me the history of each station name, finishing on an almost authoritarian note: "You really must visit Moscow, I assure you it is a very beautiful city."

Once inside the great exhibition park, built in the Stalinist style, where the agricultural exploits of each republic were on display in separate pavilions, she appeared to tire quickly. "You are young, you can carry on without me," she said after we had covered the Russian pavilion, and went off mumbling something to herself, forgetting to arrange with me a time to come home.

In the days following, this scenario repeated itself almost without variation. We always left in a hurry. Aunt Lisa would tuck her white hair under a Russian-style neckerchief, pat her somber dress, which was too hot for the time of year, and we would leave at a gallop. Once we had arrived somewhere, at the Tretiakov Gallery or the Pushkin Museum, for example, after we had visited the first room, she would invariably pronounce the same phrase, "You are young, you can carry on without me"—and I was free for the day. This didn't altogether displease me; I preferred to go on these visits alone, but, given my problematic legal status, I couldn't help worrying and even having suspicions. Was Aunt Lisa bringing me into town to get me out of the way and discuss my fate with her sons behind my back? Sometimes, losing all sense of proportion, I went so far as to imagine that she counted on me to make a false step and was relying on the vigilant militia to deliver her family from the hindrance of my presence. It was foolish and ungrateful of me, of course, for in the event of a slipup, Aunt Lisa and my cousins would have had far more worries than I, who, after all, was young and impoverished, an escapee from Siberia, and who, as the Russians put it, "couldn't be sent back any further."

I visited Red Square, where the view of Lenin's tomb had a powerful effect on me. The large panel proclaiming "Class Brothers, Prisoners of Capitalism, Receive Our Ardent Proletarian Greetings," no longer ornamented the façade of the GUM department store, but I remembered it from a photo that my brother Alexander had shown to me in Lodz. These places symbolized the hopes born of the October Revolution. Abroad, the Revolution's adversaries, like its partisans, had never stopped talking about it, either to drag it through the mud as the "leadership of subversion" that was still reputed to sit behind the white walls of the Kremlin, or to exalt it in the name of a "better future." I was very happy to be there, and was quite taken with the beauty of the place. Political considerations aside, Moscow was an incomparably more imposing city than either Lodz or Lvov.

On my return, Aunt Lisa didn't ask a lot of questions about how I'd spent the day, but confined herself instead to commenting on the weather. Although her sense of family loyalty was obvious, and fully repaid my gamble on coming to Moscow, she seemed hardly curious at all to know how my family lived in Lodz, nor was she preoccupied with the fate of her brother under the Nazi occupation. When I spoke to her about it, she would raise her arms in the air as if to say, "What an awful world we live in," and then she would repeat one of those sayings, which I had already heard in September 1939, whose gist was that "at the start of every war the Germans win some victories, but they are always beaten in the end."

Although she subscribed to *Pravda*, *Izvestia*, and the majority of other Soviet periodicals, Aunt Lisa had in fact only one source of news: her son Stepan. The general always called at the house in civilian clothes, without any warning, during the day and in the evening alike, and replied to his mother's thousand questions about the war with an angelic patience, generally repeating in a more lively manner the news from the official dailies. Even though he dropped in almost every day, she questioned him as if she hadn't seen him for months. He would come from the nearby Sklifasovski Clinic, where he was undergoing physiotherapy for his right leg, which had been fractured the previous winter. Plump, always good-humored, often bringing cakes that he ate for the most part himself, Stepan was, in my view, an accomplished liar. Knowing full well that his mother was against the Germans—what Jew was not?—he very clearly favored in his reports the British and their American allies (who still hadn't entered the war). Reassured, Aunt Lisa nevertheless pointed to my testimony on the strength of the Wehrmacht, and he then replied invariably that in the eyes of a mouse, a cat appeared to be the most frightening animal in the world, which didn't flatter me at all. The general didn't tell the truth about his private life, either; in this regard, in my opinion, he lied without apparent reason.

One evening he brought me to the opera, to a branch of the Bolshoi, to see *Rigoletto*, after having announced to his mother that he would take advantage of the occasion to introduce me to a useful friend. The friend proved to be a very pretty, short-haired young blond woman who had a harsh look about her and a slightly martial bearing. Her presence had a decidedly more military air to it than Stepan's, which had something irremediably civilian in its gestures and expressions. Not only was he plump, he also accompanied his jokes with contortions of his physiognomy ill befitting the solemn rank of general.

"What a mess!" he said to the blond woman. "We come especially to see Lemyechev, and it isn't him after all who is playing the role of the Duke of Mantua. What a pity, eh?"

"Yes," she replied, taut as a rope, "he's our favorite tenor and he's the best in the show." They left the box soon afterward, leaving me alone. Their story seemed a transparent ploy.

Yet, three days later, we returned to the same box; this time Lemyechev was to sing for sure, and once again they left, under one pretext or another. When they repeated their quiet walkout a third time, I became a solitary patron of *Rigoletto*, almost certainly judged to be a fervent music student by the usherettes. I didn't mind. I observed the stage, the hall, the Soviet theatrical costumes; I noted the popular character of the audience, so different from that which frequented the theatrical entertainments in Lodz—where there was no opera. But something in Stepan's behavior eluded my understanding. Why did he need to close me up in this box—always the same one, and always for *Rigoletto*—when in fact he was free to go wherever he liked with this young blond woman of martial aspect? After all, he wasn't answerable to his mother, since he didn't live in her apartment or in her neighborhood. No doubt he had had a reason for wanting to show me to the blond woman, but I didn't discover it then—and I am still not sure of it today. Fortunately, on my return from each performance, Aunt Lisa didn't ask me what I had seen, but only about the audience, the toilets, and the weather.

If my sojourn in Moscow had been prolonged, I would surely have gotten to know my aunt and cousins better, and the mysteries surrounding them, which are engraved in my memory, would have disappeared without trace. Barely two weeks after my arrival, though, General Stepan cordially and firmly invited me to leave—not, however, in search of the adventure that his timorous brothers had proposed. He advised me to go to Rostov, to present myself to a certain Ivanov in the local NKVD leadership, and to tell him that I had come from Lvov, without the proper papers, admittedly, but moved by the irresistible desire to get to know my family's hometown. I was to give as my new home the address of my other aunt, who was even older than my aunt in Moscow, and without means—she had had three daughters, none of whom had succeeded in life—but I wasn't to worry about means of support: Each month I would receive a money order for 150 rubles sent anonymously from Moscow. In dealing with Ivanov of the NKVD, I was not to cite any name or to offer references for testimonials; in particular, I was to avoid all mention of either Moscow or Siberia.

The general didn't explain why I had to see precisely this Ivanov, but he suggested to me that in my new life I should ask fewer questions and listen a bit more to official talk and opinions. My future, he said, hinged on a detail upon which he had been unable to shed any light: whether or not the authorities in Western Siberia had judged it necessary to issue a search warrant concerning me. If they had, neither Ivanov nor any other NKVD leader could do anything about it, and I would be returned. If such a warrant hadn't been issued, then Ivanov would have two options: either to send me back to Lvov—which wouldn't be such a disaster after all—or to grant me the permission necessary to reside in Rostov, in which case the Department of National Education would hasten to come to my aid. I could take it or leave it—or rather I could only take it, since my opinion in the matter was not in any way solicited.

The plan dreamed up by my cousin Stepan, doubtless with the help of his brothers, had been worked out with marvelous precision, including its financial aspects. For the ten months that followed, until the Soviet declaration of war, I received a money order through the mail each month. I never saw Aunt Lisa again, however; she died on the eve of the evacuation of Moscow, during the winter of 1941. Her first-floor neighbors gave me the news in 1944, but they didn't have the address of her daughter Maria, who was a refugee somewhere in central Asia, or that of General Stepan Vladimirovich, who was off at the front.

The contest between the NKVD and me ended in September 1940 in a draw. The secret police had scored a goal in Lvov, by shoving me inside a *tyeplushka*, but I evened the score in Rostov, by palming off on them the version of this great journey quietly suggested by cousin Stepan. Given the renown of my adversaries and the fact that I had been playing on their home turf, far from my Lodz supporters, this result was more than honorable. Still, perhaps my equalizing the score wasn't entirely the result of my own talent. I had the suspicion that Ivanov, the NKVD goalkeeper in Rostov, had been a little absentminded, perhaps even bribed. Perhaps the game had been rigged.

Ivanov was only a captain in the NKVD, a fair-haired man of about thirty, who didn't seem well disposed toward me. When I told him that I had come secretly from Lvov to Rostov out of overpowering love for this town, he gave me a grim look as if to say, "This idiot is completely crazy." He then left me in a small office adjoining his own, but his threatening air seemed to say, "You will leave here this very day, my boy, and I'll teach you once and for all never again to break the laws of the Soviet Union." I expected him to return with an escort that would take me back again either to Western Siberia or to Lvov.

In fact, he came back after two or three hours, accompanied only by a certain Vlasov, a civilian from the OBLONO (the acronym for the Department of National Education). He was a former student of the University of Warsaw and he was able to translate my Polish documents for Ivanov, who began to relax a little. Soon he spoke to me without further hostility, as if he had begun to understand the nobility of sentiment that had brought me to Rostov. Able to relax in my turn, I noticed then that he resembled slightly the young blond woman who had accompanied General Stepan to the performances of *Rigoletto*. Here is the key, I concluded, to the mystery of the opera box in Moscow. To find out if this wasn't pure fantasy on my part, it would have been necessary to ask, "Comrade Captain, do you have a sister who is a great admirer of Lemyechev and who is a great friend of General Stepan Vladimirovich in Moscow?" The rules of the game precluded any such question, any indiscretion, and I wasn't willing to risk a penalty in Rostov in order to satisfy my curiosity.

Ivanov asked me to write out my curriculum vitae and to complete various administrative forms. "Take your time, there is no hurry," he advised me, as if he sensed that at the age of sixteen years and one month, I already had a lengthy biography. It didn't conform closely to Soviet criteria, truth to tell. My parents were not proletarians, my education was suspect, and the Lodz high school bore the name of a priest who had fought against the Bolsheviks. What, finally, could I say about my participation in 1939 in the defense of Poland, against the Third Reich, the ally of the USSR? From another point of view, though, what did this Ivanov know about the Polish careers of my parents, or of the Abbot Skorupka's death on the Vistula? I could just as easily have been born into a workers' family and attended a school dedicated to the memory of a heretic who had been excommunicated by the Roman Catholic Church. To say that would have been to cheat, like scoring a goal from offside, with no regard at all for fair play. I chose, therefore, to make my parents office workers or clerks, belonging to the class of the exploited, who, under the hegemony of the proletariat, play a positive role in the anti-capitalist struggle. Next, while admitting to the Catholic character of my high school and deploring it, I emphasized strongly the intransigent atheism of all my family, myself included. Finally I said that I had lost my right eye in the course of a bombing raid in 1939, and having given details of neither the place nor the date, I wasn't actually lying. The village where I was wounded had been bombarded by mortar and artillery fire. Ivanov read my script with interest, and passed it to Vlasov, who decided it was very well written; neither one of them asked me for any additional details, and I heard the resounding applause of an imaginary audience; my shot had gone straight into the net. "Look. Envy me, I am a citizen of the Soviet Union!" as Mayakovsky had put it. The passport that Ivanov then issued to me did not have the same qualities as those of the poet, but of this fact I was going to become aware only much later.

A second contest began soon afterward, against the OBLONO, a much weaker opponent than the NKVD. Before awarding me a grant, they wanted to be satisfied that I was capable of following sixth-form classes and of making up for lost ground, in Russian literature and the history of the USSR in particular. Vlasov agreed only to give me a "trial run" at School No. 44 in Rostov. Now, one month later, I was already running so well that the rest of the class had difficulty keeping up with me.

Was I satisfied and proud to have scored so many goals this year, to be the best in all disciplines, Russian literature included? Having been lazy in Lodz, threatened more than once with having to retake examinations, I had made a thorough study of the career of other idlers who, like Adam Mickiewicz, the Polish national poet, later became famous. On the other hand, I knew nothing about those who placed first in their classes. I had observed that teachers' pets are appreciated by their instructors but are rarely liked by their peers; in Rostov, I almost felt at fault each time I found the correct answer while the others froze up, beginning with my neighbor Klava. In my defense, I must say that I became a "professional" in my studies because in Rostov I really had nothing else to do: no family obligations, practically no athletic activity, and, alas, no political life.

It was for want of protagonists that political discussions disappeared from my life. The thread was broken at a stroke, immediately after my forced departure from Lvov. Western Siberia was far away, too far to allow oneself any interest in the rest of the country, let alone the rest of the world.

In certain Siberian localities the people apparently learned of the German attack on the USSR only several weeks after the fact. That explains why, in the immense wooded expanse between Tyumen and Omsk, we were totally unaware of the Battle of Britain and of other trifling matters that were unfolding in faraway Europe. Later, in Moscow, I managed to fill in these gaps when, at Aunt Lisa's, I sat in on General Stepan's briefing sessions, but their conversation never went very far, and didn't touch upon any fundamental questions.

It is hardly better in Rostov. None of the friends who adopted me, beginning with the mathematician Motya, is troubled by the catastrophic turn taken by the war. "As long as it doesn't reach as far as us," is their sole thought, and thus they give genuine approval to the policy of "neutrality" adopted by Stalin. However, in the *kine-kroniki*—the newsreels shown in theaters before the feature films—the Secretary of the Communist Party of the Ukraine, Nikita Khrushchev, could be seen on a friendly visit to the *Gauleiter* Frank in Krakow, or Molotov could be seen in Berlin, while one never saw any Soviet leader in London or Washington. This discrepancy would make for an interesting discussion among friends, and I am surprised that cultivated people such as Motya's colleagues, whom I admire to the extent of attending their mathematics classes without understanding what goes on in them, never make any allusion to it. Neither the "finest hour" of British history, nor Churchill, who is alone in confronting Hitler, really concerns them.

During my Siberian summer the USSR annexed, in June, the Baltic countries (Estonia, Latvia, and Lithuania), and in August, Bessarabia and Bukovina, which had belonged to Romania. In Rostov each of these events was registered and approved in the course of meetings, but in mid-September after my arrival, very few still recall them. Misha, my best friend—the one who would like to travel around the world—believes that "Stalin has advanced our frontiers" the better to parry an eventual surprise attack by the capitalist powers. Misha's father, a supervisor at Rosselmach, a large agricultural machinery factory, has supplied him with this unofficial version of events. But when I eat with Misha's very hospitable family, his father only repeats the editorials from *Molot* ("The Hammer"), the Communist Party newspaper in Rostov.

"Nikolai Stepanovich, do you think there is a danger of war?" I ask him to try to get him to commit himself.

"You must always be prepared," he replies, breaking into a few bars of a song then in fashion: "If war should come tomorrow, be ready from today."

I am satisfied with Misha's hypothesis. In this region the USSR can feel threatened only by the Third Reich; if it is taking measures against this danger, it is because it doesn't believe in the solidity of the pact with Hitler. Reading *Molot* nevertheless never fails to bring me disagreeable surprises. It argues, for example, that the war undertaken by Britain in Europe is only a continuation of the previous conflict between imperialists, a kind of prolongation of the First World War. I would really like to write a letter to the editor to reestablish the truth about the facts of September 1939, and to protest against putting democratic Great Britain on a par with the Hitlerite monsters. The instinct of self-preservation carries the day, however, and I refrain from revealing the truth to the readers of *Molot*.

Although I am concerned by the world situation, I recognize that my school friends have other legitimate everyday worries. As a rule, both of their parents work, and delegate to them a weighty part of the household chores, including care of the youngest children. It is for this reason, it seems to me, that School No. 44's program is much less onerous than the one in my school in Lodz, and that we are given very little homework. Even Russian literature, which ought to have been a handicap to me, is studied here only in anthologies of selected pieces and not in the original works. In my parents' library I had had the opportunity to cover all the books listed in the syllabus and many more besides, from Dostoyevsky to Bunin. As for the famous political indoctrination that was talked about so much in Poland, I am obliged to note that none of Marx's writings circulates in School No. 44, not even *The Eighteenth Brumaire, The Civil War in France*, or other generally accessible works. All that we ever do is regurgitate in all its forms the *History of the CPSU (Bolsheviks)*.

In January 1941, at the end of term, I am awarded the title of *otlichnik*, the best pupil in the upper sixth form. A *lineika* is organized—a sort of school general assembly—and the head teacher, accompanied by the secretary of the Party organization, holds me up as a shining example, with a rain of praise that would have turned my head were it not that I understood that circumstances alone had made a model pupil of me. I accept, however, the responsibility of helping those who have fallen behind by working with them in the evenings. Klava is the first on this list because she has poor marks in physics and in Russian literature.

Klava is the most decorative girl in the class, with her even-featured face lit by lovely green eyes. To be really attractive, how-

ever, she would have to be taller and physically more mature—as is
the case already with some of her classmates. She still has the air of a
young girl, which doesn't incite a young man's thoughts to courtship.
I suppose that the head teacher of School No. 44 put me on the same
bench with her to show me that the sixth-form girls may be pretty, but
they are also very serious. He chose the one on whom he could rely
not to distract me from my duty, which was allegedly to make up for
lost ground in specifically Soviet matters. Recalling the many Western films that I saw in Lodz, I associate Klava with Rose Marie, a
"flower of the scented prairies," but, unlike the disconcerting
Jeanette MacDonald, she inspires only the most chaste of dreams.

Thus I go to her home without any ulterior motive; she lives in an
isolated wooden maisonette near the railroad station, a little similar to
but larger than that of the Tyumen railway worker. Klava has her own
room but she receives me in the dining room in the presence of her
parents, Emilyan and Maria, who remain patient and silent throughout our reading and discussions of texts. They are very courteous
toward me and always thank me for helping their only daughter (she is
the baby of the family, her three brothers having already left school),
but they do not seem willing to leave me alone with her, even to study
the Fourierist utopias of Vera Pavlovna, the protagonist of Cherny-
shevsky's *What Is to Be Done?*

Curiously, the prohibition on our being alone together applies only
under her roof, for in other circumstances Klava often comes with me
as far as the tramway and we sometimes go to the movies or theater
together. What, then, is the meaning of this partial surveillance?
Klava thinks she is explaining everything with a single phrase when
she says, *"Ya Cosachka"* ("I am a Cossack"). She seems neither
proud nor ashamed of this fact, but she thinks that I ought to understand what it signifies, since my parents, in their time, lived in the
"special region of the army of the Don." Originally nomadic horsemen, the Cossacks were given an entire territory that became famous
for its autonomy, its atamans (chieftains) who resided in Novocherkassk, and for its unique customs. That was a long time ago,
however, and the storm of the October Revolution ought not merely to

have swept away the privileges and the artificial status of this former Czarist praetorian guard, but also to have changed their habits of mind. Why should a young girl like Klava feel herself to be different in a society that has overturned everything and that has been constructing the future for the past quarter of a century?

I can't criticize her on this subject; she doesn't claim anything, but merely alerts me to a fact. On the other hand, in my class, Arkady and Alexander in particular have already drummed into me their theories concerning the Cossacks' superiority over the Russians, and still more over the Ukrainians, whose plain inferiority has been generally acknowledged since the dawn of time. At first I even believed that they weren't being serious because the Cossacks satisfied none of the criteria used by Stalin in *The National Question* to define a nation: Didn't they speak the same language as the Russians, and didn't they belong historically to the same culture and to the same territory? But when I ask Arkady politely, "Okay, you are the strongest, but tell me, how do you tell yourselves apart from others?" he replies proudly, "Simple; any fucker off the streets can become Russian, but to be a Cossack of the Don, you have to be born one."

I encounter the myth of privileges inherited at birth not just among the Cossacks; my own family in Rostov has some similar surprises in store for me. Aunt Lisa's sister, Raya, is older than she, and has an even poorer memory. Her husband, David, who is also retired, is short and bald; neither of them recalls having received a letter from me sent from Lvov. It is not important now, since, according to General Stepan, they have simply to supply me with an address for Ivanov of the NKVD. Otherwise, they live frugally and have few resources; they can neither put me up nor help me financially. In any case, they are not to find out about how I have come to Rostov, or that I receive a monthly money order from relatives in Moscow.

Despite his short memory with respect to the mail, Uncle David remembers an old, still-unsettled score with my father. You would even think that he has been awaiting my arrival for a quarter of a century to get it off his chest, and so he attacks me on the theme, "Your father is not a good Jew." He accuses him of having sold his

soul to the *goyim* of Finland (for whose stationery industry he had
apparently acted as the representative in South Russia). My father
had thus betrayed the mission that God had assigned to the Jewish
people. If you were to believe Uncle David on the matter, my father's
current misfortunes in Lodz, like his earlier loss of wealth, were the
direct reward of treason, and proof that God didn't easily forgive.

This notion of a "chosen people" seems to me an abstraction at
least as strange as that of the would-be heirs of the Cossacks, but it is
absolutely impossible to discuss this with Uncle David. This pious
little man places himself on the transcendental biblical terrain and
doesn't want to understand that real Jews like those of Lodz or Lebedovka, divided among innumerable spiritual families and political
tendencies, cannot, in terms of simple logic, accomplish all together
a single and identical mission ordained by God.

After this dialogue of the deaf I decide to speak with his daughter
Genia, who works at the Karl Marx Library and who is always extremely kind to me; she even bends the rules a little to allow me to
take books home. When I press her to comment on the zealous
religiosity and excessive Judaism of her parents, she finds, like the
Cossacks, no argument other than that of birth: "You can't understand these things, for you were born into a family of atheists."

The problem of my origins, which preoccupied me very little until
then, acquires a fresh relevance in Rostov when I see Pudovkin's film
on Suvorov. When the Czarist hangman Suvorov in this grade-B
movie is acclaimed by his troops to the cry of *"Slava, slava, slava
Warszawa, slava, slava, slava Ismail!"* ("Glory, glory, glory for Warsaw, glory, glory, glory for Ismail!") I find that it is too much to
stomach. Let him glorify this butcher for other victories—and it is a
shame that Pudovkin does it at all—but not for having crushed the
rising of a people fighting for its freedom from the enormous empire of
the Czars! And suddenly, despite my internationalist and Russophile
education, I say to myself, "These Russians are bastards to make
films like this." The same night Sister Kunegunda comes and repeats
to me in my dream, *"Badz Polakiem! Badz Polakiem!"* ("Be Polish!")

On waking, I am pervaded by an infinite sadness. How is it that the old rivalries persist in this society where there are no longer either capitalists or landowners, but Russians against Cossacks, Jews against Poles, each with their own mission, the result of which is always to denigrate, always to despise the others? Thus I am in the throes of a crisis of national identity when the cuckold militiaman in whose house I am living interrupts my reflections. I cry out too much in Polish during the night, he says. I like it better that way; if I shout in Russian, he would have a fine report to make on my negative attitude toward the "great Suvorov."

Joining the Komsomol was the key event of my life during my year in Rostov. It played a determining role in my future career in the Red Army, and even in my first loves. I have therefore never underestimated or forgotten what the *Komsomolski billet* brought me, this membership card whose very name seems to contain the promise of a ticket for a voyage.

At the beginning of February 1941, in the middle of a German lesson, the *Partorg* (the secretary of the Communist Party branch at the school) sends for me with an urgent message. The *Partorg*, whose name is Borisov, is a man of considerable importance and he occupies an office that is larger than the teachers' staff room. Loyal to tradition, he always dresses in the Bolshevik style: a *cosovorotka*—a long shirt worn over the trousers with a belt—and army boots. To understand his importance, you need only meditate on the slogan that adorns the walls of our town: "Let Us Close Ranks Around the Glorious Bolshevik Party, the Steely Nucleus of the Soviet People." The *Partorg* is a particle of this nucleus, illuminated by Stalin, "our sun," around which, as in the solar system, the planets called NKVD or Komsomol revolve.

The *Partorg* can send for whomever he wishes, whenever he likes. He explains to me that, having followed my school career closely, he knows I can skip a German lesson without difficulty. (The Wehrmacht jail wasn't entirely useless.) He talks about my excellent grades and then informs me that it is usual for students who place first in their classes to join the Komsomol. He understands, however, that I am still unfamiliar with the customs, but doesn't interpret unfavorably my apparent lack of zeal. The enthusiasm that I show in my studies sufficiently demonstrates that I am animated by a noble ideal, he says, and that I aspire to serve the socialist Fatherland and the great Stalin. He has no doubt that my place is firmly in the Komsomol, and has already arranged everything so that I can join with a minimum of fuss. Every candidate needs two sponsors, and he hands me an application for membership signed by himself and by the *Komsorg* (the secretary of the Komsomol), whose name is Soburov, nicknamed "the Blond" because of his fair hair. It only remains for me to thank him because, if the procedure now appears to me to be somewhat expeditious, I am not any the less flattered by the praise heaped on me by this member of the "steely nucleus" and by the confidence that he shows in me. I tell myself that perhaps he is right after all, and that my good grades must have a political significance that I have somehow overlooked because of my ideological immaturity.

While escorting me back to my class, the *Partorg* gives me some advice: I am to memorize the regulations of the Komsomol, and to follow national and international affairs closely because my application for membership, once approved by the relevant committee of this organization, has to be ratified by an assembly of all Komsomol members in our school, and on this occasion the candidate is often asked questions to check the level of his ideological formation. Convinced that I will pass this test, he nevertheless alerts me to possible pitfalls. Only ten days remain before the general assembly.

The worst of idlers wouldn't have needed more than half a day to assimilate the little book of statutes explaining the rights and duties of a Young Communist. Therefore I devote myself entirely to a more attentive reading of the Soviet press—which is, in any case, the only means of following the news.

Now *Molot* as well as *Pravda* have agreeable surprises in store: I learn that German air raids over England are declining, that fewer and fewer towns are being bombed, while Luftwaffe losses are mounting; and that in Africa it is the British who are making clear progress in Cyrenaica—a name that means nothing to me—and especially in

Abyssinia,* which instantly reminds me of my past in Lodz. It happens that I am very attached to this country because I cut my first political teeth, as it were, on the occasion of the demonstrations organized in my hometown against the invasion of Haile Selassie's empire by Fascist Italy. The entire left, for once, was unanimous in protesting this act of aggression: my social-democratic mother, my Communist brother, my dear geography teacher at the high school who was so impassioned that he would drop whatever material he was supposed to be teaching in order to talk to us at length about this proud African country attacked in such cowardly fashion by the Fascists and abandoned by the European Pontius Pilates.

In 1941 the English, it seems to me, are finally making amends for their crimes of default in 1935, when the League of Nations voted sanctions against Italy, without ever succeeding in having them enforced. Better still, I am pleased to discover a short dispatch on the inside back page of *Molot*, announcing that British troops are being actively aided by Abyssinian partisans in their march on Addis Ababa. On the other hand, I am not blind to the historical misdeeds of Great Britain in Africa, to a colonial past that would allow one to interpret England's landing in Ethiopia as an episode in the struggle between imperialists for the division of the colonies. Something tells me—I don't know what—that it is on this point that I am going to be questioned, and so, considering that the subject is at once delicate and symbolic, I draft a very personal and emotionally charged exposé, as if, before going to the Komsomol, I would have to learn a text by heart each time.

The candidates for membership—there are about twenty of us— are not admitted to the plenary session right away. We have to wait in the antechamber until the meeting goes through its agenda and comes to "any other business." Only then are we summoned one by one, and those who are accepted as members are asked to remain in the hall when they return from the assembly. I am among the first to be called,

* The name used by the Italians for the Ethiopian Empire, which allowed them to speak of "the Abyssinians" as a people without either a history or a right to independent existence.

and I head with a firm step for the platform, where, besides some Komsomols from my school, several representatives of the GORKOM (Urban Committee) are seated. Among those present I recognize many faces, some of them very young—one can join the Komsomol starting at fourteen years of age—who look at me with a certain respect. Wishing to save as much time as possible for the discussion on Abyssinia or any other such theme chosen by my examiners, I make my declaration of adherence quite brief. But the problem of Abyssinia interests no one, and I am asked only two elementary questions about the number of medals that have been awarded to the Komsomol, before a vote of raised hands decides in favor of my membership. In less than five minutes I have become a member of the Leninist Communist Youth of the Soviet Union. For the other candidates, matters don't drag either; some of them go through it even more quickly than I do, and in the space of an hour, the Komsomol has been enlarged by a score of new members. The next day *Molot* honors us with a report: Its columns explain that the tremendous élan of Soviet youth, just at the very time of the forthcoming Red Army holiday, pushes the best of them to rally to the ranks of Communist youth.

On the eve of the five-kilometer march planned in homage to our army, the wind from the Don stops blowing and there is a thaw that is very unusual at this time of year. We set out, therefore, in snow that has become a kind of muddy soup, in rows of four, singing "If war should come tomorrow . . . ," but after half an hour of it our shoes are completely soaked, and here and there, you can start to see gaps in our columns: Komsomols or not, certain comrades cut their losses and take French leave. Despite wanting to show my mettle with all my heart, I manage with great difficulty to get only just beyond the tank-shaped theater in the center of town. I don't feel I have the strength to go as far as Rosselmach, the factory where the march is supposed to finish. I have a bad conscience about deserting, but it is not a sports club that I have just joined, and this march could not in any way be seen as the test of my worth to the Komsomol. How many, in any case, stayed until the end? The next day *Molot* publishes only one photo of the march, taken as we were about to set off when we were still very numerous; Klava believes she can recognize me in this crowd, and thinks that I ought to keep the newspaper photo, which she has cut out as a souvenir.

Despite my not having finished the march, I am a very good Komsomol because I like to hang around in the GORKOM premises, where, after classes, one meets pupils from other schools and even young workers, all of them *udarniki,* "the workers' vanguard." Thus do I profitably enlarge my circle of acquaintances. I refuse no task, I spend time at the House of Pioneers—a large palace at the center of the Sadovaya. I help to organize cultural activities, such as film shows for our school, or outings to theater performances. I am quickly promoted, becoming a member of Komsomol committees in my school and then in the neighborhood, and I am well liked at the GORKOM. Obviously the Komsomol secretary in a large town like Rostov is too busy to chatter with a young man like me, but I am sure that without my knowing it, he follows my work closely, just as the *Partorg* at School No. 44 had done before I was acclaimed as first in my class.

What worries me is that Motya seems to suspect me of being some sort of careerist. Not that he says anything to offend me; on the contrary, my attempts to discipline the "pioneers," youngsters less than fourteen years old, make him burst out laughing, and even the beautiful but reticent Clarissa jokes once or twice on this subject. Motya insists on the priority that I ought to give to the sciences, and his words seem to me to be laden with implications: "It's the best career for you," he repeats, as if he fears that I might become a Komsomol official.

There is obviously no question of it in my view, but at the approach of the end of the school year the problem of each person's vocation urgently presents itself. In the USSR, all the higher-education establishments do not enjoy the same status. The degree of state subsidy varies greatly, as does the quality of the refectories and student accommodations provided. In certain schools, the *otlichniki* are accepted without examination; in others, the mere fact of being an *otlichnik* or even of having a recommendation from the Komsomol is not sufficient. At the Mifli, the Moscow Institute of Philosophy, Literature, and History, and its Leningrad homologue, the Lifli, for example, competition is obligatory, even after a preliminary selection. Russians have a mania for abridging the names of their institutions and the titles of their functionaries that sometimes baffles the novice, but the *Komsorg* ("the Blond" from the color of his hair) explains to me that the Mifli and the Lifli are formidable universities; if you succeed in getting into them, you have it made for life. I continue to promise Motya that I will go to his faculty of sciences at Rostov, but the name Mifli rings in my ears as if it were the name of a pretty girl. Moreover, if I were to pass the entrance examination to the Mifli, I could go back to my Aunt Lisa's. I would like to see then the expression on the face of my cousin who had made the figure zero with his fingers to show what little chance I had of obtaining permission to live in Moscow!

Today, when I recall these youthful plans that occupied my mind during the last spring of peacetime in Rostov, I realize that no one was really expecting the German attack, no one thought that war was imminent. It is striking that a country so seriously threatened as was the USSR had done nothing to prepare the opinion of its people for such a calamity. We were led to believe to the very last that the conflict then raging in Europe, Africa, and China didn't concern us, as though we were assured of following it from afar, merely as spectators. In my own case, having counted on the war to make it possible for me to rejoin my family, I had been deluded by this soothing atmosphere. I had decided that I would first bring my studies to a brilliant conclusion at the Mifli or in Rostov, and only then would I try to find my mother. I imagined that she would be proud of my diplomas. My main worry, in the midst of this collective myopia, was that my anti-Communist mother would not be very pleased to learn that I was now a member in good standing of the Komsomol.

For Alexander Blok, the greatest Russian poet of this century, according to Motya, Russia is a land of *taina*—secrets or mystery— now a sphinx of many faces, now a world hidden behind "its girdle of rivers and encircled by its forests." On this day, June 22, 1941, however, toward midday, upon hearing Molotov announce the news of the German attack, the USSR chiefly gives the impression of a giant transfixed by fear. You might say that even its rivers stop flowing for a time, that nothing moves in its forests and that the only perceptible trickling sound is that of the tears that flow down the cheeks of Blok's imaginary sphinx. The Soviet people have been living as if anesthetized since the signing of the pact with Hitler's Reich, put to sleep by their own leaders, who repeated to them just ten days before the start of hostilities that the Nazis would respect their treaty commitment to refrain from any aggression. Nothing gave anyone cause to suspect an immediate contest. The war seemed to be far away, and without any relation to the current of affairs.

Yet here is Molotov suddenly speaking about a real war, and denouncing Hitler because he didn't declare it in good and proper form and because, without warning, he has had fifty Soviet towns and cities bombed. Next, in order to explain our troops' retreat, he informs us in his dreary official's voice that the Germans have concentrated 170 (or even more, I no longer remember) of their best divisions along our frontiers, without counting their gigantic air force, which is saturating our airspace. And our leaders? How is it that they haven't had the foresight to prevent the arrival of this fantastic army at our doors? And Stalin? Too many questions assail our minds for Molotov's final promise—"the enemy will be crushed, our cause is just and we shall conquer"—to be credible. People who, like me, hear his speech broadcast in the street, disperse without any commentary, without offering each other a single word of hope. Convinced as I am of the ineluctable defeat of Hitler, I nevertheless hear, behind the music of the "Internationale," the sober voice of Blok's "Guardian Angel" as recited by Motya: "Is the fire or the mist before us? Are we going to perish? Are we going to die?"

In the days following the German attack, the official decrees multiply and the men set off. There is a general mobilization; all wireless sets are confiscated (they are to be handed in to the militia within twenty-four hours); a war directorate presided over by Stalin is formed in Moscow; and a "Sovinformbureau" is established to relay the communiqués of our military high command. Motya is one of the first to leave, and at the station I witness the heartrending lamentations of women who accompany their nearest and dearest, as if these were to be definitive adieux. Mysterious Russia, sphinxlike, has a presentiment already, perhaps, that she will obtain victory at the price of twenty million dead, and she weeps for them in advance.

Then finally on July 3, 1941, Stalin speaks. He addresses us as "brothers and sisters." It is the most remarkable speech of his career, the only really moving one, and it reaches straight to the heart. Later, at the time of the Twentieth Party Congress in 1956, Khrushchev will say that he had been skeptical, and allege that since he was the only one able to speak, Stalin had no merit even on this occasion. It is a mistake, though, to judge people as all black or all white; I have never written anything whatever to extol Stalin, but I maintain without hesitation that his speech of July 3 was a masterpiece, better than Churchill's "blood and tears" speech, because I saw with my own eyes how it raised the morale of a whole country, and mine in particular.

Some who heard it on good wireless sets, and not like me in the street, would later allege (during the Khrushchev era) that Stalin was so terrified that at times you could hear his teeth chattering. But perhaps it isn't such a bad thing to know that the Supreme Commander-in-Chief shares your sentiments. It makes him more human and brings him closer to his people. It was the technique used by Roosevelt in his famous "fireside chats"; in order to be understood, you have to enter the homes of your listeners, sit at their tables, be one of them. Although I personally didn't hear Stalin's teeth chatter, if they did I'm sure it was done to better convince us that he was one of us. And it worked. From this day forth, all of Russia appears to unite to make war.

What does he say to reassure us, to reassure me? Nothing very original. He explains, arguing from history, that there is no such thing as an invincible army, and that Hitler's army will be beaten as Napoleon's had been in another time. The parallel between these two invaders emerges bit by bit, didactically but discreetly, throughout his reasoning: The more the Wehrmacht penetrates into the immensity that is Russia, the more thoroughly it will be crushed. This time, though, it is not a matter of an ordinary war between two countries and two armies, but a trial of strength between two visions of the world; therefore the Red Army fights not only to defend its own soil, but for the freedom of all peoples who "groan under the yoke of German fascism." Ever since my crossing of the frozen Bug, I have been waiting to hear exactly that, no more and no less. Blok's poem "Guardian Angel" asks, "Shall we revive?" In my mind, as of July 3, the Soviet Union is already beginning to recover.

Toward the end of July, I leave with a brigade of Komsomols to help with the harvest in a *kolkhoz* near Salsk, six hours by train from Rostov, in the steppes of the Don region. The night is half gone by the time we are ready to leave Rostov's station. All the lights are switched off, and my comrades don't sing or even talk for fear the noise might draw German bombers down on us. It is an absurd fear, but I don't blame my companions; hadn't I, in 1939, seen a professional soldier order a peasant woman to strangle her child to keep it quiet? We leave in a blacked-out train in silence, like conspirators, and by the next morning we have already started work in one of the richest agricultural regions of the country.

There is only one older person among us—Grisha Voronov. His title in the GORKOM of the Komsomol is so long—*Zamzavkomprop*, assistant to the president of the propaganda committee—that it is silly to use it in daily relations with him. Among ourselves we call him simply "Senior," and we address him with the respect due to a superior. I am one of his four assistants, representing the former and prospective candidates for the baccalaureat at School No. 44, who form more than a third of our brigade. The Blond, the school *Komsorg*, is another of Senior's assistants.

My closest friends unfortunately haven't come with us; Misha has gone to work in a factory since his father was mobilized, and Klava has stayed at home with her parents, who have been badly shaken by the departure of their three sons. I would have preferred to go off with them myself, but no volunteers were being taken. Being too young in any case, my only chance of getting enlisted is through the help of the Komsomol. At the GORKOM I have been promised that my case will be examined on my return from the *kolkhoz*, when I will at least have crossed the threshold of my seventeenth birthday (August 4) and given proof of my political capacities.

Which is to say that I take my role in the brigade very seriously. Resolved upon conducting myself like a man of steel, as a fit compatriot and heir of Felix Dzerzhinksy, I am obliged to admit, less than a week after our arrival, that I am not of this stamp of men. It is a young literature student, Olga Alexeyevna Spodina, who, by her sudden— although very agreeable—entrance into my life shows me that it is illusory to sketch great plans in Russia without taking account of the amorous designs of Russian women.

Olga is not as pretty as the blond-haired woman of martial aspect in Moscow, and she has neither Clarissa's elegance nor her class. Her gait can appear clumsy or peasantlike, the more so as she always runs about barefoot, without worrying much about the details of her clothes. She has a snub nose, which can often displease—"an acquired taste," as my friend Kola will say to me later. Finally, her resounding laugh is almost embarrassingly loud. Nevertheless, there is not a man in the brigade or among the *kolkhozniki* who, when she appears, doesn't stare at her as she goes by. And this tall blond girl doesn't lower her eyes before their unabashed stares. She seems quite sure of herself, and capable of defending herself in any circumstances.

One evening, Senior summons her in front of the small executive committee that manages the brigade's affairs, to talk to her about both her lack of enthusiasm at work and her occasional absenteeism. Senior isn't really a bad sort. He is thirty years old, a graduate of some obscure history institute; he knows how to involve us in making decisions, but he is tiresome and complicates matters by stuffing his already slow sentences with quotations from Stalin that everyone knows by heart. Instead of saying "Okay, Olya [the diminutive of

Olga], what's going on?" he starts with the stiff and formal "Comrade Olga Alexeyevna Spodina," and then cites Stalin on the need to abandon the "insouciance" of peacetime and to organize one's work in awareness of the danger, in military fashion. "I am not insouciant," she replies with aplomb. "I'm not feeling well. I was badly sunburned yesterday and it left me feeling terrible."

Senior launches off again, without acrimony, into an interminable speech on the war, the enemy's atrocities, the duties of Komsomols, and a string of verities having no connection at all with sunburn. Olga listens, calm and distant. Her blue eyes wander across our faces as if to gauge our disposition toward her. Then she takes us all by surprise. "If the comrades of the committee don't want to believe me, they have only to look." And, quickly, she removes the bodice of her dress. "Touch my back," she says to me, "it's on fire."

In principle, the suggestive power of striptease is based on the slow quality of the movements. We are also accustomed to seeing girls in their bras, because it is very hot at this time of year and many comrades work with their blouses off. Nevertheless, Olga's sudden gesture has an overwhelming effect on me. Even before touching her shoulders, I think I can feel their heat.

"Obviously she can't work in the sun in this state. Go on home, Olga, and when you are better you will return to the fields." I say this with an air of authority, even though nothing authorizes me to make such a decision. No one contradicts me, though, and Olga, as calm as can be, takes all the time in the world to readjust her bodice and to say good-bye to each of us. As she shakes my hand, she sketches the merest smile of gratitude, which makes me melt even more. I have an irresistible desire to leave with her, to accompany her, to try my chances with her. But you don't leave a meeting like that, especially in my situation, when my military future depends on my good leadership record.

The rest of the meeting is all the more difficult. Senior lectures another comrade who is supposed to have tormented some bulls with blows from a pitchfork in order to get them to run, and is even said to have organized a cart race, to the great indignation of the kolkhozniki.

The accused defends himself badly, alleging that he has to arrive as quickly as possible at scattered work sites, which, in this enormous *kolkhoz*, are often very far apart. He claims he has done no harm to these stupid animals, which understand perfectly well when the *kolkhozniki* order them to the left or to the right, but which remain deaf to our orders, except when we prod them gently in the backsides. Who could possibly be interested in this interminable discussion on bovine intelligence when he thinks he has a semi-rendezvous with the fair-haired Olga?

Around midnight the meeting finally breaks up, and we go our separate ways. Olga doesn't live at the school but, like nearly all the girls, with a private family. To find her I would need a personal radar. In Poland, in the villages, each farm is clearly recognizable: The enclosures are never identical, the stables and granaries vary in shape and size, thus there are plenty of markers to guide you. Here, the same bare maisonette, without either granary or stable, duplicates another similar maisonette one hundred meters farther on, all of them in confusion, and there are no streets. I walk at random in the silence of the village, convinced that even if by some miracle I manage to remember where Olga has been lodged, she will surely be fast asleep at this time of night, exhausted from sunstroke.

Suddenly, Olga emerges from the darkness, and slips her arm under mine. "I knew that you would come. No, this way. Let's get away from the village."

With more expert hands than mine she takes all the initiatives. When finally the time comes for talk, she manages a flattering reproach: "Is that how you get to know each other in Poland?"—as though she hadn't noticed that I have just tasted the pleasures of the flesh for the first time, in this haystack she has picked out. I play along and proclaim that it is not Polish habit but rather her exceptional beauty and her frankness that have moved me to act so boldly and that explain why I feel so happy in her arms. But, persuaded that my body has had nothing to do with my good fortune, I admit my astonishment at having seduced her so rapidly. Is it to thank me for my decision at the meeting that she has given herself to me, or because I am a member of the committee? "You please me because you aren't like the others," she says simply. "Our men are thick brutes [*grubyé*], and drunkards as well; you are different, subtle."

The next day, on an oxcart, forgetting the comrades who surround me and even forgetting the war, I can't refrain from an immense smile of satisfaction at the thought that I have the most beautiful girl in the brigade. I no longer doubt that it is I who have conquered her, and I strut about it to the point of crowing. Astonished at my obvious joy, the others ask me what has happened, and I hide behind the first excuse that comes to mind: it is "something I can't talk about."

At the end of three or four days, however, the entire brigade knows about it. It is partly the result of communal life, and perhaps also partly a result of Olga's free and easy manner; she still pretends to be ill, and I can't resist the temptation to worry about (and to ask after) her health, even during the day. In fact, Olga likes to sew and she does a lot of small jobs for her friends, repairing clothes they have torn, for they are unused to working in the fields and often tear skirts and bodices. It is obvious that she prefers to work at home, and this suits everyone—except Senior. Nevertheless, I hear the others sing behind my back the well-known lyric from a Tchaikovsky opera: "I love you, Olga! I love you, Olga!" Or perhaps *"Za Rodinu, Za Spodinu!"* ("To the fight for the Fatherland, to the fight for Spodina!"—whereas, in the song, the words are "to the fight for Stalin!").

My authority is clearly eroding, although Senior has said nothing and I miss out on none of my duties. It is true that I no longer think of anything but Olga. Not only do I have her "under my skin," as they say, but her personality and ideas fascinate me. She is lively and observant, and talks easily and well: "The Komsomol is not a monastery; nowhere is it written that we are a religious order," she says to me categorically, when I confide to her my fears about having problems because of us. "Don't let yourself be contaminated by these hypocrites who pretend to live only for the Party; my father is one of them. If I had ten rubles for every time that he was unfaithful to my mother, I would be a millionaire in the land of the Soviets."

Suddenly everything comes to a head. Senior calls a general as-

sembly early one morning to tell us that our work will be remuner-
ated, even though we are volunteers. He puts me in charge of a
commission that, with the help of the *kolkhoz* accountant, will determine the rewards of each person and the method of payment in
agricultural products. Expressions of joy are widespread; in these bad
times, flour, corn, and eggs will make valuable and unexpected
presents for the families back in Rostov. Olga applauds too, but at the
moment of the final hurrah her enthusiasm singularly dries up as
Senior adds in a deadpan voice a postscript on loafers, such as
Comrade Spodina, for example, who think they are on vacation. All
eyes turn toward her as if expecting a contrite self-criticism, but Olga
refuses to get riled; she seems invulnerable. "Have me summoned to
the committee this evening," she whispers to me before we separate
for the day.

Confused, I turn for help to the Blond, because I haven't the
courage to confront Senior alone; nor do I have the power to summon
Olga on my own initiative to attend a meeting of our committee. The
Blond is not a friend; we have never associated, even at School No.
44, but as one of my "sponsors" at the time I joined the Komsomol,
his interest in my good conduct coincides with mine. I find him near
one of those giant combines made at Rosselmach, which reap the
corn magnificently while creating a great cloud of dust, but which
also often break down. We sit down at the edge of the field as if to
discuss business; I tell him about my liaison with Olga, and ask for
his help to summon her the same evening. He doesn't answer immediately.

"Listen," he says finally, "you have adapted yourself well among
us, you are already one of us. But with us, nothing is ever guaranteed. The least false step can compromise everything. I advise you to
drop Olga, since she will only create problems for you. She is an
individualist and pigheaded. She thinks also that she has the right to
choose whichever man she wants. With us, things don't happen like
that. The last thing you want to do is link yourself with her in a battle
with an official like Senior. Especially not you!"

It is a harsh recall to reality and no doubt timely. The Blond is right, perhaps, to think of me as not quite like the others, but after what Olga has told me of the hypocrisy of the organization men, of the "steely nucleus," I don't consider for a moment behaving like them. It is not a question of love but of dignity. "Please, I beg you, summon her." He shrugs his shoulders: "Okay, but watch out or women will be the end of you." The Blond tosses off this bitter prediction clearly without any malice, but the future will show that he is no more of a prophet than the functionary in Lvov who announced that I would never join the Komsomol. My Russian girlfriends, far from leading me to my ruin, were more than once to give me a helping hand in difficult moments ahead.

That evening, toward the end of another tedious committee meeting, Olga enters the little room where we are gathered. She looks pleased with herself, almost gay. She greets us in turn and chatters away about the weather as if to excite our impatience. She has dressed to effect this evening, and has even put on high-heeled shoes in order not to appear in a position of inferiority before this men-only tribunal. I have the impression that she has calculated everything, that she is conscious of being more beautiful and disquieting than ever, but I still don't understand what she hopes to achieve by it.

To Senior she says, as if in passing, "You reprimanded me this morning in the middle of a full assembly. Yet didn't you agree, the other day, that I shouldn't have to work for a few days? You will kindly give me the satisfaction of removing this extract from the minutes of the assembly, because I refuse to accept an undeserved reprimand in my dossier."

Senior, who always speaks slowly, on this occasion puts strange spaces between each of his words: There is a war going on, entire regions of our country are devastated, and Stalin has alerted us against carelessness at work or work carried out without enthusiasm. She listens, smiling, almost amused.

"You haven't answered my question, Comrade *Zamzavkomprop* Grigori Vassilyevich Voronov. Yes or no, did you exempt me from work for a few days?"

This time Senior replies more rapidly: "I am not answerable to you."

"Ah! I see," she says, laughing, "you are directly answerable only to Moscow. To whom, then, tell me if you please, to Stalin or to Mikhailov [the Secretary General of the Komsomol]? So you don't condescend to discuss with the simple comrades at the base, is that right? We shall see, we shall soon see about that when we get back to Rostov."

Olga is tough, no doubt about it, but I tell myself that she must have more than one trick up her sleeve, and that her father, whether a hypocrite or not, probably occupies a post that counts in the Party.

I try to rush to Olga's aid, ready to testify that her back is peeling like a baked apple and that by sewing at home she performs a much greater service to the brigade than by sorting out grain in the sun; but the Blond stops me:

"Come, now. Let's not fight among ourselves. Our country is at war. Go back to work starting tomorrow, Olga, even if you aren't completely cured, and everything will be forgotten. If you agree, the comments by Grisha will have no need to figure in the minutes of the assembly, and there will be no reprimand."

We adopt this suggestion almost without discussion, and all of us leave together, good friends. And to put an end to any secrecy, Olga takes me by the arm and leads me quietly away. "It was terrific of you to get me called this evening. In fact I don't give a damn about their reprimand, but I don't like their digs below the belt; don't let them walk over you, that's my principle."

Our precarious idyll will continue until the end of the stay on the farm. Olga works in the kitchen, and in the evening she transforms my old trousers into a bag to carry all the provisions I receive as payment. Since I have no family, she will carry double portions to her parents. Or at least, so we thought; in fact, no one will carry off any of their earnings in nature's currency to Rostov. In the course of a final general assembly, Senior "suggests" to us that we contribute it all to the Red Army supply stocks. "It's decided unanimously, then," he announces officially, without having consulted anyone, not even our little directorate committee. These Russians definitely haven't got many democratic habits, I decide, and their manner of imposing things is even stupid, for it removes all motivation from people. After all, the majority of us would surely have supported a last-minute patriotic resolution and we wouldn't be left with this bitter taste of having been fooled by false promises. Olga laughs at my disappointment: "We've ruined your trousers for nothing, but don't worry, you will receive a diploma of merit." I don't find it funny at all. Back in Rostov we hardly see each other again, since she lives at the other end of town and even to meet is a problem. It is out of the question for me to go to her home or for her to come to my little room in the militiaman's house.

For its part, the GORKOM of the Komsomol is as good as its word and obtains a post for me in the political services of the Soviet air force. The date of my departure is not yet fixed, but already thoughts of Olga have begun to fade. Anyway, didn't she tell me herself, at the outset, that our affair wasn't destined to last?

I remember Olga, however, because of a subsequent episode that occurred after the war, in 1945 or 1946. After having been deported to Germany during the Nazi occupation of Rostov in 1942, she was placed on her return to Russia in a "verification-of-identity camp" near Rostov. Although the camp was really quite close, she didn't have the right to come to town. One of her friends, a former member of our brigade, contacted me to ask me to go and see her, without specifying a reason. As I was married at the time, I needed to deal tactfully with my wife; my approaching departure for Poland was enough of a strain on her. And because Olga had been deported against her will and hadn't gone to Nazi Germany to volunteer to help Hitler, I believed that her release was imminent. Any bureaucratic problems that remained could be cleared up on the spot, in Rostov. I decided not to see her, and didn't think any more about it.

Later, once I had come to the West, when I discovered that the so-called verification camps had been only a way station for the majority of former deportees or prisoners of war before their wholesale deportation to the Gulag, Olga's message took on quite another meaning. Perhaps she wanted me to see her not in memory of our old affair, but to enlist my help in escaping the tragedy that she alone knew she was facing, since neither myself nor my friends in Rostov had imagined it for a moment.

I don't know if I could have helped her, nor is it certain that she was a victim of the great wave of Stalinist deportations of the postwar period; I do know that I ought to have gone to see her, if only to honor the brief happiness she had given me during a summer of sweat and frolic in the fields and haystacks of a Soviet collective farm.

2

NIEVKA

When I return to Rostov in September 1941, the war seems quite distant. According to the Sovinformbureau communiqués, the Germans are stumbling about the Ukraine somewhere, far away, and will be forced to revise their plans because of the unexpected resistance of the Red Army. Nevertheless, Rostov begins to empty surreptitiously, shamefully, without any explicit evacuation orders. The mounting exodus is enough to persuade me that Rostov is going to fall, and to sap my morale while awaiting official word of my departure for military service. The Red Army has apparently abandoned the idea of halting the Germans' advance along the Don, one of the Soviet Union's most imposing natural defenses. Where, then, will they be stopped? On the Volga? In the Urals?

People, although visibly concerned, don't talk openly about their fears. "Defeatist" talk is forbidden in any case, and wouldn't help them one iota. Discussions center instead on the problems of food supply—an inevitable subject. Supplies pose insoluble problems because the rations bureau is proving incapable of distributing the available products fairly. Some people manage to get their provisions almost entirely from the state shops, but many others, in spite of having lined up for hours at a stretch, leave empty-handed. For these unfortunates the only recourse is the *kolkhoz* market, where prices defy imagination: The price of a kilo of bread is equivalent to a skilled worker's earnings for a week's work, and costs are spiraling upward. After three months of war the USSR thus settles into a double economy on a massive scale (which persists even today): The first, official, rather inexpensive, but marked by a penury of goods; the second, parallel to the first, better supplied and without restrictions as to how much you can buy, but characterized by galloping inflation.

Nor is it the only novelty to emerge. In the shadow of this exodus that refuses to speak its name, trafficking of all kinds thrives: Looking after Number One is raised to the dignity of a general rule. Thus it is, for example, that Olga's father is evacuated along with his organization—and his latest mistress—while his wife and daughter remain behind, "for the moment." The *kolkhoz* market and the flea market experience considerable growth, creating an outlet for a great many entrepreneurial talents hitherto repressed. Small dealers buy, at low prices, the goods of those in a hurry to leave, and resell them calmly at a large markup to those who stay behind. One would have to be blind not to see that there is something suspicious in these deals, but the authorities close their eyes to them. Indeed, preoccupied with their own powerlessness in the face of the problem of supplies, they appear to encourage such practices.

Even in normal times, Rostov at night offered nothing to write home about; now its nightlife is practically extinct. As soon as the sun goes down, the town plunges into darkness and silence, and its avenues recall the streets of the Middle Ages emptied by plague.

Silence has also fallen on the cuckold militiaman's small apartment. In the room that a simple curtain separates from mine, all bustle has ceased. The militiaman and his rival are no longer there, having been impartially called up by the army on the same day. Their wife and lover, Maria Pavlovna, known as Moussia, spends her days out of doors. She has decided to make a career in the black market. In the evenings, at a loss as to how to spend her time, she at first champs at the bit but gradually regains control of her own solitude—alongside of mine—in a kind of oriental meditation, almost without moving.

One day she remembers my presence and, poking her head around the curtain, asks me whether I have eaten. She then has the idea of taking me in on half-board; in exchange she asks me for only a trifling additional contribution based on prewar prices. How can one refuse such a godsend? In accepting, however, I am half terrified by the fear that this agitated woman has inspired in me for a year now. Finding myself alone with her each evening promises to be an unnerving experience.

Moussia shows her discernment by declaring from the outset that I am a "timid young fellow," and limits herself over the first two or three meals to asking my opinion of her cooking, which is excellent. Then, bit by bit, she begins to tell me about herself in a terribly intimate manner. In the course of these chats she reveals nothing less than the joys and miseries of an honest Russian woman who has been far too much in demand with men, constantly obliged to avoid the traps set by all those who only want her for her body. By her account, men have been running after her like madmen since she was a girl, even men in "high places" and the "well educated." All of them swear that they are ready to do anything for the love of her green eyes. If most of them were liars, she has known real passion with some, combining ruptures, reconciliations, suffering, and moments of exaltation. Her life has apparently been one long chain of amorous entanglements—now painful, now happy—eclipsing all the rest, notably her material difficulties and, obviously, politics.

I am somewhat taken aback, but the spontaneous confidences of this Soviet woman, if not of the same value as Hollywood romances, are not without interest. Moussia speaks of love as though it were a boxing match, but without a referee to penalize the opponents for any punches struck below the belt. She had barely turned fifteen when a supervisor in her factory "cornered" her and, being ignorant of the rules of the game, she had let herself be abused. Since then, being better armed and having learned to calculate her distance and to counterattack, she had learned how to "neutralize" far more imposing adversaries. In her husband, the militiaman, she recognizes a loyal combatant, a regular guy who is really attached to her. That goes also for her current lover, a good man who, without her, would have foundered in misfortune and vodka. In this three-cornered match, however, it is she who runs the show, dealing as best she can with each of her men.

All of these stories, punctuated by assorted stillbirths and abortions that she tells about matter-of-factly, leave me a little flabbergasted nonetheless, especially since Moussia doesn't have the physique that might have made them more plausible. Packed solidly on her short legs, "sweeping the floor with her backside," as she puts it, she is neither very pretty nor very carefully looked after; her modest budget does not allow her to aim for elegance. How is it that so many men have fallen "sick with love" for her? Is it the lot of all women? She admits having had more problems in this respect than other women. But these are things that can't be explained; it's a question of nature.

I don't count in this connection. She situates me in a sort of sexual no-man's-land; I am too young to be treated as a man. Moussia remains evasive about her own age, but that doesn't prevent me from making my own calculations: She is getting on, at least thirty. Nothing, therefore, can happen between us; and after each dinner, I withdraw behind the curtain.

It was only much later—she was then far away—that the idea scrambled up the staircase of my mind that Moussia had actually tried to provoke me to behave with her "as a man." Certain of her gestures and words came back to me, prompting the disagreeable sensation of a "missed opportunity." In my dreams, images often appeared of Moussia and of our beds separated by a simple curtain, while Olga, with whom I had had a real affair, practically never entered them. From afar, Moussia punished me in this way for having doubted that men could desire her so much.

In September 1941, however, during our period of chaste companionship, the big problem remains the career that she pursues on the black market. For the first time in the USSR, I am living under the same roof in cordial complicity with someone who is breaking the law, albeit in a minor way. The bulk of Moussia's income derives from a percentage on the sale of new food ration cards, which one of her former suitors procures for her each week. She makes no secret of it. On the contrary, the loyalty of her supplier consoles her: She can always count on those who, at some stage, have been "sick with love" for her. It is flagrantly obvious, though, that their joint venture is a straightforward offense; and each time Moussia speaks to me about it, I half picture a swarm of Siberian mosquitoes buzzing around her curly, chestnut-brown hair. (At the time I still believed that Western Siberia was the worst of punishment centers.)

To persuade her to give up a practice that I think is dangerous, I try to appeal to her conscience. Is she unaware of the plight of her fellow citizens who, armed with official food rationing cards and unable to find anything in the shops, haven't enough money to purchase provisions at the *kolkhoz* market? Or of the fact that the more surplus cards there are—those in particular that she and her accomplice are putting into circulation—the more people in Rostov suffer?

Moussia lets me have my say; a light smile forms comic little wrinkles only on the left side of her nose. Certainly, she says, she feels sorry for the unfortunates who cannot obtain their rations, but she calmly points out that all of this is a long-standing practice. In Russia, the people have been familiar with rationing since the beginning of time. With the exception of newcomers like me, people know very well from experience that a ticket represents the hope of a food ration, but that it doesn't in any way guarantee it. As to the food rationing cards, they represent a kind of supplementary currency that one uses at will. A citizen short of rubles has never hesitated to sell his monthly card, knowing he is perfectly free, some days later, to buy another, depending on availability. Sometimes he makes a small profit, since the price of cards fluctuates. Moussia even argues that the surplus cards that she puts onto the market tend to lower the prices. And when her supplier—who might be pressed for money— brings her a more voluminous packet of cards than usual, she even goes so far as to flood the market with cards at giveaway prices, thereby provoking a temporary collapse in the going price, from which all buyers gain a profit. Therefore, she performs a genuine service. In any case, she adds, her customers come from all walks of life—even men in uniform. Her conscience is easy.

Momentarily defeated, I remind her that she is the wife of a militia-man, a representative of socialist order. At this she laughs openly and wrinkles appear on both sides of her nose. First, she retorts, she married a man, not the militia; second, the members of the militia are just like everyone else; they don't hesitate to sell their ration cards, which, she remarks in passing, are not among those most sought after. "Here, we are all in the same boat, and that means you too. In this dinner we have just eaten, everything came from the black market. You knew that and yet it didn't cramp your appetite. Live like us, like we do, and you'll get by like the rest of us." She says it without any hint of reproach or anger, but she makes it very clear: Whatever I may think of it, she sees more of the black market in my future. I don't reply. She has a stronger stomach than I have for dealing with matters of social conscience.

In any case, our conversations end when I finally receive my orders to leave for military service in Kislovodsk. Moussia, deaf to the danger, has decided not to move. There is no way to make her change her mind. I haven't enough authority; I am only a youngster from the sexual no-man's-land. When I warn her that she is running the risk of suffering atrocities at the hands of the Germans, she replies very patriotically that Russians are the strongest of peoples precisely because they know how to suffer. Dear Moussia! At the time of my departure she refuses what I owe her in rent for the month of September, and secretly places some newly pressed underwear in my suitcase. I don't notice it until I arrive in Kislovodsk, and I am not too sure how to interpret the fact that she has systematically chosen it two sizes larger than mine.

We saw each other only once more, in 1944—at Rostov market, where else? Her house had been destroyed so she couldn't invite me to dinner, but she was now selling borscht instead of ration cards, and more than once she treated me to some while refusing payment. We chatted about this and that, and promised to arrange a proper evening together, at the earliest opportunity, to talk at greater length about our war years. The opportunity never arose. I know only that Moussia was furious at the Red Army, which hadn't granted a single furlough to either of "her men," both of whom were still living and burned with the desire to be reunited with her.

My adjustment to the Soviet armed forces was rather like my dinners with Moussia: apprehension followed by relaxation and contentment, and finally a certain frustration.

It is futile to dwell on my apprehension; everyone feels it at the moment when his life goes through a major upheaval. I needn't have worried. Everything went very well for me at Kislovodsk: rather agreeable company, decent food, indifferent but tolerable accommodations. Moreover, my tasks in the political department of the air force had to do with cultural activities and recreation rather than surveillance or indoctrination. I was among young people hardly older than myself, just out of sixth form or students in some cases, and all of them excited by the prospect of their future as pilots. My frustration derived from the fact that, for a "politico" like me, there could be no question of flying.

Everything started with my meeting with Andrei Byelokonyenko, my commissar. This former worker from the Ukraine, around forty years old, gave me the feeling from our first contact that my life in Kislovodsk would unfold beneath the sign of the unexpected and without an excessive amount of military rigor. He was rather thickset but taller than I, a robust, blond-haired man, graying at the temples. He read through my enthusiastic recommendations from the Komsomol without betraying the slightest interest, limiting himself to murmuring by way of welcome, "You will tell everyone here that you are twenty years old; we are not running a kindergarten." Next he shut his eyes, as if afflicted by the sight of me, or as if seized by an irresistible somnolence. Finally, at the end of several long minutes, he said, "Let's go to the park, I have to speak with you," and doubtless to make up for lost time, he hastily seized his peaked cap, hurried down the staircase, and broke into a kind of jog, marching at such a furious pace that I had difficulty keeping up with him. I heard him therefore mainly from behind, for he preceded me by a good meter.

It didn't bother him. He spoke, apparently, for himself, and talked of the trees and about Lermontov, pretending to situate, with a precision that is absent from the text, the actions of the protagonists of *A Hero of Our Time*. What could all this mean? Malicious tongues in the first squadron of the air force would tell me later that because he was an autodidact he liked to pass himself off as erudite, and that his strolls in the park were a Ukrainian style of coping with hangovers.

I didn't find this very convincing. In my view, our commissar's taste for Kislovodsk Park was perfectly justified. It is an incomparable spot, one of the marvels of Russia, a splendid sample of mountainous forest with waterfalls and even a river, preserved in the middle of a town. From the first day it took my breath away. To move at a stroke from the sad, wartime atmosphere of Rostov to this "pearl of the Northern Caucasus," and to have this singular military chief as a guide, seemed marvelous.

He explained that we belonged, as cadres of the political service, to a separate "vertical" structure, operating throughout the Soviet armed forces, but that at the same time we had to identify ourselves unreservedly with the branch to which we were attached and to share its esprit de corps. Though we might not be pilots, we were supposed to defend above all the honor of the air force. Even though Byelokonyenko was no expert on airplanes, he nevertheless knew enough about Soviet planning in this field to affect me greatly. My morale, which had been sagging in Rostov, suddenly became extremely buoyant. Since I am unable to recall exactly what he told me, I shall limit myself to recounting what I know today about the evolution of the Soviet air force in this period.

During the first three months of the war, each of the Soviet armies at the front, broadly speaking, exercised control over its air support, its armored divisions, and its artillery. With this unwieldy system a lot of planes were lost without striking a serious blow at the Nazis. Therefore, in September 1941, the Stavka—the GHQ—which Byelokonyenko sometimes called the "armed forces Politburo," decided to consign the unified command of all air forces to the air staff. After having thus won or reconquered their autonomy, the latter wanted to give a special status to long-range strategic aviation, foreseeing a primary role for it in the second phase of the war.

The father of this special force was Lieutenant-General Anatoly Golovanov, later promoted to the rank of Air Marshal. A former airline pilot, he understood that long-distance navigation required careful and precise preparation.

A certain number of training schools were therefore created—that of Kislovodsk bore the number 11, but I believe that there were at least thirty of them—to train over the next two years the future strategic air staff (for that, in fact, is what it was). It was called ADR, the Russian initials for Long-Range Aviation. In 1944, however, a backlash is thought to have taken place within the air force general staff against this "separatism," and particularly against the real or imagined privileges enjoyed by this special section, and it was rebaptized Marshal Golovanov's 18th Air Force.

Former Kislovodsk trainees continued to believe, however, that from the beginning, since 1941, they had belonged to the prestigious crème de la crème, for the seventeen other air force sections comprised only very ordinary tactical aviation outfits.

Commissar Byelokonyenko limited his remarks to telling me how our trainee pilots, in two or three years' time, would bomb "the German beast in his own lair." It was this capacity to engage in long-term planning for the war that made a striking impression on me. After all, in Poland in 1939, or in France in 1940, it would have been unthinkable to "program" what was going to happen in two or three years' time, at the height of the German offensive. Russia, I told myself, despite appearances, wasn't collapsing. A brief calculation deepened my conviction: Our school in Kislovodsk was training 450 pilots; and since there were at least thirty other such schools, that meant some 15,000 trainees, not counting the teaching personnel. An entire elite, in short, was being put in reserve—in spite of the urgent exigencies of war—in order to inflict decisive blows later on against these damned Nazis. These Russians were decidedly not short of breath; and I found myself swelling with pride in thinking about it.

But it was at this precise moment, according to historians, that the USSR really was on the brink of defeat! The Soviet command had sent out distress signals at the time almost in broad daylight. To cite only one episode over which much ink flows nowadays: On October 16, 1941, seeing their government—and Stalin himself, apparently—fall back to Kuybyshev, the people of Moscow crowded into the train stations in panic to leave, and many people were killed in the resulting crush. It is possible that my Aunt Lisa, who died at this time (though she had been healthy enough the year before) was one of the victims. Four days later, in an appeal for the defense of the capital, the Soviet High Command strongly advised against "any panic." If I had possessed a minimum of good sense, this exhortation would have aroused my suspicions. In the course of a war, panic is never mentioned unless it is in reference to the enemy camp. The Allied powers, though they didn't hide their defeats, strictly observed this unwritten law. Therefore, some truly terrible things must have happened in Moscow on this fatal day to prompt the Soviets to violate it.

On the other hand, Russia is a big country where information is slow to spread. News of the events of October 16 in Moscow wouldn't have reached Kislovodsk before two months had gone by, at the earliest, and then only through the intermediary of the wounded from the front. Meanwhile, Stalin, back in the capital, had celebrated the anniversary of the October Revolution in full public view, and presided over a military parade from the height of Lenin's mausoleum on November 7. (The troops left Red Square for the front, just a few kilometers away, directly afterward.) The Red Army finally went on the counteroffensive on December 6, inflicting on the Germans their first great defeat of the Second World War.

This victory reinforced once more my tendency to optimism. I had had a lucky break in having been sent to the "pearl of the Northern Caucasus," the sunniest spa-town of the region, which never suffered even an air-raid alert.

Kislovodsk enjoyed other advantages as well. It was given priority with respect to food supplies and entertainment, for its sanatoria and its hotels had been converted into hospitals where a swarm of friendly and charming nurses tended the wounded. The great tragedy of the autumn unfolded far away from us; we certainly heard the echoes of it, but we didn't suffer it. For eleven months we were sheltered, and it was a bit of good fortune that we were able to appreciate properly only after it had run out.

Among the changes wrought by the war, a celebrated title born with the Revolution and the Red Army would undergo a difficult metamorphosis: The political commissar would henceforward be merely a *zampolit*, an abbreviation of the Russian expression "replacement for political affairs." The well-known commissars' deputies, the *politruki*, would be even less well favored: they would be designated by the frankly ridiculous and unmartial *pompolit*, or "political assistant." All of this would happen after our forced departure from Kislovodsk, but it throws some light on our problems of this period.

The great reorganization was to take place in October 1942, during the critical phase of the Battle of Stalingrad. A decree would proclaim that the political consciousness of commanders had reached a level such that they no longer needed commissars to give them lessons. They would survive only with the title of *zampolit*. By a reverse process, Red Army commanders would become "officers" once more, a rank banished since the Revolution, and, in doing so, would don magnificent uniforms gleaming with epaulettes, resembling precisely those of the Imperial Army of His Majesty the Czar of all the Russias. Let us note, in fairness, that the politicos—the *zampolity* and the *pompolity*—enjoyed the same sartorial privileges, which enables us to admire in certain photographs today the martial bearing of Khrushchev or Brezhnev.

This decree of October 1942 (which hasn't received the attention it deserves in the West) offered, however, somewhat perfidious explanations for these reversals of "protocol" in the Red Army.

This revolution—or counterrevolution, if you prefer—was allegedly indispensable to "reinforce discipline," and to strengthen the patriotic motivation of the combat troops. You would have deduced from it logically that the commissars and their ilk had, until that time, sapped discipline and put a brake on the ardor of the troops.

Of course the decree did not formulate such brutally stated conclusions; but a good advocate before an impartial tribunal—in Britain, for example—would have had no difficulty in demonstrating its defamatory character. My share of the damages thus awarded the political services of the Red Army would doubtless have been a meager sum, consistent with my minor importance, or even the slight ambiguity of my role in Kislovodsk. What in fact is the situation in Training School No. 11, the "eleventh" of the air force, at the end of 1941?

The "eleventh" regiment is composed of three squadrons, each divided into five *zveno* (or chains) of thirty men; it is provided with one commissar assisted by three *politruki*, all of them seasoned members of the Communist Party, and lecturers in Marxism-Leninism and other serious matters. There are also in each squadron simple "political workers" such as myself, sent by the Komsomol to take charge of routine daily tasks. Without wishing to prejudice the reputation of the *politruki*, I think it can safely be said that they serve no practical function while the ordinary politicals like myself are very useful; even when, as in my case, they don't automatically contribute to reinforcing discipline.

The *politruki* tirelessly rehearse the course based on the *History of the CPSU (Bolsheviks)*, which all of the trainee pilots have already learned at school in order to pass their baccalaureats. What's more, since the beginning of the war this course hardly corresponds any longer to the actual doctrine of the country, which puts the struggle of the Slavs at the forefront—with Russians at their head—and relegates that of the proletarians to the shadows somewhat. Still, the ritual lessons in Marxism-Leninism are very popular in Kislovodsk. They allow the trainees to rest and to doze in the heat (they will not be examined in the subject this time), and it will be conceded that it is more sensible to rest comfortably in the shade than to trail along in the mud or the dust under the orders of a sergeant-major with clear sadistic tendencies.

My work, in contrast, doesn't deal with indoctrination. I have to

take part, with everyone else, in military training not directly connected with training in aviation—there is far too much of it for my
taste—and busy myself next with the cultural life of my companions.
I put on film shows for them at least once a week, arranging for the
films to come from Stavropol, the nearest large city. I obtain reading
matter for them also, on request, by searching through the town
library for it, and finally I convene small meetings of Komsomols in
order to read *Pravda* with them, or the daily paper from Stavropol. My
recreational program meets with only limited success. The vast majority of the members of the first squadron organize their favorite sport
for themselves—chasing after nurses. These future pilots perfectly
exemplify Moussia's description of the behavior of Russian men,
these "frantic skirt-chasers."

As for the nurses, they appear to behave just as Moussia herself
did, in the days before she had learned to "calculate her distances
properly." This sport can only develop, however, thanks to politico-
cultural activities. It is rarely the practice in the army to leave you
with the pastime of your choice. In our case, after dinner—served
early in the evening, between five-thirty and seven o'clock—we have
to return together quickly to our dormitories at the other end of the
town, in order to think about aviation or to oil our guns. Only those
who take part in my properly scheduled meeting are allowed to stay
behind in the large, centrally located building that houses the school.
Now the duration of these meetings is unspecified and so, unless a
politruk announces that he is going to come along, which is extremely
rare, we can cut short our reading of *Pravda*. In this way we gain the
time to make a detour, returning to our barracks via the avenue called
Piatachok, where, despite the darkness, intrepid or naïve nurses are
strolling about.

Personally, I am a mediocre predator (no doubt I lack conviction
and self-confidence), but I don't wish to hinder the success of my
more gifted friends, who "latch on" to a new prey on each occasion,
and afterward recount exploits that are incredible, given the short-
ness of the time and the precariousness of the places available. We
arrive at the following *modus vivendi*: The trainees to whom I am

attached turn out in large numbers for my recreational evenings to convince the commanders of their deep interest for everything that I organize. Other meetings, on the other hand, last for only a minimum length of time—as long as it takes the last NCO to clear out. This clearly renders me an accomplice to a violation of the regulations.

None of this interests Commissar Byelokonyenko or his *politruki*: the surveillance of comings and goings at the barracks is the exclusive responsibility of usually stupid and spiteful career NCOs. Their chief, in the first squadron, Sergeant Major Orlov, understands nothing about the manuever that allows us to frequent the so-called Piatachok. He is convinced that we climb over the wall of the barracks. Therefore he reinforces the guard and organizes patrols in the surrounding area by mobilizing the unfortunates who are already excluded from the chase. Sometimes he goes so far as to sacrifice his sleep to slyly await the return of late stragglers, whereupon he inflicts punishment duties on them straightaway. And punishment is severe: We are sent in groups to Min. Vody, the railway center on the Moscow-Yerevan Transcaucasian line, to dig antitank trenches.

Orlov can only let off steam at me during exercises, and he doesn't spare himself. All my efforts to wheedle him, to persuade him to stop considering me his number-one enemy, fail completely. I am fascinated by his resemblance to Sergeant Major Bartczak in the Polish Army, particularly in his use of language. Like Bartczak, he screams automatically at the sight of an unbuttoned collar on a subaltern, "What sort of costume is this?" The similarity of their vocabulary seems to me to be explained by a linguistic phenomenon whose existence I would never have suspected without them: In these two languages that have become as different from each other as French and Spanish, the words designating the sexual organs have remained the same. Orlov's expressions, like those of Bartczak, are heavily garnished with these; and I often have the impression of finding myself two years back in time, in front of a Polish sergeant major who has only changed his accent a little.

At Kislovodsk, however, I belong to the "political vertical," a separate hierarchy, and Orlov is powerless to impose punishment on me at his pleasure. He must go through Byelokonyenko, the sole figure next to God with authority over his service. One day Orlov brings me along to the commissar's office, therefore, stands stiffly at attention, clicks the heels of his boots together, and, to underline the gravity of his indictment, delivers it in such a jerky voice that it is difficult to follow him. Byelokonyenko pretends to have understood everything; he knits his eyebrows in a frown as if he were really outraged and were ready to have me shot, then pronounces a single word: *besobrazye*, which, in the slang then current, expresses the strongest indignation. Orlov, for his part, doesn't dare say, "It is not enough to say *besobrazye*, he ought to be punished." A sergeant major, fanatically respectful of the hierarchy, cannot permit himself to suggest anything whatever to someone who wears the insignia of a colonel, even if the rank is primarily political.

After three or four fruitless attempts, therefore, my persecutor gives up on his sinister design: to have me sent to dig antitank trenches. And I no longer risk very much by going for a walk along the Piatachok, or even, later, when the nurse Nievka has arrived in Kislovodsk, by actually sleeping away from my barracks.

I still haven't explained what the Piatachok was exactly. In Rostov, as I have already said, the main avenue, straight as a stretched thread, bore the name Friedrich Engels; but for the population and even for us Komsomols, it was the Sadovaya, from the word for "garden." In Kislovodsk, the avenue that descended abruptly from the railway station, and then described a semicircle before dividing up into several boulevards, bore the name Karl Marx. The slightly unusual shape of this avenue resembled the figure five, which is *piat* in Russian—hence the general tendency to refer to it as the Piatachok, the "little five," and for the prestigious name Karl Marx to vanish altogether. The centrally located building housing the "eleventh school" of the air force was close by, situated in a street giving onto Lenin Boulevard, which itself opened onto the Piatachok. This admirably placed street was simply called Green Alley, in honor of its trees. I never did learn its real name, no doubt taken from among the martyrs of the workers' movement.

Today I am struck by this curious coincidence: In the two Russian towns where I lived, Rostov and Kislovodsk, the most popular places were dedicated to Marx and Engels, but in practice they were referred to by quite different names. Russians, it seems, have always preferred descriptive titles—whether of trees, shapes, or colors—to the abstraction of great names.

One day the commissar orders me to keep an eye on Kola P. Why? What has he done? "Nothing. Don't ask stupid questions. I am not asking you to set a trap for him, or to put him away; we are not the military police."

I didn't know it then, but it was thanks to this order that Kola P. was to become my best friend for the rest of my stay in the Soviet Union.

Kola is invariably called "the Herring" by his comrades. This nickname has nothing prestigious about it, and in Russian it is even a bit ungracious. Kola is admittedly very thin and of a very ordinary appearance. He doesn't distinguish himself in any way from the average trainee pilot, and hasn't any great ambition. He is neither very agile during exercises nor very gifted in theoretical matters. Yet this "herring," this apparent waif, is inexplicably a remarkable leader of men. He has established himself as a leader in the first squadron, and that is what worries Byelokonyenko.

In fact, in my view, these two men in other circumstances would have gotten along very well together. My commissar is one of the rare Soviet citizens to resemble the Communists or left-wing socialists in Poland. Neither the dogmas of the *History of the CPSU (Bolsheviks)* nor the vicissitudes of life have crushed in him the need to think about the future society, of how to construct real communism. These notions interest Kola too, in spite of his cynical airs and his obvious interest in day-to-day survival. In addition, both of them share an aversion to the nationalist prejudices that are so widespread among the members of our squadron.

Kola's merits in this regard are far superior to those of the commissar. He is a Cossack, in fact, like the great majority of the first squadron; he is even descended, it appears, from an illustrious family of the former "special region of the army of the Don." Byelokonyenko comes from the Ukraine. Now the Ukrainians are held in open contempt by the Cossacks, who describe them as *khokoly*—an untranslatable term—or *gady*, meaning snakes. By declaring that these prejudices don't mean anything to him, Kola deliberately goes against the herd, and incidentally lends a hand to the commissar, who faces a crowd of Cossacks in the squadron over which he presides.

Since June 22, 1941, the Cossacks have once again found a place of honor in the USSR. As soon as war broke out, giant posters were put up in Rostov showing these fierce cavalrymen in their uniform of yesteryear, sabers held high, galloping to the front under the slogan, "Cossacks of the Peaceful Don, Crush the German Invaders as Your Ancestors Crushed Napoleon!"

These posters at first send chills down my spine: In the Polish films I saw as a child, it was this cavalry in these same uniforms who hunted our compatriots and smashed strikes; for me they were savages, the Czarist praetorian guard. A Soviet Communist could also recoil at such propaganda by simply recalling that the Cossacks' brave ancestors had not only crushed Napoleon but had come close to inflicting the same fate on Lenin and the Bolsheviks. Hadn't their ataman, Krasnov, struck at the gates of Leningrad with the declared intention of hanging all the Reds?

To be truthful, the Cossacks in our squadron ask only to have their national identity recognized; they simply want to be considered as different from the Russians—just as Klava had wanted back at School No. 44 in Rostov. They don't seem to know how to affirm themselves, however, except through their contempt for others. Nevertheless, no Russian in our squadron dreams of ruffling the thin-skinned pride of the Cossacks, given the general political line, but they also know that no Cossack will ever serve as commander. It is impossible for the simple reason that there aren't any: until the advent of the 1936 constitution, the Cossacks were deprived of certain rights, particularly the right to make a career in the army. Nothing can be done; the commander of the "eleventh" is a Russian, terribly

Russian in fact: Colonel Leonid Vasilyevich Ganachek, commonly
called Lionka Swiste, "little whistling Leonid," because of the pitch
of his voice; the chief instructor, Colonel Gerch Yakovlevich Zlotnikov, is Jewish, and it will readily be guessed that he is generally
referred to as a "dirty Yid"; as for the commissar, he is regularly
called a serpent, like all Ukrainians.

It is in this context that Kola's unique courage needs to be appreciated when he declares against all comers that he cares as much about
being Cossack as he does about his first pair of long pants—that, all
things considered, he would prefer to be Polish or Jewish. And why
not? These people, in his view, travel more, have broader horizons.
And when Kola says something, whether he is a "herring" or not, it
counts for something. It counts first of all for his three loyal clan
followers from Myechotka, a Cossack *stanitsa*, where they were born
and spent a hard childhood together. These three are endowed with
nicknames that leave no doubt as to each one's importance. Vassya is
Slon or "Elephant," and in the squadron there is neither a "lion" nor
a "tiger" to contest his prowess. Next comes Volodya, "the Singer,"
and when one becomes aware of the privileged place that song occupies in the real or supposed identity of the Cossacks, all further
commentary becomes superfluous. Finally there is Kostya, the last of
the clan and the closest to Kola, a solid cheerful type, but as shrewd
as a monkey, and who, because of his slightly projecting cheekbones,
is called "the Khan"—one of those of Asian extraction who, for
centuries, have dominated the whole of Russia. Certainly the Myechotka clan has neither the ambition nor the power to put an end to
the Cossacks' anti-Semitism and anti-Ukrainianism, but Kola and his
friends succeed in moderating their effects, which simplifies the lives
of the non-Cossack trainee pilots, not to mention that of the com-
manding personnel, the commissar included.

It isn't easy, though, for me to speak about it to Byelokonyenko.
The barrier of hierarchy separates us, despite the understanding that
he seems to show toward me. He is also of another generation, if I am
to judge by his tired blue gaze, that of a man who has lived through
much and who fears that everything he has built might collapse with

the war. In the nationalistic gossip in the barracks he sees only a survival of the old world, which was supposed to disappear thanks to the progress of industrialization, after the completion of three or four five-year plans. It is as if this schema were now suspended; instead of building, everything in the Ukraine, in Russia, is being destroyed; and when the Germans haven't done it, we have had to do it ourselves, in the name of the "scorched earth" tactic, more discreetly described as "active, in-depth defense." My commissar worries a lot. He was more at ease when the motor of history was the class struggle, rather than this "great, patriotic Russian people." After all, he has been a worker himself and isn't a Russian anyway.

Kola, despite Byelokonyenko's persistence in designating him as the "mischievous spirit" of the first squadron, is actually rather fond of him. In his eyes, our commissar possesses, among his innumerable eccentricities, a quality that redeems all of them: He is not at all repressive. And, Kola adds, it is not from either weakness or stupidity; on the contrary, it is the attribute of an intelligence that has never let itself be drowned in vodka. Byelokonyenko, though, drinks a lot, and so does Kola; it is another point they have in common. So, for that matter, do I—I even manage to keep up with them without too much difficulty.

In December, at the time of the Soviet victory at Moscow, Nievka arrives in Kislovodsk. Her real name is Natalia, but, having been born twenty-three years earlier in the quasi-Venetian district of Leningrad where the Nievka River joins in confluence with the Neva to form the majestic river so frequently evoked in Russia's literary classics, she had uttered the name "Nievka" even before "mama" or "papa." To her parents, therefore, Natalia became Nievka, and so it is as Nievka that she introduces herself.

There is a certain snobbery implicit in Nievka's insistence on being called by her nickname. Only the families of important Communists live in her area of the city, heirs in this respect of the former aristocracy. What's more, Natalia Trofimovna makes no secret of it. She takes no pains to conceal the fact that her father is a man of consequence: He is sufficiently friendly with Andrei Zhdanov for the latter to have approved personally, it seems, of her nickname, and for Zhdanov to have taken her on his knee more than once when she was a child. It was thanks to him—or so I imagine—that she was one of the very elect few to be evacuated from an encircled Leningrad. She is none the prouder of herself for that, and she enlisted in the army as a simple nurse when, as a third-year medical student, she could have taken quiet refuge in a good faculty to finish her studies in peace.

Nievka is very beautiful, rather tall, and unquestionably very thin. In the West she could certainly have made a fortune as a model. Her arrival is a gift from the heavens for me. This is hardly an overstatement, for her evacuation from Leningrad is nothing short of a miracle. At the time, Nievka explains, the only access to the town was across Lake Ladoga, but the flotilla of ferryboats that usually serviced the lake was practically out of action and the lake was swept by German artillery fire. As soon as it froze over, however—and the winter of 1941 was both premature and severely cold—Zhdanov had a "lifeline" cut across it. Trucks carrying vital supplies began to arrive at night; on their return trips they evacuated mainly children and the sick. In the truck that took Nievka, children had been packed together like sardines under a tarpaulin in an attempt to keep them warm. During the night, Nievka and another student, Rosa, clung to the outside of the cabin, buffeted by the frigid wind that blew at thirty degrees below zero. To avoid artillery fire the convoy also had to leave the track and to make an interminable detour before ending up at a military post where, of course, there was no one waiting for them. It must have been an awful journey.

I don't meet Nievka for the first time on the Piatachok—she isn't the type to let herself get picked up on the street—but at the hospital where she is working, in Kislovodsk's former sanatorium. It is in the upper quarters of the town, near the ruins of a former fortress built by the Russians to fight the Ciscaucasians (or by the latter to fight the Russians, I am no longer sure). When I go there, it is on an errand for Byelokonyenko, who uses me as his man Friday. He needs a dossier or some information concerning a wounded man who comes from his

hometown of Zaporozhye. Nievka—luck leads me straight to her—
knows nothing about him; she has just arrived. She asks a junior
nurse to go off and find out what she can, and in the meantime asks
me about Kislovodsk and about my handsome uniform; she didn't
know that there were airmen here. Then, by a second miracle, this
stylish and very classy young woman, having still not located the
dossier, offers to bring it to me in town the next day. It is only a
business rendezvous, but it is a rendezvous all the same. We arrange
to meet near the columns of the main entry to the park, at the
beginning of the afternoon. At that time of day there is almost no one
there.

The next day Nievka arrives for the rendezvous with military punc-
tuality, attractively wrapped up in an infantry commander's cape, and
wearing a discreet military cap—but in fur—finely matching her
short black hair, and a pair of boots of supple leather. For my part, I
have mobilized all my sartorial resources; I even put on dress boots
belonging to Kostya the Khan. A business rendezvous doesn't perhaps require such an effort at stylishness, but in any case there was
no longer any business matter to see to, since the dossier concerning
the man from Zaporozhye had been sent a long time before to the
hospital administration of the Caucasian military region, which is on
Green Alley, only a few steps from my commissar's office. So we go
for a stroll in the park, and Nievka, with perfect naturalness, takes
me by the arm. I play the role of guide, repeating word for word
Byelokonyenko's commentaries on the splendors of the place, and in
this way we arrive at the large waterfall—a favorite spot, according to
my commissar, for ladies and gentlemen of good society in the previous century. The sun is setting after a clear December day and the
site is bathed in a mild, romantic light fit to inspire poets and to bring
young souls together. After enjoying the view in silence, Nievka
stiffens suddenly and, tears in her eyes, presses herself against me;
but it is her Leningrad that she talks about instead of Lermontovian
phantoms.

"You don't realize what is happening there. It's awful. It's worse
than awful, it's a nightmare." I wipe away her tears by covering her

with timid and affectionate kisses, but we are interrupted by a group of patients in pajamas, wandering at large away from the hospital. They are wrapped up in blankets, giving them the appearance of vagrants, and they begin to hurl vulgar taunts at us. In Mikhail Lermontov's day, I would surely have challenged them to a duel, but we leave without saying a word. In 1941 the "heroes of our time" wear pajamas and are as indifferent to fine language as they are to courtesy.

Nievka, in all innocence, invites me to have tea with her at her home. If she is not exactly privileged, she has at least been very lucky in that she has been allocated a beautiful room with independent access, on the ground floor of a building surrounded by a small garden, to the south of the town, in the sunniest zone. She shares it with Rosa, her companion from Leningrad. It isn't very far from the town's center; nothing is very far, for that matter, in a town of fifty thousand inhabitants.

The furniture and fittings in this room are at once spartan and bizarre: Two iron beds stand at opposite walls, and between them a large Persian carpet covers the floor; there is only one chair and a battered old armchair. We choose, inevitably, to sit on the carpet. Nievka, however, keeps her distance. But we enter a stream of conversation that flows all night; among other things there is much talk between us of a strong and sincere love through which we can help each other surmount the trials of war, just as one encounters in the classics of romantic Russian literature. Later we will always look back upon this night, during which we dreamed aloud, with a hint of nostalgia, as we would upon a wonderful, shared secret.

Although news travels very slowly throughout Russia as a whole, it spreads at astonishing speed within Kislovodsk. In relation to my *nuit blanche* with Nievka, it is hardly a surprise. Kola's bunk is next door to mine. He is delighted to see that I have spent the night away. He and his three Cossack comrades—the four Musketeers of Myechotka—have already given up the chase for more stable relationships; it was high time that I did the same. My principal enemy,

Sergeant Major Orlov, has noted my absence too, and marches me off to the commissar's office.

Byelokonyenko, however, listens to him this time with barely disguised impatience. Skipping completely over my absence from the barracks, he asks me instead for suggestions for the upcoming New Year's celebrations. In his view, things are going well in the international arena. After Pearl Harbor the United States is determined to enter the fray, and on January 1, under its aegis, twenty-six countries, including the USSR, are due to sign in Washington a declaration of total war on the Axis powers, and principally on Nazi Germany. It is important, therefore, to celebrate the event and the new year by organizing something better than a film show—even though, in my view, a good American movie would be entirely appropriate—a concert, for example, a theatrical evening, or even a dance. Obviously he reserves for himself the job of delivering a lengthy speech for the occasion.

His friend, Captain Pyetya Danilov, the *zavkhoze*, or senior figure in the quartermaster's department, and a native of Zaporozhye himself, suddenly arrives. He quickly becomes involved in the conversation on America. It is a tiny bit upsetting for an Anglophile like myself, but these Russians really have an extraordinary liking for the United States; they are fascinated by this country that is so similar in size to their own and is not (yet) classified as imperialist because it hasn't officially any colonies. Moreover, Stalin, in the course of his speech on the anniversary of the Revolution, has said, "The war of today is a war of engines, and it will be won by whoever has a crushing superiority in engines." This statement made a powerful impression on my commissar and his friend Captain Danilov, both of whom associate the United States with the automobile industry. Byelokonyenko goes as far as calculating on the basis of approximate statistics the combined level of steel production of the twenty-six countries in the anti-Axis coalition who are to sign the declaration in Washington on New Year's Day.

Despite my personal preference for Churchill, who was one of the first and most resolute of Hitler's adversaries in the West, I gladly drink a bumper measure of vodka to the health of Franklin D. Roosevelt, while paying tribute to the political perspicacity of my commissar and of Captain Danilov. The idea of a New Year's Eve party with internationalist overtones pleases me a lot too.

More immediately, however, I have to confront a more private party: one organized by the Musketeers of Myechotka, who have evolved from the stage of nomadic wandering to the historically more advanced sedentary life. The first to give up the chase was Vassya the Elephant, who fell for an incomparably beautiful local nurse, Raya, who has a room in a communal apartment to which she can invite as many people as she likes. Raya has a pronounced Mediterranean personality, enhanced by amazing, bright eyes. She has a sunny disposition, and enjoys singing magnificent duos with Volodya, the Singer. She is the first to organize an evening for us, at her place, and she gives us a taste of more intimate domestic pleasures.

Next is Kola, who finds himself a local schoolteacher, Maroussia, who also has a room. Although of average appearance, Maroussia is as accomplished a hustler as the Herring. They discover together, from practice, that in Kislovodsk men in uniform are served before other customers in the food stores. It is, of course, greedy of us— aren't we already lodged and fed by the air force?—to take advantage of their discovery, but it is very helpful for our collective dinners. Our military uniforms allow us to buy at low prices the majority of products needed for good Russian cuisine. Kola and Maroussia don't confine themselves simply to the role of quartermasters, however; they see to more ethereal pleasures by reciting for us a large repertoire of poetry ranging from the classics to more recent works. They provide vocal support to Raya and Volodya, whose singing is the principal attraction of our evenings.

The Singer has linked up with Tania. They met, like most, along the Piatachok and liked the look of each other. Volodya had been hoping to meet a nurse but in fact met someone much better placed; Tania works in a vodka factory. It is a wholly unexpected stroke of luck, even though the kindly Tania, because of searches at the factory exit, takes a lot of risks to earn her our title of "Honorary

Supplier." She too is from the town and has a two-room flat—her parents'—but only on Wednesdays, because once a week they leave for Min. Vody for twenty-four hours.

Finally, Kostya the Khan begins to see Vera, a fair-haired nurse from Rostov, who is very Russian-looking with her braided plaits, even though she says she is half Cossack. She is stuck in a dormitory and cannot contribute anything on the logistical front, and frets a little because of it, the more so because at twenty-four she is the oldest in our group. Vera compensates, however, by throwing herself with a will into the cooking; she makes an excellent "vinaigrette"—a large salad with a base of marinated cabbage—and mushroom *piroshki* worthy of a deluxe restaurant. She tries to find a nurse for me—I am the only one who is not yet fixed up—but in vain; I don't suit her friends, nor do they suit me.

Into this little setting comes the news that I have slept away from the barracks. I am expected, therefore, at the next evening get-together, to appear with my "girlfriend." No one has a shadow of a doubt as to the character of my relations with her; what else could we have done throughout a whole night? My "wedding" celebration coincides with the Khan's twentieth birthday; the evening thus acquires great importance. Nievka joyfully accepts the invitation and even finds a present for the Khan, a belt from Leningrad. I am ill at ease, however, because of my not-so-matrimonial situation. I also have a vague feeling that somehow Nievka will not fit in.

In Raya's room, with ten of us present, we really are a little bit crowded together. The boys remain perched on the bed so as not to get in the way, while the girls, including Nievka, busy themselves with the cooking. Then the fatal moment arrives; as soon as they have sat down, everyone helps himself or herself to a vodka—except Nievka, who, undaunted, fills her glass with mineral water. Consternation. What kind of provocation is this? So Leningrad is no longer in Russia? They haven't heard of vodka there? Nievka, in a serene voice, in her lovely northern Russian accent, soft and musical, tells the story of her trip across Lake Ladoga and adds to it a final episode: In the military post where there had been no one waiting for them, there was nothing to help her warm up; someone massaged her legs with some eau de cologne and made her drink the rest of the bottle. It twisted her insides, and ever since, the least taste of alcohol has made her sick. Silence falls. Incredulity follows. A vast debate develops on the difference between cologne and vodka; in vain. The nurse from the North doesn't change her mind; she merely sketches her pretty smile to inform us that she never prevents others from drinking, especially not on someone's birthday. Honestly. Thanks all the same.

The ambience is shattered. Relations between vodka enthusiasts and those who drink mineral water have always called to mind the class struggle. Amiable arrangements do not serve any great purpose; you can't get quietly pissed under the allegedly indulgent gaze of the abstemious. To save what I take to be our common honor, I try to drink for the two of us, until Nievka pulls me forcefully by the arm and orders me to take her home straightaway. Once we are out in the street she gives me an earful as though I were personally responsible for the generalized consumption of the *prokliataya vodka* (damnable vodka) in her country. Back at her place she allows me to stretch out on the Persian carpet, makes some tea, and, good nurse that she is, calmly explains that vodka is no good for "people like us." This plural pronoun reassures me as to the state of our relations. I remain more reserved as to the possibility of weaning myself away from alcohol in the context of the "eleventh school" of the air force.

With the Myechotka Musketeers, things subsequently took a more serious turn for the worse, but for a reason that I had hardly foreseen: These fine connoisseurs of women didn't appreciate my Nievka because she had small breasts. To them she was "flat-chested," a blemish that was enough to ruin the reputation of a girl, even if she did enjoy a tipple with the rest, and didn't put on airs.

The Elephant shot off, "What do you hold in your hand when you're screwing?" among other subtleties of the same genre. Kola said sulkily, "Frankly, you can do better."

No way. I chose Nievka and divorced myself from Kola and his clan. We redivided possessions that we had shared, and cut in half several towels whose ownership was in doubt. Everything was over between us, in short. Two days afterward I took my nurse to the town theater to see *La Dame aux Camélias*, with permission from the commissar to get back late; in practice, not to return at all. Nievka, who knew nothing about my fight with the Musketeers, perhaps noticed my distress. When we got back, she no longer insisted on keeping her distance from me on the Persian carpet. It is possible that the play by Alexandre Dumas *fils* had something to do with this; in it, love is something less spiritual than it is in romantic Russian literature.

"There will be nothing for the New Year. A short assembly, a speech, and then everyone will go back to the barracks, in good order and without exception." Byelokonyenko raises himself from the table to announce this to me as if he were a judge announcing a verdict. And all this simply because of some *galushki*, the little balls of flour that floated in our soup. A few trainees, the evening before, had the bright idea of using them as projectiles to bombard some NCOs for the hell of it. For the commissar, it is going too far. And yet there is hardly anything worth getting upset about. The NCOs had taken their revenge by sending a large squad of those responsible, among whom was the Elephant, to dig antitank trenches, and it was only a bit of flour, after all; no one died from it. But Byelokonyenko wants to set an example. In his eyes we are a lost cause, irresponsible bums, instead of the stout soldiers the country needs. He is going to make sure that we smarten ourselves up properly, all of us "without exception." We are in the armed forces, not in a brothel; we are to concern ourselves with airplanes, not girls. His allusions appear to me to be more and more transparent.

Have the Myechotka Musketeers denounced me to the commissar after our falling-out? From hatred of Nievka? I feel myself grow pale. The idea that Kola and his friends might have betrayed me is a terrible blow. What an informer-riddled country! Since there's no hope, I'll just run off with Nievka. Isn't that how they behave in all the best literature?

Byelokonyenko, however, is a kind of Russian version of the

drunken millionaire in Charlie Chaplin's *City Lights*. In his case, though, it isn't vodka that reverses the mood, but other less obvious factors. In my opinion he is reproaching himself for being too familiar, too tolerant toward us, and to reestablish his authority, he tosses off these terrible threats that he regrets almost as soon as they are made. And then he begins again from zero. The threats fade by the next day. Kola is innocent, flight is useless, and my commissar, for the New Year assembly and celebration, orders me to find a good performing artist at the town theater to recite the highly acclaimed poem of the year, "Kirov with Us," by Nikolai Tikhonov, who, like Nievka, is from Leningrad.

As I'm on the way to the door, Byelokonyenko adds, "On January 1, after the assembly, you are authorized to slip away; go and join your nurse, but discreetly, without drawing attention to yourself." A real Charlie Chaplin character, this commissar. Does he also know who my nurse really is? And if so, from whom? I am terribly suspicious; my continuing separation from the Myechotka Musketeers has me very worried.

"Tell me some *dyetskye skazki* [fairy tales]."

"Oh, Nievka, we are too old for that, and besides, I don't remember any now."

"Of course you do. Think hard and you will surely remember at least one Polish fairy tale."

I find more than one, but in the Karl Marx Library of Kislovodsk, where Grimm, Andersen, and Afanasiev replace my studious reading of Korneichuk and Ehrenburg, to the great amazement of the librarians. Then, as soon as the occasion offers, I dazzle Nievka with my *dyetskye skazki* by pretending that they are coming back to me spontaneously. If she suspects the deceit, she doesn't show it—maybe so as not to break the spell. In difficult times, escapist fiction is as necessary for adults as it is for children.

But why is Nievka so much in need of fairy tales? To see her, with her determined step and satisfied smile, you would think she was the most stable of human beings. I sense that she is fragile, however, and decide that she is too much of a "mama's girl," never having had the experience of living alone. I am convinced that adulthood begins with separation from the family, and Nievka, who has barely just gone through the experience, is two years behind me in this. On the other hand, she is very much the "liberated woman," very sure of her right to a love life of her choice. Unlike me, she doesn't care in the least about what wagging tongues might have to say about us. Immediately after the night we see *La Dame aux Camélias*, she succeeds in obtaining a double bed and a second armchair. Quite openly, she goes about the business of refurnishing the room, as if the better to inform the whole building, which is occupied by Party functionaries, of the real reasons for the visits of the "young airman."

The sexual mores not only of Nievka and Olga, but also of the girlfriends of Kola's clan, were, in my view, living proof of the enduring ideas about free love preached by Alexandra Kollontai after the Revolution, and proof too of their resistance to the wave of puritanism summoned by Stalin. In this, Soviet women were ahead of their sisters in the West, who were still imprisoned in bourgeois family morality and the religious concept of sin. Even my own sister Alicia, although she was an atheist, had decided to remain a virgin until she was married.

Emancipated, materially independent, often highly cultivated Russian women were, like Nievka, still haunted by the fear of being "without a man," as if they felt the irresistible need of a masculine arm in order to feel stronger, or to realize their potential. I am struck by the unaffected way in which Nievka often says to me, "You're the man. It is for you to make the decisions." Similarly, she finds it normal to take responsibility for all the domestic chores and to get up at dawn to make tea for me, so that I arrive at work promptly at seven o'clock. Because the time I spend with Nievka, over and above the leave to which I am entitled once a week, is "stolen" from my regular duties, and is therefore difficult to plan in advance, she always waits at home for me and goes out as little as possible during her time off, in order to be at home on the off-chance I'm free. Her devotion overwhelms me and, I need hardly add, I am in love with her.

Except when I drink too much, Nievka "doesn't want to lose me" and says it to me openly, as if she believes she can't find any other man than me, which is clearly absurd because she is both beautiful and highly cultured. Her mother teaches German literature at the Lifli and thanks to her, Nievka knows by heart a good part of the work of Heinrich Heine, in the original as well as in translation. Her father was a history teacher before becoming a Party functionary, so that her cultural baggage far exceeds mine and that of my friends. She doesn't talk very much about her feelings, though, thinking that we have said enough about this subject to each other and that the very fact of being lovers proves that we love each other. But I would like to talk of love and to pursue forever the torrent of tender words that began on the Persian carpet.

What surprises me most, however, is Nievka's behavior when we are alone together. She is terribly shy and asks me not to look at her while she undresses, as if she were ashamed of her body. Once we are in bed, I see her naked; she has a splendid body, soft skin, very soft, infinitely more pleasing to touch than Olga's—my sole point of comparison—softer, I imagine, than the silk of all the dresses of Alexander Blok's "Nyeznakomka."

Nievka also has a holy terror of becoming pregnant, although abortion is freely available in the USSR. I suspect this anxiety undermines her sensuality and obliges her to control her desires to the point of blunting them. She makes love only during her "safe" days, and since the safest are those during her periods, she ends up inculcating in me completely false ideas concerning the sexual behavior of women. Nievka's ideal—though she doesn't admit it in so many words—is to wrap herself around me under the sheets, and talk passionately, softly, about the distress of her native Leningrad, about literature, listening next to some *dyetskye skazki* for consolation, and then going to sleep, without running any of the risks of carnal love.

I don't reproach Nievka, however; I am as happy as a king with her and I think of no one else from morning to night, during military exercises or while carrying out my politico-cultural tasks. When, therefore, my commissar makes a vague reference to me about the forthcoming formation of a Polish Army in the USSR—following the Stalin-Sikorski agreement in December 1941—I am seized with panic and instantly declare, "I am staying in the Red Army."

Pleased as punch, he concludes, *"Ty nach."* ("You are one of us.") He congratulates me on my irremediably Russian "consciousness and culture."

In fact my "consciousness and culture" have nothing to do with it. I am simply crazy about this tall girl from Leningrad who speaks with such a bewitching Russian accent, makes almost horizontal plaits with her short hair before going to sleep, and stares at me with her big, green, astonished eyes when I tell her fairy tales.

I made up with Kola and Kostya first, and then with Vassya and Volodya. Kola, who is objective, comes to recognize that Nievka isn't flat-chested, but simply has breasts "in proportion to her build." It is just as well, for I need his help to fight against the campaign of denigration directed at me in the first squadron, on the theme "A Polish *pan*, a king into the bargain, found for his *karoleva* [queen] a mute, flat-chested duchess from Leningrad." Nievka is called a mute because when she is accosted in the street she refuses to answer or even to utter a word. In our detractors' little songs there are other couplets of such vulgarity that, even forty-five years later, they are not fit to be written down.

The taunts with which I am assailed leave me neither hot nor cold. I am called *polski pan*, for example, even though I have explained a thousand times that in Poland anybody is a *pan*, that it doesn't constitute a title, but is a term equivalent to "Mister" or "Monsieur." My colleagues in the "eleventh" of the air force don't want to believe me. They are victims of a stupid propaganda campaign against the *panska Polcha* (the Poland of the *pans*), which has persuaded them that in Poland it is only the rich and the oppressors who are called *pan*. They persist in singing an anti-Polish refrain behind my back: *"Perepil vseh polskiy pan, v bardakye on jest ulan."* ("The Polish *pan* has drunk more than everyone else, he plays the hussar in the whorehouse.") Now this is not without a certain salty humor, for in order to *perepil* these inveterate Russian drinkers, you really would have to start out early in the morning, and if someone *could* open a brothel in the USSR, he would become rich overnight, because these Russian men think of nothing else: It's their dream. I keep cool, even when they toss at me, *"Pan, gliadi v oba"* ("Look with your two eyes"), a not-so-subtle allusion to my blindness in one eye; on the other hand, I can't stomach this little song of the king and his mute, flat-chested queen; it sends me foolishly into a rage. Kola is probably the only one who, thanks to his authority, is able to ensure that it is excluded from the repertoire of the first squadron.

We talk about it one evening, after a meeting, as we are returning to the barracks. Suddenly, in the darkness, a shadow cries out, "Halt!" There is no mistaking it: the voice is clearly military. A silly reflex, born of habit, sends us running off at full speed to save ourselves. The shadow gives chase and, good runners though we are, manages to catch up. We stop. After all, for once we are not violating the regulations! We turn around. Facing us is Colonel Gerch Yakovlevich Zlotnikov, chief instructor and pilot emeritus, the commander most feared for his intransigence and severity. Our explanations are in vain, as is a discreet allusion to my membership in the political "vertical." "Hardest fatigue duty for both of you," he says. "I will arrange it with the commissar personally." The very next day Kola and I are ordered to dig antitank trenches in Min. Vody.

It is an unending building site on a snow-covered plain where mainly women, muffled from head to foot, are assigned to work. The supervisor who stamps our papers and gives us our picks is also a woman, ugly and shrill-voiced and used to welcoming trainees on punishment duty from the "eleventh" of the air force. She tells us straight off that we are going to have to "move our butts" and warns us against "acting up." We pick away conscientiously at the frozen earth, chiefly to warm ourselves. January 1942 will long be remembered for its record cold temperatures.

Kola is so incensed by the injustice of it all that he issues an endless litany on the vile, irredeemable stupidity of the Russians. "And for starters, what use can these idiotic trenches serve?" he asks, observing with good sense that the Germans hadn't come to the USSR to practice mountain climbing in the Caucasus or to plant the swastika at the summit of the Elbrus; and then, if they were to get as far as here, it would mean that the war was lost and that the trenches had been dug in the wrong place. He is terribly persuasive. This mini–Maginot Line makes no sense. They are constructing it only to torment us and these unfortunate women whose husbands have already quit them for the army. Events are going to prove us partly wrong, however. The Germans will occupy all of this region some months later. But our trenches will not slow down in the slightest their advance toward the great chain of the Caucasus.

In the last *electrichka*—a self-powered carriage on a narrow-gauge track—which brings us back to Kislovodsk after this harsh day out, we are in the mood for confidences. Kola begins with some general considerations on the aptitude of the Russians and Cossacks for suffering and for imposing suffering.

"What were my parents' first words to me? Guess if you can." Without waiting, he hits me with his answer: " 'Suffer, Cossack, and you will become ataman.' Today, though, the title of ataman no longer means anything. And in the past, how many of these lousy atamans were there, anyway? Hardly one per generation, while the votaries of suffering were numbered in their thousands. They all suffered, my father, my grandfather, everyone. A great competition in suffering. There you have the historic contribution of the Cossacks. Let them piss off without me from now on, for I have suffered my bit.

"Unfortunately, the Russians and Bolsheviks too are great specialists in suffering. This time, of course, it is in the name of collective progress and productive forces, while with the Cossacks the competition is strictly individual, but it is of just as little use to me. I am a member of the Komsomol, sure, but I have just about had it up to the teeth with sacrificing myself for the happiness of my grandchildren. I am barely twenty years old, and as far as sacrifices are concerned, I have already exceeded a reasonably calculated norm for a long lifetime."

I can no longer hold back. I talk about all of my misfortunes. I tell everything to Kola, even about Western Siberia, although some days earlier I had taken him for an informer and, until then, had carefully concealed my Siberian sojourn.

"You are twenty years old too, because your last two years count as double," he says approvingly, like a good accountant of dangers. "You were able to react, to defend yourself, while in our case we could only suffer without being able to do a great deal. I have been separated from my parents for a very long time; I don't even know where they are, perhaps even in Western Siberia. And your fine *mastyer* in Zavodoukovsk could have been my father. After the war, though, all of that will have to change—is going to change—and I am not the only one to think so."

We are stirred like long-lost brothers who find each other as if by a miracle. As luck would have it, we are able to celebrate the event immediately. It is Wednesday, the day the Musketeers meet regularly at Tania's house. When we get there the clan and their girlfriends have eaten almost everything; the girls had not foreseen our return, but there is plenty left to drink, and Kola, who normally holds his liquor very well, gets awfully drunk. His story of suffering, like nausea, rises up once more. He mutters strange things that we can't hear properly. "What are you saying, Kola, my love?" Maroussia, who genuinely loves him, finally asks.

"I am saying that they are all fascists, Hitler and Stalin, Churchill and Roosevelt, and that I have had it up to here with them, and that everything here will have to change." Maroussia prudently leads him off into the next room.

For me, however, the evening passes with cheerful, drunken abandon. All of us recover quickly and fully, however, with a minimum of hangover; at seven o'clock the next morning, all five of us are in our places in the squadron's column, which strikes up: "Stand up, enormous country/Stand up for a fight to the death!"

I sing along with the others, as far as Green Alley. Then, in the afternoon, I make a detour via Nievka's place to announce that we would once again be taking part in the Myechotkians' social evenings. She declares herself delighted by the news, but it is perhaps only out of a spirit of submission, because "the man has to decide."

In our latitudes, love is like the weather: the fairest rarely lasts. From the spring of 1942 on, the first storms break between Nievka and I.

It's because we have inherited from our respective parents—she from her mother, me from my father—a pronounced propensity for jealousy. We don't think for a moment, however, of putting an end to our turbulent love affair and of leaving each other; on the contrary, precisely because of it we decide to ask the authorities for permission to live together. The only definite result of this foolhardy initiative—though I have no way of knowing it at the time—is to reopen hostilities between the NKVD and me. Our blunder is perhaps explained by the bizarre political and military climate of this period.

Our watches are set at 1812, as Stalin has suggested in giving to us our glorious nineteenth-century ancestors as a model. At that time, though, Napoleon's campaign only lasted for a single summer, since his army proved unable to survive the Russian winter. Hitler, on the other hand, fell back only some two hundred kilometers during the periods of deepest cold, and his troops are still here. What is going to happen in the spring?

Above us, the sun rises higher each day, the months pass—March, April, even May—but the war front doesn't move at all. Neither side seems to be committed to a decisive breakthrough. The Soviet press sees proof in this that the Germans were not stopped at the gates of Moscow merely by "General Winter"—as they were alleging—and that it is really the Red Army that has beaten them. Not content with this boast, the Sovinformbureau affirms that the Wehrmacht has exhausted its capacities for offensive action once and for all because of the enormous losses it has suffered: 10 million dead, wounded, and taken prisoner; 30,500 tanks and 20,000 aircraft destroyed. Presented with such figures, who can resist concluding that the German danger no longer exists? Safe in Kislovodsk, "the pearl of the Northern Caucasus," I come to believe that the war will pass us by and that, in these conditions, we might as well arrange our future as best we can.

Nievka, however, doesn't believe that the Wehrmacht is exhausted. This is not because of any inherent skepticism; Nievka is, after all, a "believer," one of the Party faithful, a candidate-member of the Communist Party, and not a simple Komsomol like me. But in her hospital she faces every day the harsh reality of the wounded. The latter have a lot to say, and they contradict our official communiqués. Nievka relays everything to me but swears me to secrecy, insisting each time on my "Komsomol's word" not to tell any of it to anyone, especially not to Commissar Byelokonyenko or to Kola.

Of course, I would never dream of repeating to my commissar these stories about the poor functioning of the Red Army medical services, or the disturbing news that Nievka has gleaned from the wounded who have come from the Crimea and from the southern front in general. For Byelokonyenko is convinced that our army's general offensive is imminent and that it is going to coincide with the advance of a second front to the West, which our Anglo-Saxon allies are about to open in Normandy or elsewhere. He doesn't say from what source he has this news, but I know that he receives confidential reports from the leadership of the political services, in addition to the Tass news agency special bulletin that includes dispatches from Western news agencies not destined for publication in our press. He must, therefore, have an overall idea of how the war is going; Nievka bases what she says merely on partial testimony. The problem is that my commissar limits himself to optimistic generalities ("The Nazis' goose is cooked; they will be caught in a pincer grip between East and West"), while Nievka cites pessimistic but individual and irrefutable testimony. Wouldn't it be a good idea to put the two of them together and to discuss the war situation at length?

Chance arranges it well. One hot day in May, Nievka and I are stretched out in a discreet and sheltered spot on the edge of a small river that crosses Kislovodsk; the water is too cold to bathe in, but you can paddle your feet for a few moments at a time. It is in this position—with our feet in the water—that Byelokonyenko surprises us. I shouldn't be here at this time of day (nor should he, for that matter). Without my shoes on and with my trousers rolled up I must present a fairly ridiculous sight. Unsure how to deal with the situation, I introduce him very ceremoniously to Natalia Trofimovna G., who is sitting half-paralyzed and doesn't even dare remove her pretty legs from the stream. Byelokonyenko, to my surprise, is delighted:

"You aren't by any chance the daughter of Trofime Stepanovich G., of Leningrad?"

It's really a small world. Byelokonyenko and Nievka's father had met ten years before at the time of God-knows-what national meeting on transport productivity (of all things!), and have seen each other often since then. They are more than good acquaintances; they are "comrades-in-arms." "What an old fox, though, Trofime is," Byelokonyenko carries on. "He never told me that he had such a pretty daughter. There's no hurry; let's sit down and chat for a while; it's cooler here than in town."

After this promising beginning we have an opportunity to compare notes on the war's progress. But there is no such talk. I might as well have gone home, for Byelokonyenko and Nievka babble on without allowing me to put a word in edgewise. He speaks fervently of Hitler's ineluctable capitulation. She declares herself in agreement with everything he says. What strikes me especially, however, is the ease with which she engages in conversation, an ease quite at odds with the reserve that she maintains in the course of our social evenings with the Musketeers. Byelokonyenko, for his part, doesn't spare the compliments, and it hardly escapes my notice that he is examining my Nievka in detail with a frankly concupiscent eye.

When we get back and are finally alone on the Persian carpet, I tell her that the commissar fancies her. By way of a reassuring reply, Nievka explains, citing physiological reasons, that it is impossible for a woman of her age to make love with a man who is old enough to be her father. A fine joke! How then could I have come into the world, if women of twenty-three years couldn't sleep with men who were twenty years older? I am not about to commit myself on this terrain, however, and I reproach her bitterly for not having taken advantage of the chance to say a few words about the grievances of her wounded charges. The argument ends when she bursts into tears, gets up from the carpet, and throws herself on the bed, cursing the fate that has thrust her into the arms of such an intolerable person as I am. To crown everything, she accuses me, between sobs, of defeatism. That's the limit! I have been consoling her for months, struggling

against the avalanche of her depressing confidences, and it is I who
am defeatist!

I don't have time to argue at length. I must get back to Green
Alley. I don't wish to leave her moping on the bed, however, and so I
make a little speech of reconciliation—not without a touch of irony.
"You said that in bad faith, Nievka, but it's not your fault, you didn't
do it on purpose. For me, you will remain Cassandra. The two of us,
in spite of everything, will know how things are really evolving."

She relents—my irony having escaped her—and recovers her
smile. I am to come back this evening, after my last meeting. I am
almost at the door when she cries, "Don't eat any of their filth, I shall
get dinner ready here." Again, this Russian mania for referring to
"them," even when in this case it applies to the Red Army, which she
holds in such high esteem! I let it go, however: The food Nievka
prepares is incontestably better than that prepared by our squadron's
canteen cook.

After the episode of the bare feet, my commissar seems to promote me
also to the rank of "comrade-in-arms." He completely exempts me
from Sergeant Major Orlov's exercises. So that I shouldn't become
altogether idle, though, he often lends me to Captain Danilov, to
escort the supply truck. At every opportunity, sometimes twice a day,
he asks for news of "the ravishing daughter of my friend Trofime, of
Leningrad." He even reproaches me for having hidden her from him.
Despite this familiarity, he is very careful not to invite us to his home
to introduce us to his wife, Jara (a large Ukrainian mama). It is
obvious what's going on: Byelokonyenko has secret designs on
Nievka. He appears to me already as a dangerous rival.

Having witnessed the scenes my father used to create with my
mother, I swore resolutely that I would never give in to jealousy. In
present circumstances, though, I would have needed an exceptional
self-control that was out of character; I would also have had to love a
girl who didn't work in an army hospital, where relations between the
wounded and nurses are—it appears—very unhealthy. It is not simply a matter of my imagination; Nievka herself measures the progress

of the cure by the yardstick of their sexual appetite. When they arrive
in the surgery department where Nievka works, they are usually
delirious or screaming against our incapacity to prosecute the war,
but hardly have they recovered their spirits than they begin to make
indecent propositions to the nurses; the latter are relatively plentiful,
and some of them who are young and incompetent seem to have
enrolled in the medical services only because the food is better than
what can be had by civilians. At this stage, Nievka pretends no
longer to have much contact with them because she remains attached
to the surgical ward and to the seriously wounded. Nevertheless, she
spends a lot of time at the hospital, crosses the communal halls, and
is often called at in passing, sometimes very crudely. "Hey, you,
Miss Stuck-up, give us at least a sniff of your big ass." It is Nievka
herself who relates this to me.

Certainly, soldiers everywhere are slobs, in Russia perhaps more
than elsewhere; there is nothing in that to get excited over. Nievka,
though—so it seems to me—shows an excessive indulgence toward
her wounded. "They have spilled their blood for the Fatherland and
are only asking for a bit of human warmth."

"And suppose one of them, in search of 'human warmth,' should
try to sleep with you?"

"Where? How? You can't be serious," she replies.

Now in fact she spends two or three nights per week at the surgery
department; the problem of where and how cannot be insurmountable.

In April, because of an inspection by General Golovanov—the
future Air Marshal—I find it impossible to leave the barracks for a
period of ten days, and when finally, relieved and delighted, I head
for Nievka's, she greets me with a fearful scene: "Admit it, you filthy
drunkard, you took advantage of it to sleep with girls with big tits!"

Had this been said in a bantering tone, it might have been rather
flattering. But she isn't joking at all; she is livid with anger. She
knows all about it; she has proof; someone has seen me; they have
told her everything; we have to tell each other the truth; and so on.
Anger has the effect of making her lose her fine Leningrad accent,

and she hits out at the *tsytsatye baby,* these "girls with big tits." Her performance is worthy of a Cossack. It takes hours to calm her down and to resume a normal dialogue. Slowly I learn in sequence, first, that Nievka's mother, allegedly because of her small chest, was outrageously deceived by her husband; next, that in Russia the men are maniacs for big breasts and that, although I am Polish, I ogle Raya's chest in a very suspect manner; and finally, that during these last ten days she had become convinced that I would never come back to her.

To put an end to our mutual suspicions and frequent arguments, she decides there's no alternative but to live together. As it happens, Nievka's roommate, Rosa, is about to move out—to live with her lover, a Captain Pojarski. "Now we can stop tormenting each other with our jealousies," Nievka concludes. I have only to move in with her. But only commanders have the right to live in town; I have no official rank, and my mission as a Komsomol special envoy is precisely to live alongside the ranks.

"No excuses, please. You have only to speak about it with the commissar," she says with assurance. "You are not asking permission to live just anywhere in town, but at the home of Natalia Trofimovna G. And if you won't do it, I'll speak to him about it myself." She doesn't take herself for a commoner, my Nievka, but for a great lady of Leningrad society. We agree that I shall take the necessary steps; it is more logical for me to do it. Moreover, I don't want to give Byelokonyenko the opportunity of a face-to-face meeting with Nievka.

I couldn't have chosen a better day to raise the matter with my commissar. The night before, an exhilarating storm freshened the atmosphere and purified the air; it is so clear that from the upper part of town you can clearly see the great chain of the Caucasus and the majestic Elbrus. Byelokonyenko is also in a good mood: We are in the process of signing, after the Pact of London, a decisive agreement in Washington on American deliveries. Large quantities of engines supplied on credit are already under way or will be in no time; with this aid, even if there is a short delay in the opening of the second front, we'll show the Germans what's what next winter. With the aid of the formidable cold, Hitler will be beaten. I seize the moment to explain Nievka's and my plan to live together. As I do so, Byelokonyenko's good humor gives way to embarrassment. There are regulations in the armed forces: each one to his place. Someone of my rank cannot enjoy the same privileges accorded a commander. And anyway, who would do my work within the ranks on behalf of the Komsomol? I would have to be promoted and a replacement would have to be found for me, and all of that takes time. My promises to carry on doing everything as before, in spite of changing my living arrangements, don't carry much weight. He continues, however, thinking out loud: He cannot, on reflection, give cause to upset Natalia Trofimovna, the daughter of a "comrade-in-arms." I slip in the fact that she is called Nievka, and for good measure the fact that Andrei Zhdanov himself used to bounce her on his knee when she was a little girl. "Natalia isn't a bad name either," he says casually, but the information has been duly noted.

A lengthy, silent meditation follows. At last my commissar recovers the use of his voice and proposes a compromise; I can move in with Natalia Trofimovna—"Nievka" is decidedly too familiar—but on condition that I return to the barracks two or three nights per week, to show my face and make my presence felt, and to share the life of my comrades. Byelokonyenko also promises to look after my *propiska*—my residence permit—for Kislovodsk. All those who live in town are obliged to have one; it is the law. He will have to withdraw my passport from my Red Army dossier, have it stamped by the NKVD, and then return it to its place. "It is a mere formality," he says.

Three or four days later, just as I am about to go to bed, someone comes to look for me at the barracks: I am to go immediately to Byelokonyenko's home, in town. He lives at the far end of Kislovodsk, off an alley. In the daytime I can find it easily enough, but at night it is another matter. I hear the chimes of midnight when I finally enter his small apartment, after having passed Captain Pyetya Danilov on the stairway, a little the worse for a drink or two.

Byelokonyenko is in a foul mood. His wife is sleeping in the other room and he asks me to lower my voice, but he can hardly control his own as he cries out, "Wretched creature, what terrible wrong have you done in your life?" as if he didn't recognize me. I fear the worst, the discovery of my Siberian past or something of the kind. I wasn't born yesterday, however, and I wait for him to show his hand. He repeats the question; I repeat my silence. "Do you know, wretch," he continues finally, "what sort of passport you have?" I continue to say nothing because I don't know how to answer; he repeats his question several times. At last he answers it himself: "You hold a passport that is issued only to persons who are not allowed to change their place of residence, who are thereby declared undesirable everywhere else. It is notably the case for *prostitutki*; do you understand what I'm saying?" And he insists on repeating this provocative word ten, twenty, or thirty times.

What is there to say? I am not going to explain that a certain Ivanov in the NKVD in Rostov has apparently played a dirty trick on me, and that this hypocritical Soviet bureaucracy disgusts me. I confess only to my puzzlement; this passport has been inspected a hundred times in the Komsomol and in the Red Army—which keeps it in its own files—and no one, any more than I did, noticed the fact that I was marked down in it as a prostitute or any other sort of undesirable. "It's because the NKVD men are the only ones to recognize certain coded paragraphs; it's their way of communicating," my commissar replies, with an ease that persuades me he is recovering the use of his faculties. I call upon him therefore to witness the injustice done to me: I came to Rostov through love of this town, and to defend the USSR; by what right do they dare to add paragraphs to my passport as if I were a prostitute?

The score is tied: Byelokonyenko has me sit down and brings out the vodka; the atmosphere is one of détente. "It's true, you don't deserve it. Our secret police are awful characters, and you're not the first to find this out. On the other hand, there is nothing to be done about it; we cannot do without them, for there are too many authentic enemies to fight against. Later, after the war, when we approach the

112 BETWEEN TWO WORLDS

phase of communism, we will no longer need the NKVD; everything will be socialized. Do you understand what I'm saying?" No, I am interested in the here and now, and want to know if I can move in with Nievka. "At present it's impossible. You would have to move heaven and earth to get your passport changed, because they hold against you also the fact of your Polish nationality, which is suspect by definition. You ought to have declared yourself a Russian since your parents come from Rostov, but now it's too late. Do you understand what I'm saying?" Of course I understand, and I shall remember. "Don't pull a face, take a drink. Relax!" And now, completely drunk, the stout Ukrainian promises to favor in any way he can my relations with Natalia Trofimovna, "a wonderful girl." At this stage of drunkenness, his speech, which is laced with hiccups, becomes almost unintelligible. He doesn't even hear me as I withdraw, leaving him to mutter to himself.

Back at the barracks, I can't go to sleep; this discovery that the NKVD have been communicating with signs behind my back weighs too heavily on me. I wake Kola up to talk about it. He is thunderstruck; I had told him nothing about my plan to change addresses, so as not to admit my intention of betraying the Musketeers for Nievka. I spin a long yarn for him about the sacrifice I had been ready to make for Nievka's sake, to console her for her troubles at the hospital, and I spill out everything that I was not supposed to say—Komsomol's word—on the Red Army medical services and the situation on the southern front.

It takes Kola some time to orient himself in this confusing mess; then he decrees, with the good sense of a man of the South: "You are sleeping at Nievka's place three nights a week anyway. After moving house it would amount to the same thing, since on the other three nights she is at the hospital!" The truth of what he says is obvious, and the absurdity of our undertaking is apparent. We have stirred up the shit with the NKVD to no purpose. As for the passport, it is of no importance, since it is kept in the Red Army's files somewhere, and no one will bother with it until the end of the war. Afterward, things will have changed, and we'll see.

Then we change the subject to Nievka. Kola is almost touched to learn that she takes the misfortunes of the wounded so much to heart. "I would never have believed it of her," he says. "She is rather stuck up sometimes, you'll admit, and her background is very different from ours. You'll have to explain to her that people like us are used to *tyeplushki*; it's our Russian way of traveling. But we're not really a people of travelers and our railways are practically nonexistent; as for our roads, all it takes is for a cow to piss on them to bring traffic to a halt. All this is terrible for the transport of the wounded, but the Germans have the same problems with evacuating theirs. In this way our handicaps become trump cards; she ought to understand that. But don't do anything to harden her heart or to make her indifferent; we have to make sure she stays on the side of the enemies of suffering."

The next day I tell Nievka about the incident with the passport, without any sourness or reproach for this scheme of hers, which had earned me a humiliating refusal, not to mention the designation *prostitutka*. I watch the blood rise to her cheeks, however, as it does during her worst fits of anger. "They will pay me for this," she says, stressing each word. "Just wait until the blockade of Leningrad is broken, and we shall see who is strongest. I shall go to see Zhdanov and I shall have their heads. Who do these NKVD shitheads think they are?"

At the front, everything is going badly. There is no need of Nievka's wounded to know about it; it is enough to listen carefully every evening at seven o'clock to the Sovinformbureau's communiqués on Radio Moscow. The Red Army is falling back from all its lines of defense in the south and southwest, from the Black Sea coast to Voronezh. Our propaganda takes account of this with the usual lag. On June 22, on the occasion of the anniversary of the war, Colonel Zlotnikov still affirms: "The enemy is trying to hurl itself forward, but the intensity of its attacks diminishes day by day." This is the swan song of the argument about the Wehrmacht's incapacity for offensive action.

Beginning in July, the tone changes: *Pravda* exalts the heroism of

the defenders of Sevastopol and alleges that, despite the fall of the
city, we have carried off a moral victory; but it also seems to acknowledge and adopt as its own the revelations that Nievka has been
making to me in the preceding months. Certainly there is no question
of criticizing the medical services, but the incompetence of certain
commanders is obvious. So too is the lack of discipline among the
troops. Still more revealing are the denunciations in *Pravda* of those
promoting "panic" and "capitulation." The best pens in the country,
those of Ilya Ehrenburg, Alexis Tolstoy, and Mikhail Sholokhov, are
now mobilized to arouse hatred for the Germans.

This seems to contradict the speech in which Stalin himself the
previous year absolved the German people from the crimes of the
Nazis. Our troops, however, are probably not sufficiently motivated
ideologically, and so in addition, they are warned that "captivity in
Germany is worse than death." For love of our Russian mothers, each
of us must kill at least his or her German. But why should we avenge
only Russian mothers? Why not Ukrainians, Cossacks, Jews, or
Poles?

The scene at Byelokonyenko's has triggered within me a rejection
of this Russian world and its deceitful practices. I have felt this once
before, in Western Siberia; but this time it is stronger, almost irrational, because at bottom Kola is right: I am not the victim of any
injustice, I have simply been denied a privilege that I had arrogated
to myself. What's more, my commissar is as good as his word: he
facilitates my relations with Nievka and turns a blind eye when I
report late to work. The thing is stronger than I, though; I need to
drown this scene in vodka. I no longer even look for company to drink
with; I often hide myself behind a tree in the park, like a thief. Lying
there alone, I close my eyes hoping to forget everything, but straightaway I hear again the drunken voice of my commissar, and the word
prostitutki resounds in my ears.

Nievka is convinced that I have lapsed into alcoholism. She
preaches at me endlessly, even on the days when I am sober. At least
she has given up her attempts at blackmail: "It is either me or the
vodka." Now she no longer threatens to throw me out, and when I turn

up at her home, after a tankful, she undresses me with the skill of
Russian women who are well used to drunkards. She applies cold
compresses to my forehead and wraps herself around me as if to calm
me down. Early the next morning, though, while serving the tea, she
resumes her litany: "Vodka will be the death of you, wretch. I even
feel pity for you. If you don't stop drinking you will be ruined," and so
on. "Nievka," I say to her, "on August 4 I will be twenty-one years
old, and I am old enough to live my own life." In fact I will be only
eighteen, but I have always lied to her about my age.

On August 1, listening to Radio Moscow, we learn that the Germans have taken Novocherkassk, the historic capital of the Cossacks,
and have even captured Rostov. *Pravda* publishes a solemn appeal
from Stalin: "Not a step backwards." Consternation prevails in the
first squadron. We are wasting our time in Kislovodsk, while the
krauts occupy the region dearest to us. Kola does what he can to look
at the bright side. "It's not a war between Hitler and the Cossacks,"
he says. "He has the whole of the USSR against him, and on the
Moscow front he is hardly advancing at all." That boosts our morale a
little. Kola is right: The Germans have taken Rostov before, in 1917,
and once again a year later, and on neither occasion did Russia
collapse because of it. It is Moscow that counts; and there their
advance is blocked.

Our Komsomol meetings are much longer from this time onward, so
intense is the interest generated by the reading of *Pravda* and the *Red
Star* (the newspaper of the armed forces). Late in the evening I arrive
at Nievka's, as sober as an ascetic, and another surprise awaits me:
Rosa's bed has been replaced by a long peasant-style table surrounded by eight old chairs. "It's for your birthday. I have already
arranged everything, don't worry about a thing." She explains that
she has invited all the Musketeers from our evenings together, except
for that "cheap tart" Raya, whose big breasts have often caught my
eye. Rosa will be there, and can keep Vassya company. "Your commissar is also coming," Nievka adds, after a brief hesitation. "What?
Have you seen him, then?" No, she has invited him in writing, and

hands me his reply. "Charming Nievka"—that's how he addresses himself to her, this satyr who, in front of me, ceremoniously calls her Natalia Trofimovna! He will be delighted to see her again—not a word, of course, about my birthday—and he explains that his wife is unfortunately busy on that evening. He will come alone, therefore. Nievka, Nievka, this will never do.

"Nievka, you are as naïve as a child; the commissar is making eyes at you because he wants to screw you. That's why he's coming!"

"It doesn't bother me at all to be stared at," she says, laughing. "I'll dress to the nines. But your Byelokonyenko will not screw me either here or anywhere else. I have already told you that I am incapable of sleeping with an old man."

"Okay, let's not go on about it, but Byelokonyenko isn't aware of your tastes. He is going to try his luck and I will be forced to punch him and finish my military career in prison."

It is destiny. In this Lermontovian spot, I have always had the feeling that everything would end in a duel; the setting requires it.

This birthday will be the most memorable of my life. It is barely eleven o'clock—and both the night and party are still young—when someone comes to fetch the commissar, who sets out staggering slightly, but is perfectly capable of understanding that something urgent is afoot. An hour later it is Nievka and Rosa's turn; they are summoned to the hospital immediately. Something is clearly wrong, but what? The Germans? According to our communiqués, they have hardly reached Rostov. Whatever the "intensity" of their attack, they can't have been able realistically to cover six hundred kilometers in two days. Logically, it must be something else.

It is our propaganda, however, that is lacking in logic. Very early in the morning the general alert is given and we have to pack in an atmosphere of catastrophe. The enemy has already occupied the railway center at Min. Vody and has cut off our retreat in the direction of the Caspian Sea and Transcaucasia. We have to save ourselves by going through Pyatigorsk, on condition that we get there before the krauts do, and then follow the mountain routes toward Nalchik and Vladicaucasia. Before leaving, however, we have to destroy all industrial installations, including the vodka factory. And thus it is that on August 4, 1942, the day of my eighteenth birthday, the "damnable drink" flows in floods in the gutters of Kislovodsk, and the citizens, flat on their bellies, drink it as if it were water from a mountain spring.

My commissar orders me to escort the usual supply truck driven by a civilian chauffeur with a small mustache, but authorizes me to take only three men: Kola, Vassya, and Volodya. Kostya will take the *electrichka* with the others. We'll meet up again in Pyatigorsk. As soon as we are on the road, I ask the driver to make a detour via Nievka's hospital.

"You're going to bring her with you?" Kola asks approvingly.

"You won't be doing her any favors," Vassya objects. "The commissar will force her off in Pyatigorsk."

"You're kidding, sunshine! It's more likely that he'll force you off! She's coming with us!" I say categorically.

Chaos reigns in front of the hospital. The wounded are trying to escape in their pajamas, some with their heads bandaged, their limbs in plaster, leaping about on their crutches. They clutch at our truck, begging us to let them aboard. "Brothers, show us some Russian sympathy, or the Huns will certainly finish us off." It is awful, but we can do nothing for them. We have no right to take anyone at all, and if we even take Nievka, we are sticking our necks out. Vassya brutally thrusts back those who are trying to climb on; Kola and Volodya do their best to help him. Insults fly on all sides.

Finally Nievka appears on the main porch steps and announces, "I am not leaving."

Fury overcomes me and I call her an ingrate without conscience. I recover just enough cool to reason with her. "Everyone knows that you are a candidate-member of the Party, and that Zhdanov held you on his knee when you were a child. You are exactly the type of Communist the Germans are looking for, your own wounded have told you so a thousand times. Nievka, come with us, come quickly, we are already dangerously late."

She doesn't answer; silence is her weapon on those occasions when she is most annoyed or upset. I run through my mea culpas, beg her forgiveness for ever having glanced at large-breasted girls, for having caressed her friend Rosa once or twice when I was drunk.

"I'll be kind to you, I'll never make you unhappy again, but let us leave now, let's leave quickly; look at what's going on around you." She remains fixed, erect as a statue, pale as her nurse's blouse; she doesn't even seem to be listening to me. The truck's horn sounds, my friends are calling me; they risk being overwhelmed by the patients. So much the worse; I'm off, I can't stand around arguing until the krauts arrive.

I am already climbing into the cabin when Nievka catches up with me. She holds me tightly, very tightly in her arms. Her voice, choking with sobs, is so feeble that I can hardly hear her: "I don't want to abandon the wounded, I cannot, and it just isn't done. But don't worry, I will defend myself. I'll get out of it. But you, *malchik moy* [my lad], take care, be prudent, and promise me not to drink anymore." We cover each other with kisses, on the forehead, the eyes, the nose, just as at the time of our first rendezvous; we don't quite manage to detach ourselves from one another. Our friends in the truck leave us alone for a moment and stop protesting; the wounded move away, silently. Soon she is but a white point on the steps of her beloved hospital. Adieu, Nievka, Natalia, daughter of Leningrad, stubborn, anti-alcohol nurse, you have been good to me, and I will not forget you.

I never saw her again; I have never had any news of her. At the beginning I often spoke of her with Kola and Vassya. They argued that we ought to have taken her with us by force. Only after the war did I learn that Kislovodsk was savagely bombed and half-destroyed during the winter of 1942–43. The kind teacher, Maroussia, and the joyful Tania, our vodka supplier, were killed. Vera, the blond doyenne of our evenings together, survived and rejoined the Red Army medical services. Raya made it, too. Not a word, though, about Nievka. That didn't prove anything, however. Personally, I believe that Nievka is still alive.

On just one occasion, in 1945 in Rostov, were the Myechotka

Musketeers able to come together to celebrate victory. Vassya the Elephant, a captain by now, proposed a toast to the good health of "our friend Nievka." Our women companions, almost all of them Cossacks, were astonished; in the region of the Don they had never heard such a name. So I spoke at length of the nurse who had come from the North, and in order not to spoil the mood, I told them that in the end she had managed to return to Leningrad where she was now living happily and prosperously. Just as things ended in the fairy tales that she loved to hear so much.

3

THE MYECHOTKA
MUSKETEERS

Few people realize today that the loss of the Caucasus in 1942 would have been a catastrophe for the Allies. Even in the USSR, the history books dispatch the affair in a few lines and seem to regard this battle as one of little importance. At the time, it was otherwise. The Wehrmacht blitzkrieg in the region that yielded the greatest oil wealth in Europe, and that commanded access to Turkey—and beyond to Iran—was the subject of great concern among the general staffs of the anti-Nazi coalition. Churchill hurried to Moscow to discuss it with Stalin. It was the first and most difficult of their meetings; neither had the slightest good news to communicate. Some weeks earlier the British had abandoned Tobruk and were now fighting in Egypt, their backs to the Pyramids. For the Russians, things lurched from bad to worse after the fall of Sevastopol. They hadn't managed to stabilize the front either in the Kuban—their granary, near the Black Sea—or on the line of the Don.

From this moment forward, as it penetrated the Caucasus, the Wehrmacht seemed to be swooping down to meet its troops operating in Africa, under the command of General Rommel, the "desert fox." Such a junction of forces would have had disastrous consequences for the Allies. Conscious of the danger, Churchill asked Stalin in August 1942, omitting the diplomatic niceties, if his army was still capable of preventing the Wehrmacht from crossing the mountain passes of the Caucasus. (He is even supposed to have offered the aid of the

RAF, though he doesn't mention it in his memoir-history, *The Second World War*.) Stalin then unfolded a detailed map of the region onto the table—a Georgian by birth, he was familiar with the area—studied it, and decreed, "They shall not cross the passes of the Caucasus; we will stop them in the mountains."

Churchill only half-believed him, and he reported to Roosevelt that his chief of staff, General Alan Brooks, placed even less confidence in these declarations. Reading this passage in Churchill's memoirs used to fill me with a secret joy, as if, in 1942, I had personally played a fine stroke not only against the Germans, but also against these skeptical Anglo-Saxons. Today my ex-combatant's pride is less keen, and I think that the success we eventually enjoyed was only obtained thanks to the extraordinary presumption of the Wehrmacht.

I don't propose to offer here a lengthy exposition on military strategy. A brief summary of the facts of the situation after our hasty departure from Kislovodsk will, however, allow the reader to form a better picture. What is striking is that during the Churchill-Stalin discussions in Moscow, Stalingrad was never mentioned. The two leaders reasonably inferred that the Wehrmacht would hurl the bulk of its forces on the Caucasian front—where it stood to gain everything—and not on the unrewarding steppes of the Don and the Volga. In fact, the Germans did the opposite, and drove deeper into an endless space renowned for the severity of its winters. It appears that they wanted to encircle Moscow. How, though? Imagine, if you will, an army at Lille, in the far north of France, hoping to encircle Paris by making a detour through Aix-en-Provence, almost on the Mediterranean coast. On the Russian scale the distances are even greater. Perhaps these strategists with a handle to their names—von Manstein, von Kleist (perhaps the descendant of the poet of despair?), and von Paulus—pressed forward onto the steppes of the Volga for no other reason than that they met initially with very little resistance.

Their second mistake becomes clear as soon as one considers the geography of the Caucasus. Until the discovery of the oil fields in Kuybyshev and later in Western Siberia, 90 percent of Soviet oil came from Baku and Grozny. Therefore, these two basins ought to have constituted the chief prize of the battle of 1942, such was the extent of the belligerents' dependence on petroleum for their "war of engines." Now Baku is right on the coast of the Caspian Sea and Grozny on the northern foothills of the Caucasus, not far from the littoral. To reach them, the Germans were not at all obliged to secure control of all the highest mountains, and particularly the main chain. It would have been sufficient for them to have followed the path of the Moscow-Tbilisi-Yerevan Transcaucasian railway, which, after the junction at Min. Vody, threads its way through some of the lower passes and then neatly skirts the Caspian Sea. If the Wehrmacht had concentrated its best divisions along this axis, it would certainly have arrived in Grozny and Baku. General Tyulenyev, who was responsible for the defense of this sector, recognized as much himself in his memoirs published in 1960.

The noble Prussian generals, however, tried to do everything at once: they wanted the Caucasus, but also Stalingrad; oil, but also Mount Elbrus; and all of this while simultaneously encircling the adversary in order to take large numbers of prisoners to send back to Germany. It was too much. Their appetite exceeded their means, even if, to begin with, they had possessed mastery of the air and a clear superiority in armaments. After their failure at Stalingrad they were routed from the Caucasus, narrowly avoiding becoming encircled themselves. This misguided campaign didn't yield them a single drop of oil—but only the consolation of having reached the summit of Mount Elbrus.

This aspect particularly interests me—although I have a marked aversion for climbing in general—for we in the "eleventh" school of the air force came very close to losing our lives because of it. When we abandoned Kislovodsk, our commanders had reasoned sensibly enough that the Germans were going to rush along the path of the Transcaucasian, toward the oil fields, thus leaving the road to Nalchik and Vladicaucasia more or less free. These mountain towns have strategic value only for the conquest of Georgia, and, today, more than four decades later, they are still not connected to the railway network. Such an analysis neglects to take into account, however, the

Wehrmacht's taste for mountain climbing. The main chain of the Caucasus extends to the west, close to and almost paralleling the Black Sea; it is dominated by Mount Elbrus, with its peak of 5,600 meters. The Germans were bent on planting the swastika on it at any cost. As early as mid-August their press had published a clumsy photomontage showing their *Alpenjägers* on the summit of the mountain; it had immediately provoked mocking denials from the Sovinformbureau. The Germans' self-esteem having thus been wounded, they decided, no doubt, to do whatever was necessary to take some authentic snapshots.

The Red Army command, when it saw the Wehrmacht slow down its attack in the direction of the oil fields in this way, and head suddenly toward Nalchik, couldn't understand the object of the maneuver. Were the Nazis trying to cut through toward Tbilisi and from there toward Turkey? The enemy's numbers were inadequate for such an ambitious expedition. At the time it was impossible to imagine a German objective as absurd and limited as the scaling of the Elbrus. Therefore, our high command decided to defend Nalchik no matter what the cost and mobilized all available forces, notably Marshal Golovanov's future pilots, despite the investment already made in them to prepare them for still nobler tasks. This irrationality on the German side thus prompted an irrational Soviet reaction, and the "eleventh" of the air force was going to spend the second half of August 1942 defending a town of no military importance. Thanks to Churchill's *The Second World War*, I know today that we took up our battle position on the very day that Stalin declared to him, "We will stop them in the mountains."

One further remark before returning to the truck in which we are taking leave of Kislovodsk, this August 4, 1942, the day of my eighteenth birthday: In the West, since the end of the war, it has become fashionable to cover the strategists of the Wehrmacht with paeans of praise, to portray them as lucid men who were contemptuous of the former corporal, Hitler, and to imply that they were wholly unaware of the atrocities committed by their troops. Today there is a ready market for their memoirs, which sell like the most tawdry of romance novels. This is understandable; even in sports the winning team always sings the praises of its beaten opponents, the better to emphasize its own merits. Nevertheless, I would like the Western victors one day to clarify with their valiant opponents the Mount Elbrus episode. For until we are better informed, I will abide by the incontestably severe verdict of my friend Kola in 1945, that only imbeciles could have consented to expend so much effort and to weary so many people in order to climb the highest peak of the Caucasus.

Kola is not with me. He is in the back of the overloaded supply truck with Vassya and Volodya, and is discreetly inspecting the contents of the cargo. In the cabin, our civilian driver with the small mustache hardly says a word. The zigzagging mountain road is completely deserted; there isn't a vehicle in sight. We must have been the last to leave Kislovodsk, a long time after the others. Suddenly, in a little rise between two bends that form a large hairpin, the driver parks our truck at the edge of the ravine, as though not to block the traffic. We approve. It is time to "reduce the body's internal hydrostatic pressure." No sooner has the driver climbed down, however, than he moves behind the truck to the vicinity of some rocks that we have just passed by, and cries out to us, *"Gospoda russkye officery!"* ("Gentlemen, Russian officers!")

Stupefying exordium! Ever since the Revolution, there have been no "gentlemen" or "officers" in the USSR. We are all comrades; our superiors are commanders.*

After having taken up a strategic position that will allow him to take cover behind the rocks with a single leap, the driver shouts, "Gentlemen, Russian officers, come back to Kislovodsk with me! The Reds have lost the war. You mustn't sacrifice your young lives for them. Another, different Russia is soon going to be reborn, and it will need you. Come with me; I'll hide you. I will obtain civilian clothes for you. You will want for nothing. Trust me."

---

* As noted earlier, the titles of officers will only be reestablished in October 1942.

Our astonished silence obliges him to raise his voice: "Why do you want to get yourselves killed for the Bolsheviks and the Jews who have been sucking our Christian blood since their damned revolution? Don't be crazy. Come back to Kislovodsk!" Then he vanishes behind the rocks and all that we can hear is the sound of his running footsteps. He is off as fast as his legs will carry him.

None of us moves. His speech has us riveted to the spot. Today has provided us with more than our fair share of excitement: the panic departure, the tragic scene at the hospital; and now this flesh-and-blood counterrevolutionary straight out of the films on the White Guards.

"You ought to have shot him," Volodya, who is the first to pull himself together, says to me.

"Why me? You're a better shot. In fact, it's your specialty."

"Yes, but you're the politico, and the fight against capitulators is your special responsibility."

"You mean this creep's speech had no effect on you? That it's none of your business?"

"Cut it out," Kola says. "This isn't the Wehrmacht here. We don't fire on unarmed civilians. In any case, he is now far away. Let's be on our way as well. We have already wasted enough time."

Easier said than done. Which of us four knows how to drive a truck? Here the discussion sours. They reproach me for not having learned to drive, despite having escorted this damned jalopy so many times. I don't understand, I retort, how they can pretend to pilot a four-engined plane when they don't even know how to get a wretched truck to work. We outdo each other in vain recriminations. A screaming match for nothing. They plead with me to try to start it up, or else we are going to have to set off on foot. I pull the starter and depress the accelerator while at the same time releasing the hand brake, and—what a miracle!—the vehicle slowly sets off. "Bastard!" these ingrates shout at me. "You knew all along how to drive. You just wanted to be begged." But these Cossack brutes don't seem to realize that if they carry on hazing me like this, we are all going to end up in the ravine.

In fact, I keep the situation under control only because the damned truck refuses to go faster. When I press my foot on the accelerator, it simply responds with threatening noises. The traitor driver had left it in first gear—at least this is what I think today—which allowed me to start off. As I don't know how to change into second or third, however, I can't get it to run normally. Never mind. Let's go slowly, then. It is safer on this tortuous route, and it still beats going on foot.

The others don't even seem to notice that anything is amiss. Vassya the Elephant is actually snoring in the cabin beside me. Kola is also sleeping, in the back, while Volodya, sitting behind me, is singing one of his ballads from the region of the Don, in which a Cosachka offers a ring to her Cossack and promises that in a year's time she will marry him. A thousand calamities follow: wars, floods, fogs; but the chorus comes back, always the same: the Cosachka promises that in a year's time she will give herself to him. This melancholy folk song grates on my nerves. It seems to lack a conclusion. Did they sleep together? Were they happy? Did they argue? Did they die?

"That's enough, Volodya! Wake Kola up! I need advice."

"Are you thinking of running away as well?" he replies without laughing.

And to think that Volodya's best quality, in Nievka's opinion, apart from his singing voice, was his utter lack of malice. Perhaps, though, in all innocence, he thinks that I am a potential deserter? I insist that he apologize before explaining that I believe our situation is getting worse by the hour. I sense that I am in the process of destroying the truck and that it is certain that the "eleventh" school of the air force is no longer waiting for us at Pyatigorsk.

"Perhaps they will wait," says Kola. "We are carrying the grub, after all."

"But going at this speed we won't get there until late tonight. And maybe later still!"

"What's the alternative?" Kola asks, and he cites the old Russian (or Cossack) saying that "it is useless to complain about losing your hair when they are cutting your head off."

Right. If this is more or less the situation, my grumbling about the state of the truck is foolish indeed. Let's take off again in first and not talk about it any longer. What a macabre expression, though! By comparison, Volodya's melancholy ballad was an ode to joy. But Volodya is no longer singing; he is dozing like the others. They seem intent on fighting the war without losing any sleep.

In the distance, a sky filled with smoke at last announces Pyatigorsk ahead. I have pulled off a real exploit; I know how to drive a truck. I am a hero. It is incredible to what extent such a bagatelle can make a man happy. Instead of congratulating me, however, Kola and the others ask me to stop. To do what? Aren't we late already? Of course. But they are Cossacks, and they must conduct the war with cunning and discernment. They do not intend to enter a town in flames without first assuring themselves that it is in friendly hands. Volodya volunteers to go see what is happening. While waiting for him to get back, we will examine more closely the contents of the boxes of supplies that we are transporting. For once there is no argument; we are all agreed.

The news that Volodya brings back, while not entirely disastrous, is very bad. The Germans haven't yet arrived in Pyatigorsk, but our forces have already abandoned it. Easily one-quarter of the town is on fire, either as a result of aerial bombardment or because our own army had blown up industrial targets without observing due precautions. Crowds of disbanded soldiers of the 37th Army, which dispersed following the fall of Rostov on July 23 (and not on August 1, as we had been led to believe) have been left behind. These stragglers are starving and are prowling around in search of food. The krauts meanwhile are at Min. Vody, though probably in the form of a motorized column that will have to await the arrival of the bulk of their troops before advancing on Pyatigorsk. On the other hand, since the town is now practically defenseless, they might just as easily be planning an incursion at any moment, out of curiosity or to pick off the remnants of the 37th Army. We can't afford to delay; we will have to cross Pyatigorsk quickly and press on toward Nalchik. Besides, everyone is heading in the same direction.

For this very reason, however, I don't feel capable of driving our half-broken-down truck through the crowd. We need a proper driver, if we are to catch up with our unit and to avoid crushing these unfortunates on foot who have been on the go all the way from Rostov. There must be any number of drivers among them who would be happy to travel aboard a truck loaded with food. First, though, we'll stash the truck out of sight in a quiet street; it would be risky to drive at a snail's pace through these bands of armed and hungry men.

"Just a minute!" Kola says. He refuses, even in exceptional circumstances, to neglect his personal five-year plan for the elimination of suffering. He has discovered, in the back of the truck, a case containing a roll of light woolen cloth intended for commanders' summer uniforms. We cut off a good length, carefully disguise the cut, and put the remainder back in place. The spoils of war, our "strategic reserves," are calculated for five: Kola is not forgetting Kostya the Khan, even if he isn't here with us. Now we can set off into Pyatigorsk in search of a lucky streak: a quiet street and a good driver-mechanic.

It is the truck, however, that once again decides for us. At the first square it stops dead, like a horse that refuses to approach a fire. All around us there is not a soul in sight. It's crazy: This town is twice the size of Kislovodsk, and its inhabitants must be hiding somewhere instead of fighting the fires. There can be no question of leaving the truck unguarded, however. Kola and Volodya stay in the back, rifles in hand, as in a western just before the Indians attack. Vassya and I head toward the Nalchik road to try to find a driver.

Our undertaking is ridiculous. It isn't all that simple to pick a square and question passersby, one by one, asking if they know how to drive. The soldiers seem surprised by our questions and still more by the state of our uniforms. An abyss now separates those who, only the day before, were still sleeping in a bed, and these men who have been marching since July 23. We soften the shock by offering them chocolate and cigarettes that we have found in the truck.

For a retreating army, night is the most favorable time for marching, for then the sky isn't full of enemy planes. A town abandoned by the authorities, however, automatically attracts errant troops, some of whom use the respite, the vacuum of authority thus created, to rest up. It is among these soldiers that we are going to make inquiries. Vassya dismisses my objections on the risk we are taking of getting lost in these apparently identical streets. His sense of direction is "infallible," he says. So, the Cossack identity exists after all. Vassya is proof, a novice who behaves as if he had been a soldier all his life. This ghost town doesn't bother him at all. The elders of his tribe have described similar situations to him from the time he was a boy. He doesn't even flinch when I point out a slogan chalked on a wall: *Russe Kaput.* "You don't win wars by writing on walls," he observes. It is demoralizing nonetheless. Even before the Germans arrive, someone is already scribbling their slogans on the walls.

We meet a group of *chernomortzy,* Black Sea sailors. What are they doing here? Has their fleet been dispersed along with the 37th Army? It is obvious they have been doing some serious drinking. They don't seem in a hurry at all and are singing—out of tune—that "a Russian sailor never surrenders to the enemy." Vassya exchanges a few words with them, but is careful not to ask them if they know how to drive. He says he wouldn't take any *chernomortzy* with us for anything in the world, even if they were sober. They are notorious brawlers, and have a very exclusive esprit de corps. Prudence above everything: This is the ABC of the art of warfare.

"Hey, you bum! Hold on a minute!" Vassya calls out after a figure in uniform about twenty meters in front of us. The man obeys and turns around. It's a colonel. From the back Vassya couldn't identify him because the insignia of rank are worn on the collar of the tunic.* How is he going to react to this salute? A colonel without troops is only a man like any other, and in a dark street he tends to take account of the number and size of his interlocutors. Faced with the Elephant, he prefers not to be too touchy. So much the better. This is demoralizing, though. Is it still an army if you can get away with hailing colonels just like that?

* Until the reform of October 26, 1942, introduces epaulettes.

We're in luck, even so; the colonel does indeed drive, and it would suit him perfectly to travel in a truck with us. Mission accomplished. We return to the vehicle. En route we relate a lengthy story to the colonel to explain our breakdown, and pretend that we have killed the traitor driver in the way that one would put down a mad dog. He has his own worries, however. He is preoccupied by the absence of fighting spirit of certain detachments that are dispersing in the wilderness of the countryside, convinced that the sheer size of the country will be enough to defeat the enemy.

The colonel, N. N. Tretiakov, doesn't manage, despite repeated attempts, to get the engine restarted. Instead, he reverts to his habits of command and orders us to push the truck to a nearby burning house so as to see what's wrong. He has us unload most of the sacks in the bed of the truck to find the toolbox, and he gives me a thorough dressing down because, he says, I should have given the truck some water, as if it were a horse. Finally, after having decreed that the damage is irreparable—something by a mysterious name having "leaked" from the engine, causing it to freeze—he raises his voice: "Burn everything! We mustn't leave anything to the krauts. That's an order."

A short while ago he was wandering around the streets of Pyatigorsk and in the wrong direction as well, with his back to the Nalchik road, and now he has the nerve to give orders. Since we have no spare colonel, however, we are obliged to deal with N. N. Tretiakov. Kola respectfully explains that we need a written order: As our military hierarchy is in general very exacting, it will be even more so over a question of food and supplies intended for five hundred pilots. The word *food* seems to sway the colonel. He changes his tack and suggests an arrangement. He is not altogether alone; his men are sleeping in a courtyard in Pyatigorsk, near some horses that are resting. We could travel on a *telega*—a rather large wooden cart—and carry at least some of the provisions from the truck. At this he goes off in search of his men, leaving us to hold a new council of war.

Vassya is not at all impressed by Colonel Tretiakov. He's not a real soldier, Vassya says; he's an engineer who has been given his stripes on that account. His argument, though, is double-edged; it is not clear that a career soldier is better qualified than a technician to repair a truck. Volodya has another idea: We could lighten the truck of its load and tow it to Nalchik. Kola is skeptical. He suggests that I draft a written order—since I have the most readable handwriting— and to have it ready for the colonel to sign when he returns; the rest is merely idle chatter. "One day we'll get from the krauts a far better truck than this old heap," he says, proving that even if he has renounced his Cossack identity, he has shed none of its confident bravado. I lack imagination by contrast, and my pessimistic mood is only aggravated when the colonel's *telega* arrives: It is three-quarters full of baggage and is drawn by a single horse, the most skeletal specimen in all of Russia.

Where can all these servicemen have come from, wearing the colors of all the different armed forces, mounted on improvised vehicles, perched on *telegi* or walking, and advancing as slowly as a funeral procession? I imagine that these dispersed elements of the 37th Army—and of several other army divisions—flowed back toward the South, over the vast plain between Rostov and the foothills of the Caucasus, across the fields, like thousands of uncontrollable streams, before joining up in Min. Vody, in a single great river that swelled out over its banks. Because here, between Pyatigorsk and Nalchik, there is only one route, a simple country road twisting in and out of the gentle slopes that lead to the mountains. The distance to be covered is not enormous: a hundred or a hundred fifty kilometers—no one seems to know exactly—but it is obvious that at this pace, with the enemy in control of the air, this march is becoming a dangerous folly.

My experience in Poland in 1939 taught me thoroughly on this score, and my three companions are agreed. They are airmen as well as Cossacks, and they know the implacable laws of the "war of engines." Kola alone is reluctant when we discuss taking one of the small paths that link up the mountain villages. He is lazy by inclination and thinks—or hopes—that our planes will assure us of air cover along the road and allow us to arrive in two or three days, without too great an effort; our baggage and food supplies appear to him to be lighter on Colonel Tretiakov's *telega* than on our backs. In any case, we will at least need to get hold of a map of the area so as not to set out blindly into the unknown. But we search for a map in vain: Nobody has one; they are all in Nalchik, in the hands of authorized personnel. For lack of anything better, Vassya manages to get hold of a small compass in exchange for half a packet of Kazbek cigarettes.

We have the feeling, though, that there is no hurry. The hours pass by; the sun climbs higher; it is warm and the sky remains empty. Our spirits pick up. Suddenly an avalanche falls from the sky. Pilots of the Luftwaffe may not get up early, but once they start, they work with determination.

The first raid is worthy of an air show; everything is done for dazzling effect. One after the other, twelve airplanes head straight for us, making as if to land on the road, climb up again at full throttle, then, reversing their flight path, descend once again in the other direction to pass over us almost overhead. The din of their engines would awaken the dead, and among the living it creates a fair panic. Above us, these Luftwaffe aces must be chuckling at the sight of horses rearing up, carts turning over, the mad scramble of soldiers searching for cover among the bushes on the highly exposed slopes. Curiously, they don't bomb the road. It is as if they want to keep it intact for their own motorized columns. There isn't even any machine-gun fire, perhaps because they have run out of ammunition in the Pyatigorsk sector, or, more simply, do not want to damage potential prisoners.

After such a harrowing experience, order returns only slowly to our ranks. I take advantage of the pause to talk to a civilian refugee whom I have met near a *telega* full of women dressed in black, carrying children in their arms. I know from experience that a retreating army doesn't like to be restricted in its movements, and I decide to alert them to the dangers they might be facing; the Russian equivalent of Sergeant Major Bartczak would be perfectly capable of ordering one of these women to strangle her child, lest a simple cry might bring the squadrons of the Luftwaffe down on him. The man to whom I give the friendly advice not to continue along this dangerous road has a strangely young face, with an abundant white head of hair. He gives the ghost of a kindly smile, which doesn't detract from the sadness of his expression, and explains to me that they are all Jews and therefore haven't any choice.

"The Germans are killing all of us without distinction, men and women, young and old alike. In every town and city, large or small, they round up the Jews, bring them to the fields, and force them to dig communal graves, in which they are buried after being shot. It's happening everywhere in the same way: in the Ukraine, in Byelorussia, in the Don region. Everywhere the Wehrmacht passes through, they leave behind them communal graves of massacred Jews."

I feel myself go pale, as if my Jewish identity, for so long hidden in my unconscious, had suddenly revealed itself. My blood runs even colder than it did during the Luftwaffe raid. The man with the strange face doesn't seem to notice. He introduces himself and carries on with his macabre story. He is the leader of a small Jewish community in Sablinsk, a small market town near Stavropol—I am unsure whether he was a rabbi or lay president, because in the meantime, the first shock over, I am trying to find ways to doubt what he has just revealed to me. For it is nothing less than the genocide of the Jews, even if he hasn't used the word, that he has just announced to me on this August 5, 1942. Without proof, you can't accept such a horrific statement from the mouth of a stranger. To strengthen my internal resistance, and also to give courage to the man from Sablinsk, I undertake, with as much tact as possible, to explain the danger of forming a general rule on the basis of a few isolated instances. I concede that in December 1941, at the time of its offensive in eastern Crimea, the Red Army actually did discover a mass grave of the Jews of Kerch. The Soviet government revealed it immediately to the entire world and denounced the Nazis. But about the same time, in Byelorussia, the Germans raped and hanged in a public square, in front of their jubilant troops, a young girl eighteen years old, and another, younger still. We can clearly infer from this that these men are barbarians, but we cannot deduce from it that they hang all eighteen-year-old girls.

"The young girls, no. But they are killing all the Jews," the man from Sablinsk replies.

Where does his certainty come from? He can't be better informed than the entire world; Byelokonyenko, for example, received the Tass special bulletin with the dispatches of foreign news agencies. I question him politely, not wanting to give offense, and especially not to give the impression that I am trying to send him back where he came from. I help him rearrange his *telega* while listening to him speak about the witnesses to these massacres of Jews, survivors from such and such a place who have reported this horrific news to him, which he now considers irrefutable. These names don't mean anything to me—no more, for that matter, than does that of Sablinsk.

The women remain apart. They listen to the conversation without becoming involved in it. They have markedly oriental features, but their clothes, especially their way of covering the head and hiding almost all the face, make them resemble Caucasian Muslims more than Jews. The children, who tug at their mothers' long black skirts, seem very quiet for their age, as if they were afraid of crying or running about. They are on their way to Georgia, where a large Jewish community awaits them and will be able to help. Already, however, their *telegi*, about twenty in all, have become separated from each other; some have gotten lost among the crowd of soldiers. Have they at least something to eat? The man from Sablinsk thanks me and assures me that they get by. They have few needs. Their only problem is the slow pace along this congested road and, obviously, the fear of machine-gun fire. "Here at least we have a chance of escaping, whereas the Wehrmacht means certain death for us."

He has no questions of his own to ask. He addresses me formally, thinking perhaps that he is speaking to a commander because of my well-cut, dark blue uniform. Had we continued together along this road, I would certainly have told him about myself. But I see already in the distance that my friends the Musketeers are picking up their rifles and their packs from Tretiakov's *telega*. We are going to try our luck on the mountain footpaths; the decision has already been made. When I explain it to the man from Sablinsk, his face brightens up, and suddenly, in a voice that has become firm and decisive, he says, "You are defending a just cause, my friend, and God will reward you for it. You'll get out of this war unharmed."

My face reddens. Such a prediction sounds extremely encouraging. Immediately, however, the atheist materialist in me starts to laugh: These believers are extraordinary; their God is incapable of protecting them, and yet He confides the future of others to them! Later, though, in each difficult situation, the message of the man from Sablinsk was to come back to me and bring me comfort.

All four of us climb the gentle slope between the Nalchik road and the mountains. En route I describe my conversation to my Cossack companions; it has badly upset me. I tell them, "If things go badly for us, you will end up doing forced labor in Germany; for me it will be the communal grave."

Kola loses his patience and snaps at my credulity, saying that the story is farfetched and cannot be verified. Since the Germans are certainly savage, they may have massacred the Jews of Kerch for a thousand reasons that elude civilized people.

But there can be no question of their having established a system aimed at exterminating all the Jews, or any other people for that matter. In modern times, by virtue of its labor power, humanity provides the surplus value necessary to capital: To kill people systematically would be like killing the goose that lays the golden eggs.

Vassya and Volodya, who were educated in the same school, support Kola. Their history teacher at Myechotka had demonstrated, with mathematical rigor, the laws that brought wars of extermination to a halt. At a certain epoch in the terribly remote past, humanity managed to produce only the basic minimum necessary for its subsistence; thus, the winners in a war between tribes had no incentive to take prisoners, and they exterminated the vanquished tribe. Later, however, with the development of the productive forces, wars had as their objective the taking of prisoners and their transformation into slaves. The latter were squeezed like lemons, and from their suffering sprang up the Pyramids and other monuments of antiquity. Hence the inexorable if somewhat peremptory conclusion: The Nazis' plan of once more reducing conquered peoples to slavery is monstrous enough without crediting them with the intention of turning back the clock of history even further.

"You will be our Ursus, if we become slaves," I say to Vassya, who precedes me by a few steps and is almost blocking out my view of the horizon, such is the height and especially the breadth of the man. He declines the role of the hero of Sienkiewicz's *Quo Vadis?*, however, and declares instead that he will be Spartacus, a fighter and not a martyr. His quip cheers us up. Yes, we shall sell our lives dearly. We shall fight and fight, and none of us will end up in a mass grave.

In the meantime we have only one worry: We are overloaded; our guns are as heavy as they are out of date, and we are also carrying all of our winter gear—at least twenty kilos per man—poorly packed into rucksacks that press painfully against the shoulders. As we were coming away by truck, we left almost nothing behind us in Kislovodsk. I have even brought with me the outsize underwear that Moussia gave to me and, obviously, all the presents from Nievka. To throw these objects, so charged with memories, out onto the roadside would be unthinkable. It would bring us bad luck. Now to this burden is added the weight of our food supplies. We haven't taken very much, counting on the well-known hospitality of the inhabitants of the Caucasus, but even this is too much to carry. We pause every half hour, twice as often as during a normal march. At last, rising up on the horizon above us, is the outline of an *aul*, a Caucasian village. It seems to have a pleasant aspect; perhaps we will find some sacks that are better suited to our backs.

The deepest Caucasus is ours to explore, this land made famous by the stories of Tolstoy. As we plunge farther into the heart of the Caucasus, might we meet one of those Cherkess horsemen in black cape and silver-plated arms, at a turning on the path, above a rocky peak? Perhaps a Cherkessian lady of scintillating beauty would be sitting astride behind him. We would give a warm reception to this

free-spirited and audacious woman, and we wouldn't call her "shameless" as, in former times, Count Tolstoy did.

But in the *aul*, which we reach after a march of four hours, we find
only a small group of barefooted youngsters. They follow us with
curiosity but don't dare approach us. As soon as we take a step in
their direction, they scatter. The only others are some old people who
have neither the strength to run nor a great desire to talk. Who is the
village chief? What is your nationality? It is impossible to get the
slightest response. They don't understand—or no longer understand—a single word of Russian, even pronounced slowly, one syllable at a time, and accompanied by a pantomime worthy of the Moscow
Art Theater.

Kola, who is the most widely read in the literary classics, declares
that we must find the *mechet*, or mosque, the center of Caucasian
village life. But he doesn't remember how to distinguish the *mechet*
from the other dwellings. In Tolstoy, moreover, Muslims are the
protagonists of "Hadji Mourat," but not of all the stories; in some are
found the *staro-viery*, or "old believers" who refused to follow the
Orthodox Church because of its religious reforms. Vassya bursts out
laughing; he's an ignoramus where literature is concerned, but he is
certain that "these people are not *staro-viery*, or Christians of any
other persuasion."

The poverty of the place is striking. One breathes in the very air a
sense of what is later to be called the Third World. It doesn't even
occur to us to ask for food and hospitality from people who are so
poor. Nevertheless, we are at war and need information. Did the
authorities leave because of the enemy's approach? Is the enemy
coming from the west or from some other direction? Are there any
men hiding in the forest, waiting to organize a guerrilla force? Unable
to communicate with the old men, we set an ambush for a youngster
ten to twelve years old, who in theory ought to speak Russian, since
both school attendance and the teaching of Russian are compulsory.
A waste of time: The boy screams like someone possessed, and the
women of the village emerge to add to his imprecations. Even though
their faces are hidden behind veils, they don't disguise their anger.

Okay. We understand. We're going. We'll have better luck at the next village.

Unfortunately, the only track leads toward the west, whereas Nalchik is to the south. At the first fork, we take a still narrower path that we have to follow in single file and that, some kilometers farther on, disappears in the middle of a meadow. Perfidious Caucasians! You could swear that they deliberately planned these paths leading nowhere in order to waste our time and to increase our sense of insecurity. Still, our plan seems a good one, since we can no longer hear the drone of enemy aircraft. But we are too far away from the road, cut off from any news about developments in the battle, and plunged into a strangely calm, sleepy countryside.

We reach the next village, five hours' march later, at nightfall, and find two old men who reply without hesitation that they are Balkars and Muslims. After this promising beginning, their Russian dries up. In telling us their nationality, however, they at least confirm that we are on the right road, and enable us to situate ourselves within the administrative mosaic of the Russian Soviet Federated Socialist Republic, which includes the whole of the northern and central Caucasus, even though, with the exception of the spa towns of Pyatigorsk and Kislovodsk, the Russian population is conspicuous by its absence. In the name of their national identity, the indigenous peoples were given a degree of autonomy on the regional administrative level. But their Autonomous Soviet Socialist Republics are always coupled with another people's: For example, the Karachay and the Cherkess, the Kabardinos and the Balkars, the Chechen and the Ingush. No doubt this is to prevent further administrative fragmentation and to discourage any separatist temptations. In practice, however, this pairing doesn't facilitate the task of intruders, like us, who have a very poor idea of where they are and with whom they have to deal. Wouldn't it be the same in the West if countries were designated in pairs—Franco-Italian, for instance, or Spanish-Portuguese—leaving to the traveler the problem of establishing where exactly France and Spain began, or Italy and Portugal ended?

Thanks to the old men in the second village, we are now certain that we are indeed headed toward Nalchik. We even receive advice on which road to take to avoid both forests and some of the more abrupt mountain slopes. They do not invite us to spend the night in their village, however. To tell the truth, we wouldn't have accepted anyway. Vassya, always supported in this by Volodya, mistrusts these Muslims—these "Persians," as he calls them—too much to sleep with them.

Vassya takes his mistrust to the point of wanting to post a guard over our camp in the open field. Kola fortunately opposes him. "These Persians are not the enemies," he says firmly. "The Revolution happened here too." Therefore, we press close to each other in our greatcoats, and the four of us fall asleep at once.

Not for long, alas. The Caucasian mountains are a paradise for nocturnal insects. They have less bite than Siberian mosquitoes, but they are specialists at imitating the drone of German aircraft or the menacing noises of hostile men. They poison all the nights of our long march, which are punctuated by nightmares and startled awakenings. We spend only one night under cover in an abandoned hut between two villages. Even here I dream that I see Germans in front of the doorway.

Our most serious problem is lack of food. Our provisions have lasted for only forty-eight hours. From the third morning on, Vassya resorts to strongarm tactics in the villages, and manages to get us some tea, goat's milk, and a small quantity of an odd sort of crumbly cheese. Try as he might, however, for something more substantial, by waving his gun about and shouting "Boom-boom!" the Persians have nothing else to offer. Kola's attempt to exchange some winter clothes for food is a failure. The two of us enter unarmed into the Balkars' houses and come back out without even proposing a barter: The stench of mutton fat proves too much for us. Their homes rest on bare earth and seem to us to be horrendously dirty.

Our situation begins to improve when we discover vast fields of small melons. They are hardly larger than grapefruit, and we are afraid that they might not even be edible, but they turn out to be delicious. We eat loads of them, devastating each field like locusts.

The mute calm of the countryside is driving us mad. According to our calculations, we ought to be in Nalchik, or at least close enough to hear the sound of enemy aircraft. How is it that not the slightest sign of war reaches us? And suppose my bad dream was a premonition, and that the Germans, now masters of the region, are going to catch up with us at the next village or even before then? The silence of these unguarded fields and these almost deserted mountains presages nothing favorable for us four vegetarian sleepwalkers, who have left the war rather as one leaves the auditorium of a theater during the intermission. We have surely made a mistake somewhere. But where? Could our Russian-speaking Balkars have intentionally pointed out wrong paths to us in order to keep us from our objective?

We also lack a leader. In wartime, even when there are only four of you, someone has to give orders. Now Kola, a natural and undisputed leader, no longer exercises his leadership. He sulks, complaining at every opportunity that he has been against this detour across unknown countryside from the start. A situation without alternatives doesn't suit Kola's genius. He is great when it is a matter of choosing the best solution from a whole range of possibilities, and he is surrounded by a lot of people: There are some to attract; others to neutralize. In these situations his cunning never lets him down. He has flair. He knows how to think of an "easy" way out for himself and his followers. He needs, in short, a field of action and not a field of watermelons.

Our chief warrior is indisputably Vassya, a serene Elephant, sure of his strength and of his mastery of the military arts. Fatigue never catches up with him. He could march eighteen hours a day without even feeling the weight of his rucksack, his rifle, or anything else. We can't keep up with him, of course. We are not pachyderms. Volodya, the one most attached to Vassya, his shadow and best friend, permits himself occasionally to shout at him, and invites him to stop setting the pace a kilometer ahead of us. Vassya, however, is a slow-witted sort who often provokes useless fights.

On the morning of the fifth day—or is it the sixth?—a miracle happens. In a meadow, far from any village, a white horse awaits us.

It isn't grazing. It is standing upright and its gaze is an invitation. From time to time it shakes its tail to chase the insects away from its rump, but no doubt also to show, in the manner of a dog, that it is contented. In a flash, Vassya is beside it. He caresses it and checks it over. Could the animal be lame? Otherwise, why would it have been left alone and untied? No, it isn't lame, but it isn't abandoned either. A small Persian with wrinkled features, his head enveloped in a kind of turban, emerges from the other end of the field and cries out in Russian, *"Kogn moy!"* ("The horse is mine!") This doesn't deter Vassya, who replies to him with affected politeness that the animal is not a *kogn* but a *lochad*, a breed of horse suited to work in the fields rather than the kind bred for the cavalry or for racing. The other persists, for want of vocabulary, *"Kogn moy, kogn moy!"* Vassya claims that he has trailed this *lochad* all the way from his hometown of Myechotka, and protests that he is not about to leave it in this insect-infested field. The Persian is obstinate: *"Kogn moy, kogn moy!"*

Very well, then, let's fight fair. Vassya suggests a test of loyalty. They will place themselves at equal distance from the horse, each at an opposite side of the meadow, and they will call the animal. The horse will designate its legitimate owner by going toward him. The Persian understands the challenge and, having nothing to lose, accepts it. They take up the agreed positions and each calls in his own language, modulating his voice the better to attract the horse. The *kogn*, alias *lochad*, doesn't move right away. It hesitates, listens, turns its head first toward one and then the other, and then, slowly, heads toward Vassya. Hurray! It is ours, and of its own free will, too! We have defended in a Caucasian meadow the right of animals to self-determination. The poor man who had shouted *"Kogn moy!"* disappears silently.

Vassya, transported with joy, does a victory lap to thank his supporters. Then he packs our arms and baggage expertly onto the horse, and, like a commander-in-chief, orders us: "Forward, march! Day and night without a halt as far as Nalchik!"

We set off without delay, having no wish to spoil the good atmosphere. In addition, as soon as we are relieved of the weight of our rucksacks, we discover that this corner of the Caucasus is very beautiful, most appropriate to a pleasant march.

"You ought to have entered the cavalry," I say to Vassya to congratulate him.

"It's what my parents had planned for me. I was barely three years old when they put me on a horse without a saddle and had me grip it by the mane; then they set it off at a gallop."

"Oh, come on now! You're exaggerating. I've seen professional cowboys in American westerns have real problems controlling their horses in a rodeo. A three-year-old would be thrown to the ground like a sack of potatoes!"

My skepticism drives him into a fury. But what really bothers me is the feeling that perhaps we should have compensated this poor sod, left him a few rubles, some tobacco, or a warm piece of clothing. Kola argues that the circumstances hardly lent themselves to such a gesture, and that it wouldn't have changed anything. One day, after the war, we will come back and repay our debt. But in the meantime, I ask, are we simply thieves? "You mustn't exaggerate," he replies serenely. "We are also fighting for this Caucasian, which gives us certain rights. And until the coming of communism, no one can be totally honest."

A precious companion and a sturdy carrier, the handsome Balkar horse will not remain ours for long. It will leave us near Nalchik without even saying good-bye, but its bid for self-determination will enjoy a place of pride for years to come in the repertoire of our Caucasian yarns, winning widespread appreciation. We would enrich it with elements of suspense, including storms and German patrols following hot on our heels, in order to enhance the intelligence of an animal that had known how to make the right choice. The role of the man who cried *"Kogn moy!"* was impossible to ameliorate and therefore remained comic, because such, finally, is the lot of losers. A Russian would not have fared any better than had the Persian in a contest with Vassya backed up by the three of us, all armed. Our laughter, therefore, was not anti-Balkar; in fact, by repeating this popular story we became attached to its protagonist and, by extension, to his compatriots. Even Vassya, who had previously been the most mistrustful of us, ended up declaring that the Balkars had nothing in common with the Turks—his grandfather's enemies—and that on the contrary they had sought refuge in the Caucasus from the Turks. Indeed, we came to consider them "our Balkars" and sometimes raised our glasses to toast their good health at the time of victory celebrations at the end of the war.

But at that time, in 1945, the Balkars were no longer in Balkaria. Stalin had deported them one year after the battle for the Caucasus, along with the Kalmyks, the Karachay, the Chechen, and the Ingush, all of them Muslims. The operation was conducted in the greatest secrecy between September 1943 and April 1944, and involved some 800,000 persons of both sexes and all ages. Events taking place on such a scale could not pass unnoticed, and they were in fact marked by an amendment to the name of the administrative territory: the Kabardino-Balkar ASSR (Autonomous Soviet Socialist Republic) became simply the Kabardino ASSR. We were already far away by then, however, and we knew nothing about it. We spoke of "our Balkars" only to amuse our audience with this story of the horse that had been stolen by its own consent.

I learned of the tragedy of the Balkars only in 1956. Khrushchev, in his secret speech to the Twentieth Party Congress, revealed that Stalin had held the people of the northern Caucasus collectively responsible for "the hostile acts of individual persons or groups of persons," and that he had submitted all of them to a harsh regime of "misery and suffering." Khrushchev condemned this repression, which he described as inadmissible "not only [for] a Marxist-Leninist but also [for any] man of common sense." The secret report stops there; some pertinent lines on the principles of the deportation follow, but they are too short to explain what really happened in the northern Caucasus in 1943–44. Ever since 1956, silence has once again cloaked the subject; not a single book or study, not a single victim's testimony, has been published in the USSR. "Our Balkars" had the right to Moscow's official commiseration only for a single afternoon, and behind closed doors, for Khrushchev's report was never made public.

Another deported people, the Crimean Tartars, were even more badly treated. Khrushchev "forgot" to speak about them to the Twentieth Party Congress and didn't authorize them—as he did the Caucasians—to return to their homes, or to what remained of them. These "reject people" have been the only ones since that time to occasionally break through the official silence, aided by dissidents such as Aleksandr Nekrich or Pyotr Grigorenko. Their testimony is frightening: Half of their people perished during deportation. Everything leads one to fear that the story was the same for the Caucasians, and that they were all victims of a genocidal policy.

What had they done to attract Stalin's thunderbolts? We crossed Kabardino-Balkar for a period of eight days, shortly before the arrival of the Germans. Their patrols weren't hot on our heels, as we were later to pretend in order to give ourselves airs, but the Wehrmacht wasn't far away. For certain "individuals" or certain "groups" among the Balkars, in Khrushchev's words, now was the moment to commit "hostile acts." Had they been so inclined, we would not have left their villages and mountains alive. Aware in advance of the routes we were taking, and often knowing where we were going to camp for the night, they would have had no difficulty either killing us in a surprise attack or in taking us prisoner and capturing our arms. They did nothing of the kind. And the coolness that was evident, a certain degree of mistrust that the people showed toward us, is easily explained by the fact—we were witnesses to this as well—that at the moment of danger all the Soviet administrative authorities in the region had disappeared from the villages, leaving "our Balkars" to their fate.

I can't say whether they received the Germans with flowers; they certainly hadn't many reasons for liking the USSR. The great Russian Soviet Republic had only incorporated them in order to swallow them up and prolong their former colonization. It is perhaps even because these "Mohammedans" constituted the flagrant and unacceptable proof of this fact that Stalin had resolved to deport them at the first opportunity. The Christian minorities of the Caucasus went untouched; the Orthodox Church, restored to a place of honor in the name of patriotic unity, and infiltrated immediately with NKVD agents, watched over them.

In the spring of 1981, in Ordzhonikidze, in Ossetia, which had in theory been spared the roundup of 1943, violent incidents broke out in which Muslims, former deportees, fought Christians who had occupied their homes. The battle is thought to have lasted several days; troops had to intervene, and the news eventually filtered abroad. It is clear from this that the problem of the returning Muslims is still not resolved a quarter of a century after Khrushchev's secret speech, and that the victims nurse a grievance against those who benefited by their misfortune. It is possible that Stalin's attempt to "de-Islamicise" the Caucasian zones of the great Russian Soviet Republic will, in the end, lead to a war of religion in the area. And yet any "man of common sense," in Khrushchev's words, ought to understand that such great injustices scar those who have suffered them, and that they cannot consider them simply as regrettable historical aberrations, to be forgotten in silence. It is with considerable regret and pain, therefore, that I recall the part I played in stealing a handsome white horse from one of their proud people.

We can tell from the thickness of the smoke rising toward the sky that we are approaching Nalchik. We can see it from the mountain slopes at a distance of fifteen to twenty kilometers. All of the Caucasus seems to be on fire.

Suddenly, two Luftwaffe planes dive at us. Vassya runs to take cover behind a tree, first taking our baggage from the horse's back with quick, artful movements. Frightened by the noise, the animal gallops off. It passes in front of the rest of us as we lie huddled in a ditch. Go on, then, handsome Balkar horse, you served us well, but watch out because these Luftwaffe swine fire on everything that moves—*kogn* or *lochad*, it makes no difference to them! Vassya thinks that instinct will guide the animal back to its meadow and to its rightful owner.

As we get nearer to Nalchik, soldiers on the march multiply around us just as at the exit from Pyatigorsk. But Nalchik is not Pyatigorsk. Looting is forbidden here; helmeted patrols stop and question each group of soldiers; orders rain down anew; the army becomes an army once more. We button our uniform collars quickly—the vacation is over.

These patrols treat us with consideration because of our dark blue uniforms; without even asking us the number of our unit, they point out the spot where the "eleventh" school of the air force is quartered. Who would have believed that our boys were still here? Quickly, then, back into the fold. The war is a collective business after all. Fine, but my situation is not the same as that of my three companions; I am not a trainee pilot in whom the Red Army has invested a lot of money. It is from me that explanations will be demanded for the loss of the truck, since it was personally assigned to me by Commissar Andrei Byelokonyenko. It would be best if we put our heads together and agreed on a common version of the incident.

It proves impossible, though, to have one last council of war. Volodya has spotted his pretty Cosachka and seems as excited as the hero of his favorite ballad. Vassya, as usual, is already far in front. Kola alone encourages me: "Don't worry. First we'll check out with Kostya about the hierarchy's attitude toward us, and then we'll tailor an explanation to suit." His inventiveness is reawakening. The real Kola is back among us, and not the half-hearted one we had almost become accustomed to during the crossing of Balkaria.

The "eleventh" regiment is sleeping in the vast courtyard of a building that is three-quarters burned down. Our superiors are resting in rooms that were spared by the fire. The sentries don't even consider disturbing them to report our arrival. So there is no hurry. Vassya and Volodya go off to look for food. Kola and I consult with Kostya the Khan, who gives a funny account of the "eleventh's" arrival in Nalchik. They too marched on the mountain footpaths, but on the other side of the main road. Zlotnikov asserted himself as the only competent leader, earning the respect of the corps and at the same time generating some unexpectedly pro-Jewish feelings. Knowing that their fate depended on him, the comrades never hesitated,

during halts in the march, to sacrifice their own sleep to watch over
his. They took turns, discreetly, standing watch by his bedside to
chase away any insects that threatened his sleep. Among the volunteers on this unofficial guard duty was a person who, in Kislovodsk,
had always badmouthed this "dirty Yid" Zlotnikov. Kola isn't surprised; for a long time he has argued that if the army of the Don had
been commanded by Jews instead of these idiot atamans, there would
have been less suffering all around in the region.

What did the Jewish colonel's merits amount to? Zlotnikov knew
how to organize a system of intelligence and supplies, and to maintain
his little army in a state of combat alert. An airman himself, his
greatest fear was that the krauts would take advantage of their mastery of the air to drop some small decoy detachments by parachute.
He wanted to be in a position to destroy them. Convinced also that the
enemy was not advancing toward Nalchik, he preferred to sacrifice
speed to an orderly march—unquestionably the right decision. Thus
the regiment arrived in Nalchik in top condition. The military authorities took advantage of this by putting it immediately to work, assign-
ing it to the building of fortifications around the town. Zlotnikov had
nothing to do with the decision, any more than did our nominal
commander, Colonel Ganachek. They would have preferred to withdraw us as quickly as possible.

As for the hierarchy's attitude toward us four, we find that the news
is not so good. Believing at first that we had perished along with the
truck during an air raid, our commanders had planned a small ceremony in our honor, as soon as circumstances would permit. When
they learned, however, from their intelligence service that we had
been seen—without the truck—in Pyatigorsk, they probably decided
to reserve a very different kind of reception for us, to teach us how to
properly protect military matériel. On the other hand, since everyone
was now compelled to work on fortifications, it was hard to see what
more unpleasant punishment they would be able to find for us. "There
are no more jails in Nalchik," Kostya notes, laughing, since the town
has been destroyed by fire. He advises us to declare that, threatened
by the traitor driver, we had been forced to kill him; if we don't, we

will be reproached for not having forced him to drive. Kola disagrees. He thinks ahead, and doesn't want our careers to be compromised when, after the Red Army has retaken Kislovodsk, our presumed victim is found safe and sound. So we decide to be rather vague about the outcome of the incident. The driver attacked us by surprise, so we fought back, without being sure of having killed him. It is more prudent this way. Nevertheless, anxiety—or perhaps the excessive fatigue and the joy of reunion with friends—prevents us from sleeping. The next morning when we present ourselves in front of Colonel Ganachek, we are in piteous condition: exhausted, bags under the eyes, a pathetic air about us.

I would like to think that it is this that accounts for the almost insulting indifference he shows toward us. "Ah. There you are! Make out a report on the truck," he says, without even raising his voice or asking any questions about how we had acquitted ourselves. He doesn't even want to read the written order from Colonel Tretiakov, and pretends to be already acquainted with all the relevant circumstances. Since the military world is small, however, perhaps he has met Colonel Tretiakov. Fine. If he doesn't want to hear the tall story about our battle with the traitor driver, so much the better. We'll make out a report in ten lines, attaching Tretiakov's written order to it, and that will be the end of it. Meanwhile, Ganachek gives us the morning off. For me, however, the matter is not quite closed: Ganachek is not my only superior; I am also answerable to my commissar.

Byelokonyenko wakes me toward midday and invites me to sit with him. He has aged a great deal since our departure from Kislovodsk. His hair seems grayer and his shoulders sag badly, making him lose whatever little martial bearing he possessed. His demeanor worries me. My concern deepens when he doesn't suggest talking to me while walking. We remain seated in a semideserted, sinister courtyard, perched like two owls on a little wooden bench. He listens to me without budging while I recount the agreed-upon version of the incident with the driver and the story of our Balkarian escapade. As I make my report, he neither cracks the smallest smile nor utters the briefest comment.

"I am pleased that you are all safe and sound," he says finally, without much warmth, in a voice as faint as the expression on his face. "On the other hand, you have rather disappointed me." Why? Did he take me on in his service to drive heavy trucks? What, honestly, can he reproach me with? "You have let yourself be led along by the nose by Kola P., a comrade who is *nyenadiozhnyi* [untrustworthy], not to say a mischief-maker." My commissar doesn't change his spots; he still has a "fixation" on Kola.

I don't reply. In the army you don't argue with superiors; and even if we had been in civvies, a discussion on this subject would take us nowhere. I simply ask what my duties are in Nalchik, emphasizing the urgency of calling Komsomol meetings in order to raise the comrades' morale. Only then does he permit himself the ghost of an inscrutable smile that is bitter, perhaps, or ironic. After a pause, he says dryly, "You are going to work on the fortifications like everyone else." The conversation is over. He gets up and leaves the courtyard.

I am the only one of the Musketeers to be punished—deprived of my special functions and thus of any possibility of distinguishing myself in my particular field. I have to melt into the mass of trainee pilots, who face a wholly different future. However, I can't make a fuss about it; to do so would create the impression that I consider myself a privileged person, and that I am refusing to participate in the collective effort to construct fortifications, which is clearly a priority. Not even Kola sympathizes; he explains everything away by the exceptional circumstances, which are likely to be short-lived. Tomorrow the "eleventh" will be installed in Transcaucasia or on the other side of the Caspian Sea; the pilots will start to fly again, the politicos to organize meetings. It is only much later, when he analyzes Byelokonyenko's attitude toward me more seriously, that he concedes that the unexpected and undeserved punishment I received in Nalchik represented the first link in a chain of very great importance.

For the past two days the muffled sound of cannon fire has reached the hill that we are fortifying. They are our *zenitki* [antiaircraft batteries], which at long last are being used to stop the Luftwaffe, or so the optimists claim. Others think that the Germans have parachuted their decoy detachments, just as Colonel Zlotnikov foresaw, and that our 37th Army is attacking them. No one, though, is expert in artillery matters. In a school of aviation you don't learn anything about cannons, and official information is nonexistent. In Kislovodsk, while it was still far from the theater of war, the special program intended for the front line was broadcast every evening on loudspeakers: "Listen, Front. This is Moscow." In Nalchik, where the cannons are booming, there are no loudspeakers.

In the evenings we exchange impressions with comrades from other units. They claim that new armament supplies are beginning to arrive from Transcaucasia. But this proves only that the 37th Army is going to be reorganized and reequipped, not that the German attack is imminent. The only real evidence we have of new supplies is the appearance of American Studebaker trucks. The soldiers gather around them, gaping like village youngsters. They discuss the truck's four-wheel drive, its tires, and elegant design. There are even some who claim that it has been specially designed to negotiate Russia's notoriously backward road network. The Studebaker trucks are the first tangible proof that the United States, the world's leader in engine manufacture, is on our side, and this boosts our morale. Back in Kislovodsk, Byelokonyenko would not have missed this opportunity to cite Stalin's prediction of inevitable victory to our camp in the "war of engines."

We are in for a rude awakening. On the third morning of our stay, the Germans are at Nalchik's gates. We are going back up on the hill, but to fight this time and not to work. It's crazy—my comrades belong to the air force, queen of the armed forces; they aren't common infantrymen. What's more, the colors of our uniforms don't meet the requirements of camouflage; we are an outrageous blue. And what about helmets? All that we have are light peaked caps, rather stylish, but quite useless for protecting our heads against flying shrapnel.

"Quickly! Move yourselves! Take only what is necessary. There are no whores to please where we're going," our sergeant majors bawl out in their customary macho language. I sort through my belongings and leave all my souvenir possessions in the camp—those that I have brought with me from Poland and those that Nievka gave me in Kislovodsk. I will never recover them. Vassya, more prudent than I, carries off our war booty—the bolt of cloth salvaged from the truck before it was abandoned—in his lightened sack. "In war," he will explain to me one day, "you need to have everything that is dear to you within easy reach."

The three squadrons form a semicircle and Colonel Ganachek walks to the center to speak to us. He explains only our defensive positioning on the hill and says nothing to us about how long we will remain at the battle line. To avoid concentrated fire from the enemy artillery we are to keep in groups of two, seven meters apart from each other. We are familiar with the hill, since we have fortified it ourselves. We know where to find our two communication bunkers and how best to reach them across broken or shelled terrain. He closes by reminding us of the different signs through which, day and night, orders will be given to us. But we know them by heart; we have been on a thousand simulation exercises in Kislovodsk.

Ganachek disappears without even wishing us good luck, and Commissar Byelokonyenko takes his place. Silence falls; the cannonades close by stop momentarily as if in his honor. Stirred by the occasion, he mechanically removes his peaked airman's cap, feeling more at ease, perhaps, with his head bared. Byelokonyenko has never excelled in his role as orator. He has always needed notes and, on important occasions, speeches prepared in advance. This morning in Nalchik, though, he improvises. His expression is lit up in fervent emotion. He says few things about us, and little about either the importance of the battle for the Caucasus in general or about the battle for our hill in particular. He argues only for the historic role of the USSR, the beacon lighting up the path of our class brothers in their struggle to shake off the yoke of capital.

Next, my enemy, Sergeant Major Orlov, steps up to give us our orders. Our squadron is the first to leave, and when we are already en route, he decides that I will be paired with Boris T., known simply as Lovelace, and not with one of the Myechotka Musketeers. I get on well with Boris T., and in any case I can no longer invoke my status as a politico in order to question orders. I suspect that my commissar has had a hand in the decision to separate me from Kola and the others. And then I am too afraid to reason with or to become indignant over the pettiness of a sergeant major or of my commissar. I am lucid enough to realize that we have little chance of escaping from this Caucasian hornets' nest. Otherwise the farsighted air force wouldn't sacrifice its own men in an absurd land battle.

I am being evacuated to a hospital—where, I don't know. It is all too stupid for words. Nothing was happening on our hill that day. My story is straight out of *All Quiet on the Western Front*, a real plagiarism. During a period of prolonged calm, I went off to fetch some soup. Suddenly a stupefying blast hurled me several meters into the air. There had been no whistling sounds that precede incoming artillery shells. I heard the explosion only after I had been sent flying.

Fortunately, Boris T. saw me land. He alerted Sergeant Major Orlov, who contacted the medical services and signed the necessary papers for my admission to the hospital. These are required, even on the battle front. Both of them accompanied me to the ambulance truck, and Boris kept repeating, with compassion in his voice, *"Oh, kak tyebia zayobnulo,"* a Russian way of saying, "Oh! What has happened to you," but also, "You've had it, old boy!"

I don't feel myself dying, though, but the taste of earth in my mouth badly upsets me; I imagine that I will never be able to spit it out completely. I am bleeding here and there, having received scratches all over my body. I don't feel a lot of pain and I haven't lost consciousness. But you can't trust appearances. In Poland, in 1939, I also felt no pain and had ended up losing an eye.

For fifteen days we have been defending our hill near Nalchik, and the battle hasn't been without its agreeable moments. The front, at night, is sometimes very beautiful. When the artillery gunners in both camps fire at the same time, the entire sky lights up as if in a gigantic fireworks display. It takes your breath away.

I also remember very well the introduction into the battle of our *katyushe*: deafening, rocket-propelled mortar bombs. That same night, a week or so after our arrival on the hill, I understood that thanks to the *katyushe*, we were going to win the war. When we first saw their traces in the sky, we thought that these ultramodern killing machines were German, and that the Wehrmacht had surrounded us. And what can one say in praise of the terrifying and yet melodious noise of these weapons, which the enemy nicknamed "Stalin's organs," as if to advertise the powers of our Supreme Commander-in-Chief!

The next day, at dawn, advancing by several kilometers, we were able to witness the devastation they had wrought, literally sweeping away the enemy's defensive positions. Unfortunately, our adversaries were not Germans. The poor devils were Romanian; their helmets were decorated with the letter *C* in honor of their king, Carol, who had, however, been exiled well before the war. This was a great disappointment. We had learned endless poems exalting the necessity of killing Germans, but none of them mentioned Romanians. Later, when other ex-combatants boast of having killed lots of Wehrmacht soldiers, we shall be thoroughly embarrassed to admit having only ever fired on poor bastards from the Balkans. Not one among us thought for a moment of picking up a helmet in order one day to show it to his grandchildren.

When shells are raining down on all sides, it behooves everyone to maximize his chances of surviving by observing the rules of war. That much is obvious. But one also stands to gain by knowing as much as possible about destiny, about what is "predetermined."

Take the case of Boris T. He is not a Cossack but a Russian, originally from Kursk, who settled in Rostov. The son of a university professor, and therefore an atheist of unimpeachable pedigree, Boris is a very reassuring optimist, for he is convinced that he has a bright future as a pilot. By the time we arrived on the Nalchik hill, he had explained to me that we wouldn't be staying there for long, and that he would be a flight lieutenant by the end of the year. He claimed that by the end of 1943 he would be a captain and, in 1945, a squadron leader at least, or a lieutenant colonel. All of this was accompanied by exact calculations on the salary he would have earned and the medals he would have been awarded. But even the self-confident Boris T. didn't balk at crawling along the ground like a snake, under heavy cannon fire, for several kilometers, to the other end of our lines, in search of a certain Vassilchenko, a comrade of Ukrainian origin who was widely respected for his talent for palm-reading.

In my own case, I had my palm read by two different palm readers. Their predictions were favorable, but to have added reassurance I had the cards read to me, like almost everyone else, by two comrades recommended by Kola. According to them, I was a *bubnovyi karol*, the King of Diamonds, and I had nothing to fear from the krauts; I was threatened only by great disappointments with the Queen of Diamonds, a blond or red-headed woman.

The hospital is in Beslan, halfway between Nalchik and Vladicaucasia. It is an improvised building that can't be compared with the hospital in which Nievka worked in Kislovodsk. In fact it is only a first-aid post, rather large, but plunged into darkness by an electricity breakdown on the night I arrive. The wounded are lying on mattresses on the floor in a long ward. The mattresses are close together to save space. There are men lying in their underwear, on a sheet; others have their uniforms on and are covered with their greatcoats, for lack of blankets. I am among the better off; I have been washed and undressed. But I am positioned too close to the entry door, which is continually being opened. It is August, so it can't be this constant draft that gives me the shivers. I must be feverish—unless my teeth are chattering from fright because suddenly I have the feeling that I am a "goner."

A man and a woman in white overalls approach with an oil lamp, and listen to the report from the medical officer who has transported and taken care of me since collecting me in Nalchik. I can't hear very well. I think I hear him say he has given me an antitetanus shot, even though he hasn't noted any wounds caused either by bullets or shrapnel. The man leans over me and asks me to squeeze his hand with all my strength, first with the right hand, then with the left. He presses my head a little and then my legs, without hurting me.

It is now the woman's turn, and she gets right down on her knees to examine me by touch all over, before applying her stethoscope. On getting up again, she declares in a loud voice, "An attack of malaria." The other doesn't agree at all, and argues that I have lost strength in my left side as a result of a concussion to the right side of my brain. My opinion is not solicited. They discuss the matter without looking at me any further, their voices more or less drowned out by the groans of my neighbors. The two of them leave, still arguing, without informing me of their verdict.

Could there be a sedative in antitetanus injections? Why are my eyelids closing when I would like to find out first what the diagnosis is? I believe that once I have sunk into the darkness, I am in danger of never again being able to reopen my eyes. This is a very common fear, it seems, among the freshly wounded. Other casualties, according to their own accounts, draw up a balance sheet with respect to their relations and their dear ones, wondering who will suffer from their disappearance and who will rejoice over it. I simply meditate on malaria, which has always been associated in my mind with the disquieting jungles of Africa and Asia, with Tarzan and the tales of Joseph Conrad. All things considered, I prefer the concussion diagnosed by the male doctor.

The strange antics of my neighbor interrupt my thoughts. The poor man seems to be suffering atrociously, but he finds the strength to call the nurse at regular intervals and to beg her politely, "Masha, can I detain you a moment to ask about a personal matter?" And then, softly, a stream of compliments: "You are the most beautiful creature. I'm crazy about you." The woman replies each time, with great patience, that being the only nurse on the ward she is necessarily the most beautiful, that she is very pleased to hear it, and that he ought to go to sleep. But the poor man continues to beg; their dialogue begins again, unaltered, as if they were performing a play. Why beg this indifferent nurse? Is it the lot of all the wounded to lose their dignity in this way? The ward is the last place in the world to touch upon "personal matters." Somewhere in the middle of these reflections, I sink into a deep, black hole.

I find myself thinking of the man from Sablinsk and of his proph-

ecy: "You will get out of this war unharmed." He didn't say "alive";
he said "unharmed," and this word seems to indicate that in Beslan,
as opposed to my hospital experience in Radom, I will not be butch-
ered. What do these shivers matter, then, this alternation of hot and
cold, this overpowering desire to sleep? I let myself go. I lower my
guard. And after relaxing in this manner I sleep three days and nights
continuously, without thinking of anything, without hearing anything,
and without recalling anything.

The Queen of Diamonds foretold by the Nalchik fortune-tellers is
called Lyuba. Her hair is of a deep red hue, the reddest I have ever
seen. She wears it in a flamboyant style, and her face, her hands, and
perhaps her whole body are covered with freckles. With her large
green eyes, the curves beneath her nurse's uniform, and her original
hairstyle—a bun worn behind and a fringe in front falling down to her
eyes, Lyuba would be very desirable if she weren't so fierce—aggressive, even—as though she felt obliged to remind me at all times:
"Watch out. I am *bubnovaya dama* [the Queen of Diamonds], and I
will hurt you!"

However, the fortune-tellers in Nalchik were mistaken. Not only
did Lyuba not represent a danger to me; she was perhaps even the
messenger of destiny, charged with trying to prevent me from transferring to Yerevan, twenty-five kilometers from the Turkish border,
where, three months later, the intrigue against me would come to a
climax.

It is the middle of the night when I finally stir from my long sleep. I
don't know what time it is, for my watch, a precious gift from my
parents, is gone (forever, alas), but I note that all my symptoms—
fever, shivering, itching—have disappeared. I still feel rather weak,
but more as though I am convalescing, and I am able to get to my feet.
Wrapped up in my blanket, I go outside and sit down in the hospital's
courtyard, on an old tree trunk. Beslan sleeps in the darkness, in
silence. Even the noises of the large ward no longer reach me. All
around me I make out the Great Caucasus, this lacework of mountain-
tops close at hand, covered with eternal snow. We are high up, and

the air is sharp and invigorating, just the thing to dissipate the remaining traces of cloudiness in the head of someone who has slept for three days and nights. Suddenly I notice a red-haired nurse approaching, wearing a greatcoat over her white uniform.

In the large courtyard there is no shortage of tree trunks, but the nurse sits on mine, right beside me. She introduces herself—her name is Lyuba—and offers me a pouch of *makhorka*, a rough shag tobacco. The color of her hair clearly reveals her to me as the Queen of Diamonds, and so I am on my guard. I feel too weak even to think about taking advantage of our encounter. But hardly have I begun to complain about my confused medical situation and about having lost my watch than Lyuba starts vulgarly accusing me of "setting traps" for girls. Every wounded soldier tries to arouse her pity, and all of them have the same cynical motives. It is too much for me to take. I invite her to consult my medical file to persuade herself of the truth of what I'm saying; she would also be doing me a favor by reporting the final diagnosis to me.

"There can be no question of such a thing. I am not even on your ward, and nurses are never supposed to communicate such matters to the wounded," she replies aggressively. Whereupon, just as I was thinking of getting up and going elsewhere, Lyuba lays her head on my shoulder. "You mustn't be cross with me," she says. "I have so many things on my mind that I no longer get a moment's peace. Day and night, whether I work or sleep, they never stop tormenting me. Perhaps you are not like the other men—pigs, the whole lot of them. I can talk to you." And with this she begins to tell me the story of her life.

A Siberian, she fell in love at the nursing school in Tyumen—the mosquito capital of Western Siberia—with an auxiliary doctor who had been made a lieutenant upon mobilization and whom she later married. From the beginning of the war they had both belonged to an ambulance unit responsible for transporting the wounded between the first-aid posts at the front and the evacuation hospitals fifty or so kilometers behind the lines. In May, however, in the scramble of the retreat from Kharkov, their ambulance truck was machine-gunned by a German plane that had returned in a surprise attack to finish off the survivors. Only Lyuba and one medical officer survived. Her husband was killed before her eyes, riddled with bullets along with the wounded in the ambulance. They had had to bury the dead with their bare hands—she shows me hers as if they still bore the traces—in a mass grave. "I am not even sure that I will ever be able to find it again so that I may erect a decent headstone for my husband in Tyumen. I was so happy with him."

I don't know how to reply. I haven't experienced much actual combat, despite my own recent wound. To be sure, during an advance patrol while we were dug in on the Nalchik hill, I had had to bring back Churik L., one of the foursome with whom I shared a mess tin; he had been hit by a bullet in the leg and was covered with blood. But it seems indecent to speak of it to Lyuba. Having to help a wounded comrade is not the same thing as having to bury a dearly loved husband.

I ask her why she believes that men don't understand her. She straightens up immediately, in a fury, and the anger rises in her harsh voice as she tells me how men have "understood" her. Three days after the death of her husband, her new superior declared that since they were going to sleep together sooner or later, he would prefer to do it at once. She cites a long list of medical officers and wounded, all of whom, in response to her story, shortly afterward shoved their wandering hands up her skirt. "I no longer want any man, at least until the end of the war!" she shouts. She also rages against the Red Army, which won't allow her to return to Tyumen but is instead transferring her to a hospital in Krasnovodsk, on the other side of the Caspian Sea.

Tyumen, Tyumen. To everyone his own dream, but even so, there are a multitude of towns in Russia that are less infested with mosquitoes. And then, Siberia is the land of deportees; to want to go there voluntarily is something altogether beyond me. "There aren't a lot of mosquitoes in the town itself," Lyuba objects. "It is in the forest that they devour you." Ah, but no, it's not true; in Tyumen in summer, the insects reign supreme.

Astonished by the extent of my acquaintance with the matter, she only half-believes me when I tell her that I owe it to a friend. But she isn't unhappy to talk about Tyumen, and she puts her head again on my shoulder. "You can caress my hair, provided that you do it gently and don't harbor any other thoughts." I do so, convinced that she is not only the most strikingly red-haired woman I have ever seen but also one of the most bizarre. And thus we continue to while away the time talking about Siberian mosquitoes, while my hand strokes her thick hair.

The day breaks before we know it, and before our very eyes emerge the harmonious profiles of the majestic Elbrus and its rival in record European altitude, the Kazbek. It is an astonishing landscape, and at this hour of the day, beneath the mist, it is strangely soft and calming, uplifting.

The charm doesn't last. Lyuba admits that the landscape "isn't bad," but, she must leave. Work awaits her. She goes off with a firm step, despite her night of insomnia.

Some hours later an unusual noise in the ward signals Lyuba's return. On her way, she receives requests to give advice on "personal matters." After scrutinizing the faces and examining the hands of my two neighbors, Lyuba kneels down by my mattress and says in my ear, "You're lucky. I oughtn't to have done it, but I consulted your medical file. I wanted to know who you were. Your report is so good that I decided to let you know about it. You are to be sent as soon as possible to the hospital in Krasnovodsk for observation, because it is feared you may have suffered brain damage."

She is surprised that I don't understand her without further explanation: The Red Army doesn't trust this category of patient and demobilizes them much more readily than, for example, a nurse who has seen her husband killed before her very eyes.

"Who is going to fight the Germans, then, Lyuba, if everyone gets demobilized? Where would you have me go in any case, after the army? To Tyumen?"

She fixes me with her two great eyes, as if I were not so much "brain-damaged" as a madman to be tied up. Her diatribe on men's stupidity is shorter this time; we are not alone, and she hasn't the time. She leaves me without saying good-bye. Should I run after her? She would certainly accuse me of having ulterior motives. Ah, but what anguish to be alone among these groaning foreigners with the sole prospect of starting my life over somewhere on the other side of the Caspian Sea. Krasnovodsk? That night was the first time I had even heard the name. They teach geography badly in Soviet schools.

Framed in the doorway, a large silhouette appears, which could well be that of Vassya. With his back to the light, I can't see the color of his uniform clearly, but I know that it can't be him, since he is up on the hill near Nalchik. However, just in case, I cry, "Hey, Elephant!"

The soldier turns his head; it is indeed Vassya, our horseman of Balkaria. The other Musketeers are here as well, including Kostya the Khan. The members of the "eleventh," withdrawn from the front following the arrival of reinforcements from Georgia, are taking advantage of a halt to clean themselves up in Beslan. We have time to tell each other everything at leisure.

They can't get over finding me again, and in such good health. Boris T. had told them that I was stuffed full of shrapnel, as fit to burst as a turkey on Christmas Eve. Certainly, to judge from my pallor, I seem a little ill; but Napoleon himself in underpants would not have made a better impression.

Kostya has an exceptional piece of news: My commissar, consumed by remorse after my injury, wants to propose Kola for membership in the Communist Party. Membership formalities are greatly simplified at the front, and a commissar can enroll half of his troops in the Party. (It is even written about in the press at times.) Under the circumstances, it amounts to such an unexpected gesture and one so rich in implications that we find it hard to assess.

I don't bother mentioning Lyuba, but I explain that my next destination is Krasnovodsk. All of them then decree in a single voice that "observation" is fine for crazies but not for me, and that they are bringing me with them. The Elephant wants to do it on the spot, without formalities. The hospital is unguarded and they will find a uniform for me at camp. But Kola, confident in the knowledge of the commissar's offer, is for respecting the rules. Why cheat when you can do it all legally? He knows his geography: The Great Caucasus is fine to look at but difficult to cross; the hospital authorities will not hold on to a wounded man who, protected by his unit, prefers to leave of his own accord instead of being transported by the medical services.

Kola's assessment of the bureaucracy is astoundingly accurate: One hour after our decision, my papers are in order and I am free to return to the regiment. The hospital refuses only my formal complaint concerning the theft of my watch. I am given a sealed letter addressed to my superiors. Although tempted to open it, I decide finally to remit it to Byelokonyenko without cheating. It is our day of legalism.

I have already donned my dark blue uniform when Lyuba makes a noisy appearance. As she is not attached to my ward, she is not supposed to be aware of my departure. But she knows everything and suggests a private conversation. She takes me amiably by the arm but holds it so tightly that it hurts. I don't protest; I let myself be led to the quiet spot that she has chosen to avoid the other patients. Here she relaxes her grip on my arm and drops the pretense of a smile. I only have to see her flushed face to tell that she is angry and that it is not a simple matter of a good-bye kiss. "You stupid man, who do you think you're impressing by leaving here with a concussion that still hasn't been properly diagnosed or treated, and an attack of malaria on top of it all?"

I reply feebly, murmuring some empty phrases about the comradeship among men, and the "eleventh" school of the air force, which is my only family. She turns brusquely on her heel and tosses at me over her shoulder a parting "See you, soldier," meaning "Go ahead, idiot, get yourself killed!"

Byelokonyenko, closely shaven and clean as a new pin, has recovered his former self. He greets me in the way he used to in the best days in Kislovodsk, when I was almost a "comrade-in-arms." And although he doesn't suggest facilitating my entry into the Communist Party, as he did for Kola, he gives me several items of good news. I will be traveling aboard a truck with a military driver, without any risk of bother. The "eleventh" will take great care of my health. Upon recovering properly, I will have much more important tasks entrusted to me than those that I discharged in Kislovodsk. "The socialist Motherland," my commissar adds in a more personal tone, "will never forget its debt toward those who have spilled their blood for it. You, what's more . . ." But his sentence stops midway. He probably can't decide whether I deserve additional thanks in my capacity as a "class brother," or whether I deserve them because I am "consciously and culturally" Russian.

It hardly matters. What counts is that I feel myself to be a creditor of the entire USSR, and also feel that I am promised a brilliant career in the armed forces. I bear no grudge against Byelokonyenko for having sent me up onto the hill in Nalchik instead of keeping me busy in his command bunker with political scribbling. All's well that ends well; the episode having turned out to my advantage, I have no worries at all, not even about the situation of our army, which is deteriorating on practically all fronts. It is only later, when my Beslan euphoria has subsided, that I will realize that in this month of September 1942, the USSR found itself still closer to defeat than during the previous autumn at the time of the Battle of Moscow. With the Germans in the Stalingrad suburbs and in the very heart of the Caucasus, the Red Army didn't seem to have much hope of reversing the course of events.

The "eleventh" will receive contradictory orders on its destination; our departure from the Great Caucasus, which is difficult enough to cross in normal times, will be marked by several demoralizing episodes. But my memories of this journey are confused. What is certain is our arrival, at the end of the first week of September, in Makhach-kala, on the Caspian seaboard.

We are at a crossroads. From here one can go either by sea to Asia, or by rail to Transcaucasia. All of us would prefer Georgia or Armenia, which enjoyed a good reputation in Rostov. We fear, however, that the air force will send us to safe but distant destinations on the

other side of the Caspian Sea. Finally, at the beginning of the afternoon of our arrival, we hear the good news: We are ordered to assemble at five-thirty in front of the train station. Until then, we're free to
indulge our taste for tourism and barter, so we pay a quick visit to
Makhachkala to exchange our superfluous articles for some good
Caucasian grapes.

The town, for people who come from the plains, is breathtaking. It
is made up of terraces hewn out of the mountainside, which go down
in steps to the sea. Its white clay houses are surrounded by flowers
and abundant vegetation. It is a town of great beauty. The inhabitants
are clearly Muslims. (They too will be deported by Stalin in 1943,
accused of being collaborators, although their town had never even
been occupied by the Germans.)

I am among the first to go down to the station, for I lack the strength
to climb the street-paths, and I discover that the port is close to the
station, only about fifty meters away, but one terrace lower. From the
quayside, I notice almost immediately Lyuba's head of red hair on the
bridge of a boat beneath me. Standing alone, she is shading her eyes
with her right hand against the sunlight. She seems to be looking for
someone among the airmen. I hurry down, knocking over as I do so
the ticket inspectors, who are still not allowing passengers aboard.
For once, a contented smile lights up Lyuba's face. She says to me
quietly, almost tenderly, "I was waiting for you. I am pleased."

How was she able to predict that on this day and at this time I
would be at Makhachkala? Is she trying to make me understand that
destiny was, one last time, holding out a hand to me?

"Come with me," she says. And she explains that, having committed an offense in Beslan by communicating the contents of my medical report, she feels that she is to blame for my hasty departure and
for its consequences. Everything can still be made good if I go with
her to Krasnovodsk, where she herself will see to my admission to the
hospital and take care of my health. Lyuba's suggestion seems absurd
to me, almost insulting. The Soviet Union is indebted to me, and I
have great expectations of reward. How can someone suggest that I
should enter a hospital for observation and get myself demobilized?

Lyuba has a trump card, however. She has chosen her setting

perfectly—better still than in Beslan, in that dawn light in front of the Great Caucasus. The light of Makhachkala and its reflection in the calm Caspian Sea emphasize her singular, redheaded, Siberian beauty.

"You are beautiful, Lyuba," I say to her foolishly, like any novice among the wounded attempting to involve a nurse in a "personal matter."

"Cut it out. I am an ordinary girl like everybody," she replies. But think of how far we've traveled from the broadsides of invective against my "setting traps" for girls!

She insists that you have to mistrust wounds or uncured illnesses. They are like enemy aircraft; you think they have flown past and then they swoop down on you once more, brutally. And, "Bang, your goose is cooked." It was exactly like this that her husband was killed; he had prematurely relaxed his guard, believing that he was out of danger. Anything that happens to me will weigh on her conscience, so I ought to go to Krasnovodsk as much for my own good as for her peace of mind.

Is it merely a question of her peace of mind? She is no longer ferocious in the least, and says nothing more about her decision to remain chaste until after the war. But I lack boldness and I don't dare to take her in my arms. Instead of reflecting on the inner meaning of Lyuba's message, I can think only of the temptation to kiss her, and of my fear of being snubbed.

"Run to the station and ask permission from your commissar," she continues. "Tell him that your health is at stake, and we will leave together."

But I know that our convoy of *tyeplushki* is already alongside the station platform, and my comrades are getting comfortable on the carriage roofs (their favorite way of traveling). And in the calm waters of the Caspian I picture also the ironically smiling face of Nievka. "Go on, then, go with this girl with the large breasts," she whispers from the bottom of the sea. "They are the only ones you really have time for!"

That's it. The die is cast. I must stay with the regiment, with my commissar who is now finally reconciled with Kola; I must think of Nievka, and chase after the mirage of my distinguished career in Marshal Golovanov's Air Force.

"No, Lyuba. I can't go to Krasnovodsk. I'm sorry. You are a very beautiful *bubnovaya dama.*"

"So they tell me," she replies, giving to me, on a scrap of paper, all her civilian and military addresses, in Krasnovodsk and in Tyumen. "Write me if you have any problems." She makes no reference to the sort of problem that would not allow any correspondence. Even the messengers of destiny are required to observe some discretion.

4

POZHARNIK

The colonel with the Budenny-style mustache,* the commandant of the Volgalag,† a camp located in the region formerly belonging to the Volga Germans, has me brought into his office on Thursday, January 13, 1944, at 2:00 P.M. exactly. He reads out a short communication issued by the public prosecutor of the Soviet Union: "Sanction for the arrest of K. S. Karol is refused because of the absence of material evidence to support any accusation." The colonel solemnly explains, "No one can be placed under arrest in the USSR without this *sankya procurora*; the law is explicit on the matter and tolerates no exception to it." Then, revealing two rows of long white teeth, he smiles. "Therefore, comrade, your arrest in Yerevan on December 10, 1942, never took place, and we have to arrive at a clear agreement on this point."

His formula, which is worthy of the great tradition of Russian surrealism, will delight my friends in Rostov some months later. Kola will persist in searching in it, beyond its comic aspect, for the key to the future of the USSR. He will ask to hear my story a hundred times

---

* Marshal Budenny, the famous cavalry hero of the Civil War, was once described by one of his own officers as "a man with an immense mustache but a very small brain."

† *Gulag* is the Russian acronym for "Main Administration of Corrective Labor Camps," but each camp, or lager, has its own name, generally taken from the place where it is located.

over—adding to it details of his own invention—in order to demonstrate that injustices were beginning to disappear from Soviet society. He will advise me after each retelling always to begin with the end of the story of my voyage of thirteen months and three days across the Gulag Archipelago, from the prison in Yerevan in Soviet Armenia to the camp on the Volga.

This narrative ploy helped me to reassure myself and allowed me to act the swashbuckler among my friends, so that I appeared in the story as a star player who had held the big shots of the NKVD in check. It also helped me to rid myself of an embarrassing character who kept alive within me a holy terror of the camp: the *pozharnik* (firefighter) who had been stationed in a forgotten corner of the steppes of the Volga, near a red-brick barracks that housed a brigade of fifty-four women *zeki*, or prisoners. He bore no resemblance at all to the "me" of the period before my arrest, or to the "me" of the period after my return to Rostov, but for a stretch of some months, before the "historic" scene of January 13, 1944, we were one and the same person. The outlook and obsessions of the *pozharnik*, which had been conditioned by more than a year of detention, no longer concerned me. Nevertheless, he frequently appeared in my dreams to warn me that I was wrong to forget him—he and his kind who remained in the Gulag—starting with our former women neighbors in the red-brick barracks.

Today, so many years later, I shall try again to recount my itinerary through the Gulag starting at the end, not in order to obey Kola's old injunction, nor to act the swashbuckler, but to do justice to the *pozharnik*. This firefighter shared with me memories of our life "before the camp," and while he was in the camp he had secrets that I no longer recall, or perhaps he didn't register everything because of the diminution in the number of his red blood corpuscles. In addition, I no longer remember the exact sequence of events that led up to his unexpected release. What is certain is that the *pozharnik* experienced this day in two different ways, both authentic, both blurred and engraved by memory. I shall recount both.

Finally, a certain confusion reigns with respect to the dates that punctuate this final episode spent in the region that had formerly belonged to the Volga Germans (about which it used to be said, before their deportation in 1941, that it was the "garden of the Soviet Union"). I remember only that I arrived there at the end of the summer of 1943, with a convoy of *zeki* from Yerevan. As to the *pozharnik*, he made his appearance at the beginning of the winter of 1943–44, at the time of the first snowfalls.

The Armenian convoy's journey toward the Volga camp during the summer of 1943 defies imagination, first of all because of its extremely slow pace: two or three weeks for a distance that even a slow train could cover in two days. Beneath the summer sun this snail's pace alone would be enough to sorely try the passengers, who were closed up in poorly ventilated *tyeplushki*. But there is more: Fearing that someone might take advantage of the interminable halts to escape, the guards come along every three hours, day and night, and use wooden mallets to tap on the carriage exteriors and check that no one has tried to remove any boards from it. "Everyone with their things to the left," they shout; then "Everyone to the right." Now this type of movement, which is terribly disruptive during daylight, is catastrophic at night. The occupants of the *tyeplushka* bang blindly against each other, losing their bundles and the niche they had made for themselves to sleep in. They need two to three hours to recover, which is the length of time that separates one inspection from the next. In other words, we hardly sleep at all, we eat very little, and we count each drop we drink. The only commodity to spare is the appalling heat.

Once we arrive at our destination, however, the surprise is rather agreeable. The NKVD had not planned ahead for the deportation to Siberia of those who had settled on the banks of the Volga two centuries earlier. They were packed off in a hurry, without distinctions being made between the Communists and the rest. Refugees from western territories—city dwellers especially—who had fled from the Wehrmacht came here to settle. The authorities were unable to organize a population unaccustomed to agricultural work in time for the harvest, and so they called in the help of Gulag labor.

The deployment of this great labor army raised a lot of problems, though. There was no question of housing it in the comfortable villages that had belonged to the Volga Germans, or of allowing it to circulate freely. The authorities therefore opted for the creation of "provisional zones," protected by high palisades and located near the principal harvesting centers.

In Russia the "provisional" can last a long time—so long, in fact, that our convoy from Armenia, on arriving in the late summer of 1943 in the Volgalag of the former region of the Germans, finds a chaotic mess. Communication between zones is virtually nonexistent; the work brigades get to the fields only after long delays, and often have to wait for the arrival of armed NKVD guards who are lodged in the villages.

My zone has ten brigades of thirty men each, grouped according to their physical strength; but for lodging we are all in the same boat, mixed pell-mell in barracks fitted with *nary* [bunks] on three tiers. The best places are taken by those who have been here longest, the "veterans" of post-German agriculture; but in a camp, with time, these things are negotiated, conquered, and redistributed. My neighbor is a "veteran," a former professor of organic chemistry—one of the most cultivated among the *zeki* that I knew. He observes that I appear to have been exhausted by the trip from Armenia and suggests an idea that will give a new direction to my life for a whole three-month period: to have myself cared for; better still, to have myself hospitalized. I come out of my torpor to plunge myself into an obstacle race in which the prize is this dreamlike place where you sleep between sheets, eat your fill, receive vitamins, and do nothing. But in our zone there is no hospital, and I am not the only one in our camp who is suffering from exhaustion, even though I am convinced that I am more worn out than the others.

My problem is getting myself accepted for a medical visit in another zone, thirty kilometers from this bizarre agricultural penitentiary. Now, neither complaints presented to superiors nor simulation of illness is of any use whatever. What you have to do is pull strings with those with influence, and I have no money to distribute favors. Nevertheless, I have some connections among those whom my neighbor calls the "permanent delinquency." His expression strikes me as apt, because it doesn't just designate recidivists, but also conveys the cohesion of the criminal fraternity. These people are well-organized, whether in prison or outside it; they have their own hierarchy, their code of honor, and their system of communication. It is harder to be admitted into their ranks than into the Communist Party of the USSR, because they don't hold either with words or with oaths of loyalty, and they know how to recognize their own. They don't proselytize or try to corrupt the *frayer*, the term they use contemptuously to designate all the others, even though, in my view, it derives etymologically from the German and means "free man," which, all things considered, has nothing insulting about it.

The leaders of the permanent delinquency neither work nor move around—their code of honor forbids it—and the penal administration generally bows before this case of *force majeure*. On the other hand, those belonging to the next rank in importance *do* work, and even take certain responsible positions in order to protect and control the small fry, who, since they benefit from no particular consideration on the administration's part, might be in danger of losing their strength and sapping discipline. Little by little, therefore, there emerge from out of the chaos, at the head of certain brigades of my zone, some "lifers" (those who didn't work at all) who come from Yerevan. Some of them give me the nickname of "student-raconteur," in recognition of a little feat as a storyteller that I performed in a prison cell in Yerevan, where the top cons themselves, suffering from boredom, greatly appreciated the story of the adventures of the Count of Monte Cristo, which I adapted to Russian conditions and improved upon as I went along.

Of course the "lifers" with whom I am in touch weren't present themselves at this performance, and in any case their code forbids them to favor any *frayer* systematically. They show solidarity only with their own kind, and in the event of conflict between me and the least of theirs, they are capable of creating the greatest misery for me. Still, by way of acknowledging the shared experience of Yerevan, they don't mind securing a medical visit for me. In three months they manage to get me three visits. The fact remains, however, that at the hospital there are ten candidates for every available bed, at least in my category, classified as suffering from pellagra or malnutrition—"weaklings," in lay terms. To avoid favoritism and to expose fakers, the camp administration introduces a "scientific" test: The only ones admitted to the hospital are those whose red blood corpuscles, as measured by a blood count, do not exceed a certain threshold. Above this limit, access to the hospital, with its clean sheets and its vitamins, is impossible.

Even though my results "improve" from one visit to the next (meaning that my red blood corpuscle count goes down), I still am above the threshold. I am given only consolation prizes: After the first visit, I am transferred from a normal brigade to one for "weaklings of the first degree" (Slabcommanda No. 1); after the second, to the brigade for "weaklings of the second degree" (Slabcommanda No. 2); and after the third, to the post of *pozharnik* in an almost uninhabited zone of the camp. At this third failure I crack and throw in the towel. The competition is too tough; I will always have too many red blood corpuscles. You can't appeal against the verdict pronounced by the camp doctors; they alone determine what amount of red blood corpuscles correspond to what job. So off I go on a cart driven by a *zek* who is authorized to circulate freely around the whole camp, and who consoles me, "You won't have a lot of work to do, *pozharnik*; while it is under snow the steppe never catches fire."

"Why, then, do they need a firefighter?"

"There was one in the days of the Germans," he replies, as if the explanation makes any sense.

That's no explanation; aren't the Germans cruel and stupid, and aren't we at war with them? "Yes, but they know how to build. Your hut is better built and better equipped than our barracks." And, he adds, "You are lucky. You will have fifty-four women for neighbors, blondes and brunettes, young and old, beautiful and less beautiful."

An Eskimo would not feel out of place in the *pozharnik*'s hut. Outside, everything is white—snow in endless amounts. The nearest village, two kilometers away, squats behind a small rise in the road; on the opposite side there is another village beyond the horizon. The illusion of being free is perfect but cruel; there are no warders, not even a lock on the door, but where is there to go to? Near the hut, in a strange, windowless, red-brick barracks, the women's brigade is housed; they work in a canning factory in the village. The rest of the landscape is empty, without a tree, without birds—a desert where the wind shifts the hills of snow. The winter of 1943–44 is less severe than those that preceded it, and the cold is bearable. From time to time, ignoring the ban on wandering off, the *pozharnik* goes along the road to look at the village from afar. It is exhausting, but he feels himself less excluded in knowing that there is still life elsewhere.

The world inhabited by the women *zeki* seems less harsh, less unpitying than that of the male *zeki*. Officially the *pozharnik* has to keep an eye on their stoves and help them operate a water heater twice a week, but in reality they have no need of him at all. In the days of the Volga Germans, the red-brick barracks was used as a depot for flammable materials—no one is too sure what these were—which explains the water-pipe fittings and the firefighter's hut. The *nary* are arranged on only two tiers, and the space in the middle of the barracks seems almost as vast as a ballroom.

Because they aren't so crowded, the *pozharnik*'s neighbors hardly notice his presence. Their barracks is never empty, either, since, in addition to the *dezhurnaya* (day warden), there are always a few "indisposed" or absentee inmates who haven't gone to work for the day.

The brigade leader, predictably, is a foul-mouthed permanent delinquent. Her four deputies, the *naryadchitze* (distributors of work), are no novices, either, and could have taught Sergeant Major Orlov a thing or two about swearing. Toward the *pozharnik*, however, they have no reason to be aggressive; they have practically no dealings with him. Of course they insinuate, in jest, that he is a *khitryi pozharnik*, a cunning firefighter who has managed to get off working and "feasts his eyes" on fifty-four women. In fact, so little do they believe it that when a *nary* becomes free in the barracks for a night or two, they are the first to invite him to take advantage of it: "You'll be a lot warmer here than in your hut."

What surprises him most is the kindness of certain women among his neighbors, who perform services for him for nothing. Such kindness is out of keeping with his experience of the Gulag. For these are real services that require work and time, and not simply a little word in the ear of some godfather or other. Lyussia "the peasant woman" (or "the Christian woman"; in Russian these two words are almost identical) cleans his hut and brings him wood for his stove; Nadia does his washing, mends his clothes, and even cuts his hair for him. And their friends approve of their doing it.

Why do they do it? How can they allow themselves such selfless behavior in this world that never gives them something for nothing? With respect to supplies, their brigade is not particularly well favored; if anything, their food rations are rather inferior to the prevailing norm in the zone. Most of the women, as soon as they return from work, collapse from fatigue onto their bunks. They are frighteningly thin and the *pozharnik* sometimes says to himself, "These women are not long for this world." In the mornings, when the brigade goes out, some of them shout openly in the face of the *naryadchitze*, "I can't take any more of it. I'm going to end up in the morgue." The latter threaten them, "Don't play the fool or they will come to get you; they'll take you away under escort and you will end up in the dungeon." These noisy scenes are the most distressing moments of the *pozharnik*'s day.

Whether he sleeps in his hut or in the barracks, Lyussia comes each morning to check that he is still alive. She obviously doesn't admit this; she is merely bringing him a little boiling water for his breakfast. But her manner of always calling him *byednyi pozharnik* (poor firefighter), combined with her worried expression, gives him to understand that he is in danger. He will have to start the obstacle race to the hospital all over again. How, though, can he set about it? With whom can he negotiate or simply talk? Nadia is more intelligent by far than Lyussia. She rarely speaks of herself, and doesn't meddle in the lives of others. The camp effaces the past; it is not forbidden to talk about it, but you can just as easily be silent.

Style betrays nevertheless a *zek*'s origin, especially in the case of a woman. Nadia, for example, knows the folklore of the camps, but to no avail; of itself, it doesn't make her a "permanent delinquent." She sings ballads in slang, but the words don't come naturally. Blond-haired, ageless, attentive to her appearance, Nadia is also terribly thin; it is not her natural build. Before coming to the camps, she was almost certainly numbered among Nievka's rivals: the *tsytsatye baby*. It is with her that the *pozharnik* is most in sympathy, although he doubts that she can be of any use to him in the steps he hopes to take.

The best moment in the firefighter's day is when the work brigade returns; it is then that his neighbors bring him his rations for twenty-four hours from the village. He swallows straight off, in less than fifteen minutes, the mess tin of kasha intended for two meals, the three hundred grams of bread, and the half-herring. Sometimes Lyussia and Nadia make him reheat the food, and while giving in to them, his nerves are set on edge at the delay. He knows that his manner of eating is not rational, but he can do nothing about it; he is incapable of storing food. A demon stronger than his reason holds sway in his stomach, and it forces him to gorge without discernment every morsel of food that falls beneath his eyes.

This demon even dominates his dreams in which Nievka, Lyuba, and Clarissa—along with Kola and his friends—have been eclipsed by herrings. It is a distressing degradation of the ambitions of his unconscious; where will it end? In Yerevan he still dreamed about cooked dishes or Polish croissants (*rogaliki*); now he no longer sees anything but herrings.

On Thursday, January 13, 1944—a day that will end in the *pozharnik*'s unexpected release—he has gone back to sleep in his hut, after the daily uproar that precedes the departure of the women for work. Suddenly a man in uniform, wearing a fur cap, shakes him: "Hey, you, *pozharnik*; you're a real fire risk. Quickly! put out this smoking stove." He doesn't remember the man's face—but the remark, which is deeply wounding to his self-esteem, engraves itself forever on his memory. (At least, this is the first version the *pozharnik* would recount of the events of that extraordinary day.)

However, that same morning (and this is the second version) Nadia comes to look for his spare set of clothes because she is *dezhurnaya* today and is taking advantage of it to do some washing. She has promised him that afterward she will make some vegetable soup she has stolen from the canning factory.

When you haven't a bite of food to look forward to until the evening, you can't easily forget such a savory promise. The *pozharnik* settles himself down, close to Nadia in the red-brick barracks, after having helped her to place her washing saucepan on a stove. Suddenly, contrary to all her habits of discretion and reserve, she turns toward him and asks, "Did you know that I was beautiful once?" But, without awaiting his reply, she turns once more toward the saucepan and withdraws from it by means of a wooden stick a small gray thing. "Do you see these? Men have killed one another to get them off me. I was beautiful, *pozharnik*, I am not boasting; I will tell you the story one day." It is at this exact moment that the barracks door opens and the uniformed man with the fur cap makes his entry.

In both versions, he begins by addressing to the *pozharnik* the classic question asked by the secret police: "What letter does your name begin with?" They never pronounce the name of the suspect first themselves, so as to avoid any substitution of one person for another. As it happens, everything is as expected, and the *pozharnik* has to leave with him for the commandant's office.

Of course, the officer reveals nothing to him of the interrogation to come; it is contrary to camp conventions. Later, after an hour's journey in the officer's jeep, he relaxes a little and asks, "Do you remember the circumstances in which you were incarcerated?"

Does he remember them, indeed! Like a scene from a horror film. It was December 10, 1942, at dawn. Four NKVD men, along with their dog, burst into his room at the student residence in Yerevan, instilling a fear in him worse than anything he had experienced at the front. To make matters worse, he was suffering from a terrible hangover, having celebrated the previous evening with Kola and the gang. But the *pozharnik* no longer knows how to recount such a scene, and he doesn't even know how to refer to the secret police. As comrades? No. It is forbidden to *zeki*, and he was warned against it from the first day of his arrest. Well, then, four citizens with a dog? But that sounds more like a sequestration. He gives only the date, and otherwise talks only about Yerevan, of its three large avenues—Lenin, Stalin, and Akopian—the last-named of which, though he doesn't say so, is the most beautiful. His escort listens to this as if it were a rather boring geography lesson.

In both versions, the jeep arrives in the wooded courtyard of the camp's central administration building well in advance of the rendezvous. The officer offers a bath to the *pozharnik*, but he feels perfectly clean and prefers to wait alone in the antechamber of the commandant's office. There is a handsome earthenware stove in this room, like the one in his apartment in Lodz. He warms his back against the clean, lukewarm tiles and slides to the floor, where he sleeps until 2:00 P.M. exactly.

A quarter of an hour later the *pozharnik* is offered the chance of becoming a free man in a world without barbed wire. All that he has to do is to sign some forms duly prepared by the camp's commandant on the instructions of a good public prosecutor anxious about socialist legality. With a signature, a nightmare of thirteen months and three days would come to an end as suddenly as it started. Personally, I would have signed without even reading this official document. The *pozharnik*, however, sees things in a different light. He wants to recover his freedom, but he also needs a minimum of security such as he enjoyed in the firefighter's hut. Conscious of the fragility of his strength, he doesn't feel himself capable of leaving for just anywhere in any old fashion. What's more, conditioned by this harsh school of mistrust that characterizes the Gulag, he has learned to smell a trap behind every offer from a superior or a fellow prisoner. The *pozharnik*, therefore, simply says "No," and regrets that he is unable to sign anything whatever.

Although he is taken aback, the colonel is patient. (He has probably received a very elaborate communication from the public prosecutor, recommending that he handle this delicate case with tact.) He explains to the *pozharnik* the advantages that he can expect to obtain from the cancellation of his arrest and the destruction of his dossier.

His reasoning reflects the peculiarly Soviet attitude of complete confidence in the sacred authority of the written word, in history as in the destiny of individuals. We know that, by virtue of this principle, in the USSR an event that has been erased from the textbooks is considered never to have taken place. According to the colonel, a former *zek* who no longer had a dossier would no longer ever be identified as such, even by the relevant state organs.

All of his eloquence, embroidered with articles of the Code of Criminal Procedure, read out in whole paragraphs complete with pauses for indentation, is in vain. It is not even clear that the *pozharnik* has attentively followed the arguments. In the "heroic" version he would later feed to his friends in Rostov, he faces up to the colonel in the name of Justice—of Vengeance, even—but in reality he is more concerned with the immediate material advantages to be gained from the apparent goodwill of the colonel. So when the colonel, by now somewhat exasperated, asks him, "But what do you want exactly?" he replies immediately, "I want food; I haven't eaten since yesterday, and hunger is preventing me from thinking properly."

A bustle ensues at the other side of the table. The colonel, now indignant, reproaches his deputy for having left the *pozharnik* without food, and orders him to bring him some sandwiches. The scene livens up. The officer runs off to look for a secretary, who declares herself incompetent in the matter of sandwiches and who rushes off to find a cook, who, in his turn, arrives breathless and asks the *pozharnik* a question from another epoch, another world: "What would you like in your sandwiches, comrade?"

"Herrings," the *pozharnik* replies like lightning, letting himself be guided by his unconscious, which has found in this fish the sole source of protein in the *zek*'s diet. A new difficulty arises: Inexplicably, in the canteen of the administrative center of the Volgalag, there are no herrings. Someone can be sent to fetch them from the nearest zone, but it will take time. The commandant's cheeks are flushed with anger, but it is aimed at his subordinates and not at the *pozharnik*. Toward the latter he becomes more benevolent, as if he had suddenly been moved to learn of the prevalence of hunger in his camp. He has a whole tin of corned beef—better than the sandwiches—brought to the starving *pozharnik,* and while the *pozharnik* eats, he asks if the *pozharnik* has given any thought to where he will go after leaving the camp. Silence. A very hard question. The *pozharnik* sees no answer to it. "Have you any parents or family?" "In Poland." The commandant raises his hands in the air. This case seems insoluble.

A bright idea comes to him all of a sudden: "According to your dossier, you belong to the political service of the air force and you were granted six months' leave for health reasons, which expired on April 1, 1943. Go back to your post and I will see what I can do to get the public prosecutor to authorize me to enter in your military papers that you have never left it. That will extricate us from an embarrassing situation. What do you say?"

"No," the *pozharnik* persists. He isn't going to say that he no longer has the heart to organize Komsomol meetings, or to exalt the just socialist cause. Getting up, he shows the commandant his emaciated arms, his swollen legs, and declares that he can't present himself in this state in front of the elite fighter pilots of the air force. This argument sways the commandant; he orders the *pozharnik* to be placed in the camp infirmary for officers while he consults the public prosecutor on how to deal with this perplexing case.

Less than one hour later the *pozharnik* is sleeping between clean sheets, in pajamas. He has a handsome room all to himself, in the well-heated house of a Volga German who was deported in 1941. It is the most comfortable room that he has ever slept in since coming to the USSR. What's more, he is soon to enjoy a deep sense of moral satisfaction: The nurse, after taking a blood sample, reveals to him that he ought to have been hospitalized long ago, because of the very low count of his red blood corpuscles. The tests inside the camp were, as he had thought from the beginning, a con. Science has finally vindicated him.

The officers' infirmary in the Volgalag almost seems to have been designed for sleeping treatment. Around ten fairly quiet patients are in its six rooms. The double windows insulate them from outside noise, while indoors, even the nurses seem to walk on tiptoe. Minor noises occur only at mealtimes and are rather agreeable to the ear. The food is brought in but reaches the patients still hot, and compared with that in the canteens for *zeki*, it is delicious. The infrequency of medical visits doesn't worry the *pozharnik*; he is only here to rest before the discussion that he will have to have with the colonel about his future.

It would be best in these conditions, following an old Russian saying, to unplug the brain and let the time flow by. In practice, however, he would have to be possessed of unassailable serenity. Now the *pozharnik* has one point in common with me: a strong propensity to hold himself culpable for things that he thinks he has done the wrong way, or hasn't done at all. Thus he is tormented by the memory of a particular day in the prison in Yerevan, the day on which someone mentioned the public prosecutor to him for the first time. He remembers once more everything that happened before and during that day, which was so unlike the others.

Everything begins one evening in January 1943, one month after his arrest, when Captain Streltzov or Strelkunov—let's call him Strel—puts an end to his interrogation by the NKVD and accompanies him on foot to the prison in Yerevan. The town is already asleep and they walk through the empty streets like old acquaintances out for a stroll in the night air. Tall, thin, with a long bespectacled face that gives him a vaguely professorial air, Strel is convinced that he is right about everything and maintains to the end that the accused— the future *pozharnik*—has terrible crimes on his conscience that sooner or later he will admit. He tells him that in the meantime other state services are going to take his case in hand and that they will inform him of the accusations or charges against him. It would be in the accused's own interest to make a full confession, because these other services are capable of keeping him in prison or in a camp for eternity. On this note, Strel departs.

The prison in Yerevan deserves to be classed as a historic monument. A former fortress, built in the time of the Turks, it appears rather splendid from the outside, with its imposing, unscalable walls.

Inside, it is made up of vast, very somber rooms or halls. The one in which the future *pozharnik* is placed houses a whole battalion of detainees, packed against each other, sleeping on the floor. Since the ceiling is quite high, five meters at least, it should have been possible, as in other Soviet prisons, to install tiered bunks, giving them, if not exactly comfort, at least the possibility of sleeping without disturbing their neighbors. The explanation for this absence of bunks is immediately obvious: The real rulers in this place are the bedbugs, and any wooden fittings would only encourage them. During the day the detainees try to drive them up the walls toward the ceiling, but at night they come down again; the most impatient even let themselves fall right down from above, like parachutists.

Only one of the detainees deigns to raise himself in order to greet the future *pozharnik*: the *kamerkom*, commander of the *kamera* or cell.

"What are you in for?" he asks authoritatively, but without raising his voice, so as not to awaken his companions. Having neither confessed nor been confronted with any formal charges, the newcomer can only protest his innocence. His questioner points out that all of the occupants of the cell are in the same situation: "We are all innocent." To explain the specific character of his innocence, the future *pozharnik*, avoiding any mention of Captain Strel's accusations, introduces himself as a student who has problems with his papers. The *kamerkom* immediately draws from this a peremptory conclusion: "So you're a Trotskyist, eh? A Trotskyist student." It is the word "papers" that provokes this irrational reaction, and he laments aloud as if a calamity has just befallen his hitherto peaceful cell. It is impossible to clear up the misunderstanding or to persuade the cell leader to reconsider his decision to allocate to the "Trotskyist student" a minuscule place to sleep, in between the *parasha*—the tank that holds the detainees' excrement and other waste—and another tank of almost the same height that contains the supply of drinking water.

A drama erupts on the very first night: The future *pozharnik*—a restless sleeper—kicks the water tank toward the wall near which are

sleeping, in relative comfort on mattresses, the leading figures of the
"permanent delinquency." An unbelievable scrimmage immediately
follows, leading to a generalized clamor of protest against this latest
cold-blooded Trotskyist sabotage. Blows rain down on the future
pozharnik; if the *kamerkom* had been armed, the culprit would have
been executed on the spot, to the unanimous applause of the inmates.

Ostracized, he is reluctant to try his luck when the big wheels of
the "permanent delinquency" throw open a competition to the *frayer*
by inviting them to recount something of a diverting nature. The first
three candidates fail abysmally, beneath boos and thumps, and so the
future *pozharnik* opens his act in a state bordering on panic. He risks
a lot, after all; where he's concerned, they won't forgive anything.
But, thanks to Nievka's taste for *dyetskye skazki*, he knows some
stories by the Brothers Grimm that are ferocious enough to lend
themselves, with some adjustments, to the taste of this discriminating
public. The first story is listened to in silence, which is a good sign;
the second, in which a frail orphan becomes super-powerful and ends
up punishing a wicked prince—changed for the occasion into a chief
of police—by plucking out his eyes and tongue, and tearing off his
testicles, raises grunts of approval close to enthusiasm. He is asked
for more, and from the next day, the future *pozharnik* has the good
sense to go on to Alexandre Dumas *père* and *The Count of Monte
Cristo*; this serial, to be spread over fifteen or so evenings, will mark
the first great turning point—and the only happy one—in his prison
career.

The story of Edmond Dantès, a young sailor who falls victim to a
public prosecutor consumed by political ambition, but who will succeed in escaping from his dungeon, find a fabulous treasure, and
usurp the title of Monte Cristo in order to seek justice for himself,
seems to have been written expressly for the inmates of the prison in
Yerevan. To begin with, the idea that a prisoner could escape and
become immensely rich excites their imagination and their dreams;
then, too, none of them would hesitate to take ferocious reprisals
against the public prosecutors in their own cases, or the examining
magistrates of the NKVD or the criminal militia. Thus far, the credit

for the spectacular success of the future *pozharnik* belongs entirely to Alexandre Dumas, who, a century earlier, had been able to conceive a work that would go on to appear so entrancing and contemporary in the Soviet Republic of Armenia.

But that is true only of the first part of the tale—the detention of Edmond Dantès, his friendship with the Abbé Faria, another forgotten inmate of the dungeons, and his escape. The second part, devoted to his revenge, drags on—"for want of tits and ass," according to the expression used in Yerevan—therefore, Monte Cristo appears as a rather forlorn figure who doesn't know how to reconcile his legitimate thirst for vengeance with a love life more in keeping with his great wealth. The future *pozharnik* feels compelled to take increasing liberties with Dumas's story, in order to adapt it successfully to the special tastes of his captive audience in Yerevan. His adaptation is derived from two perfectly fair premises: A well-matched pair of Zorros is more efficacious than a single man, and our Monte Cristo could very well have met a Russian countess in Italy, for, in the Czarist period, the St. Petersburg nobility had a predilection for this country. All that is required is to place the treasure island in the Adriatic instead of the Tyrrhenian Sea, and to imagine that the former Edmond Dantès falls in love in Venice with his Russian accomplice-to-be, who is superbly beautiful and as Machiavellian as himself. Their first rendezvous in St. Mark's Square brings into the prison gloom in Yerevan a poetic light, and brings out the taste for romance buried in the souls of the bosses of the "permanent delinquency."

The heroine borrows first from Alexander Blok the appearance of *nyeznakomka,* the mystery woman, dressed in rustling silk, who is elusive and yet perfectly capable of inflicting a thousand torments on your average careerist prosecutor. But as the tale gradually unfolds, when the avenging couple arrive in Paris, the accomplice-wife of Monte Cristo begins increasingly to assume traits similar to those of Natasha Rostova, the heroine of *War and Peace.* This is an audacious stroke, for the beautiful Tolstoyan heroine, in the original, seems utterly incapable of inflicting cruel reprisals. At the side of Monte Cristo, however, this aspect of her character—that of the pure young girl—lulls the vigilance of those who are to be chastised. Also, she is an authentic aristocrat while they are newly ennobled. This enables the storyteller to emphasize the prestige our compatriots enjoyed as long ago as the last century, and to improvise some comic episodes ridiculing the pretensions of the French nouveau-riche Establishment.

The reader will appreciate, of course, that it is impossible to invent new wrinkles to Dumas's plot during the actual recitation itself; everything must be prepared in advance. However, it doesn't displease the future *pozharnik* to turn over these episodes in his mind, to recite them to himself, even though the place that has been given to him—between the smelly *parasha* and the leaky water tank—is not really conducive to inspiration. Fortunately, cell opinion is moving in his favor. One of the big shots, a recidivist specializing in train holdups, understands immediately the enormous injustice that has been done to the "student-raconteur," and promptly slaps the cheek of the *kamerkom*, solely because the latter has been stupid enough to call the future *pozharnik* a "Trotskyist student." The big shot's orders are irrevocable: There is to be no more mention of "Trotskyist" in relation to the student-raconteur; he is to be given a comfortable place on a mattress and he is to be properly fed, with the cream of the soup and not with the pale juice. Over the next several days, the big shot also shows a certain interest in the penal dossier of the future *pozharnik*. Unable to make either head or tail of it, he summons the *kamerkom* (the latter is merely a deputy of the power brokers of the "permanent delinquency") and orders him to arrange a meeting of the student-raconteur with a godfather versed in matters of Soviet jurisprudence who is detained in another cell block. Since moving around between cells is strictly forbidden, the *kamerkom* will have to use great ingenuity to carry out this order. But with his own position at stake, he manages to pull it off. One fine morning a warder brings the future *pozharnik* to the legal expert's cell.

This cell appears suitably imposing, as befits the prestige of a detainee of distinction: It is a former hall of arms, as vast as a railway station concourse. It is also relatively uncrowded. The man who is expecting the future *pozharnik* seems astonishingly young—no more than thirty years old. A self-assured Armenian with a harsh unsmiling face and lively eyes, he has a whole corner of the cell for himself. He indicates to the future *pozharnik* a stool near his bed, places a bowl full of grapes and oranges on a little table, and stretches out on his double mattress. "Tell me everything, keep nothing back," he says, "I can be of help to you only if you tell me the whole story with all the details." He closes his eyes, not to sleep but to concentrate.

"At the time of my arrest on December 10, 1942, I was very frightened, more than I ever was at the front. It happened at dawn, at the student residence. There was something that was both brutal and paralyzing about this intrusion of four NKVD men and their huge police dog. To top it off, I had a terrible hangover. The night before, with my friends Kola, Vassya, Volodya, and Kostya, I had celebrated our army's success at the Stalingrad front and the anniversary of my arrival in the USSR, three years earlier. We had drunk a good deal at the Intourist restaurant. . . ."

"Where? You must be crazy!" the legal expert explodes. "It is the most expensive and most closely watched place in all of the Soviet republics."

"We knew that, but for one thing we had a fair amount of money, having acquired a fine length of pure woolen cloth during the retreat from the Caucasus, and it had earned us a small fortune at the flea market in Tbilisi; for another, we didn't know where to go, our attempts at picking up girls having failed. We were fed up and we discovered that you could find everything at the Intourist, so we became regular customers of this restaurant. Besides, the waiter, whom we tipped generously, seemed to appreciate and look after us. I didn't see why I should be arrested for that.

"My conscience wasn't entirely easy, though. Because I had been wounded in Nalchik, I behaved as if I had already paid a debt to the Soviet Union, that I was now authorized to do whatever I liked, or rather no longer to do anything at all. I had obtained six months' leave from the air force to convalesce and to resume my studies, but in fact

I had no need of any further medical care and never went to the hospital. Similarly, my desire to study the Russian language and literature was less than wholehearted, and yet it was the only department that I could attend at Yerevan University, since all the other courses were in Armenian."

"There is no crime in that; a serviceman on leave has the right to do nothing. What were your official resources?" my listener asks, his eyes still closed.

"Everything was aboveboard in this respect; I continued to receive my salary and a student grant. I was housed for almost nothing in a room that I shared with a certain Oleg at the student residence. I had access to the university cafeteria and I also went sometimes to the air force mess, where I was well known and liked. Recalling the difficulties I had had in obtaining a residence permit in Kislovodsk because of my Polish origins, in Yerevan I declared that I had been born in Rostov, of Russian nationality."

"Not so fast!" the expert interrupts, asking me to tell him about the episode in Kislovodsk. The digression will be a long one, for he wants to know the details about Nievka and Commissar Byelokonyenko, as well as those concerning the papers issued to me in Rostov in 1940. Although convinced of my listener's goodwill, I avoid all mention of Western Siberia and of my Muscovite cousin General Stepan Vladimirovich.

"It seemed to me that Commissar Byelokonyenko, also recalling the distressing incident in Kislovodsk, deliberately emphasized, in the *karakteriska* he gave me for the local authorities and the university, the extent of my 'Russian consciousness and culture.' I still hesitated before making my false declaration of identity, even though I knew full well that, for the moment, the authorities would have to take my word for it. Since our papers of origin had been burned in Kislovodsk, and since Rostov remained under German occupation, they had absolutely no way of verifying what I told them. But I was also afraid of remaining stuck in Russia forever. In the future, by what right could I receive permission to return to Poland after having declared myself Russian, and having said that I was born in Rostov?

My friends from Myechotka quickly dispelled my apprehensions on this score, saying that it was simply a subterfuge, without any consequences for the future. 'On April 1, 1943,' Kola said, 'you will come back into the "eleventh," where even the kitchen mule knows that you are a *Polski pan*.'

"As ill luck would have it, all my acquaintances at Yerevan University, including Oleg, were from Rostov. They liked nothing better than to talk about their hometown, morning, noon, and night. I used to go out quite a lot with a girl named Svetlana, the daughter of a history professor, and she soon guessed that I wasn't really from Rostov. It wasn't important in her case, because Svetlana liked me and we trusted each other. With Oleg the situation was more complicated. From the first, Kola didn't like him and we never invited him to our social evenings. I wouldn't have minded inviting him; I felt sorry for him because he had lost a leg at the front, but Kola, guided in this by his sixth sense, declared that he was an informer. Whether true or not, each time I came back a little the worse for liquor, Oleg would wear me out with questions about Rostov, about girls there whom I might have known over the years. Generally I coped well with it, but on the night of December 9, after an evening of celebrations, I told Oleg to go to hell: 'I don't remember either your blond Nadia or your brunette Vera because I am Polish, and not a *kacap** like you!' This was the drink talking; such remarks were futile and could only prove insulting to an injured war veteran. His revenge, though, was swift; some hours later the four NKVD men were already searching our shared room."

"Your friend Kola was right. You can't be too careful with informers. But tell me now about your interrogation by the NKVD," the expert concludes, handing me a fine bunch of Armenian grapes.

"For the first two or three days, Captain Strel confined himself to checking details, in such a way as to make me feel that since my arrival in Yerevan, the NKVD had been keeping a close watch on me.

* A pejorative term for "Russian."

His dossier seemed more detailed than my own diary would have been, particularly with respect to my finances and my relations with Svetlana. All my expenses were meticulously noted, as were all my outings with the professor's daughter. Since our relations were platonic (through no fault of mine), Strel's corroboration of events in no way embarrassed me."

"Are you sure that this girl isn't their informer?"

"Yes, she has other failings, but not that one. Svetlana is an old-fashioned, twenty-two-year-old virgin—a daddy's girl who loves her father and wishes to become a history teacher like him.

"With the appearance of Captain Abakovmov or Abakian—we'll call him Abak—my position worsened. This little man, who spoke execrable Russian, was out for blood. 'You have left your honesty on Mount Ararat on the bulls' horns,' he said to me. I replied that Mount Ararat was in Turkey and that I had never set foot there. Then he asked me, 'How would you like to taste some Iranian sausage?' And he produced a rubber truncheon from his drawer.

"Throughout my entire interrogation—about two weeks—I kept waiting for a specific accusation against me. But nothing definite emerged. At the time of my arrest I had only about one thousand rubles left from the sale of our war treasure—hardly something over which to create a major fuss. I pretended that this sum had come from the sale of my watch, which was a mistake. They knew about everything, including the fact that my watch had been stolen in the hospital in Beslan. I had to confess, and claim sole responsibility for salvaging the woolen cloth, which had been sold in Tbilisi. They seemed indifferent, and Strel even remarked with a hint of irony that I had applied the scorched-earth tactic by leaving nothing to the enemy.

"After this, I spoke to them, unprompted, about the question of my Polish nationality, and this outburst of sincerity also made them laugh. Well informed from their dossier, they obviously knew that I had lied in order to get my residence permit in Yerevan. An unnecessary lie, in their view, for permission would have been granted to me in any case. Why, then, did they keep me locked up in this seedy little basement cell?

"Finally, when I began to get impatient and started to mention at every opportunity my claims to consideration by virtue of my military service, Strel got up and threw in my face, syllable by syllable: 'TY GER-MAN-SKAYA PROS-TI-TUT-KA!' ['You are a German prostitute!'] This vulgar invective overwhelmed me. The chill caused by an uncontrollable terror prevented me from speaking. By a violent effort of will I managed eventually to articulate in a trembling voice that I had damned near lost my life fighting the Germans at the front. 'Damned near lost my life,' he mimicked sarcastically, 'yet here you are alive and well. Spies are always above suspicion, otherwise they would easily be caught.' His spine-chilling irony was even more disturbing than his initial abusive taunts. Strel resumed his verbal assault: 'The krauts are holding your family hostage; they placed you clandestinely in Rostov; you then found cover as a Komsomol and infiltrated our air force; they have never stopped paying you and controlling you, even in the Caucasus where you feigned a concussion. In Yerevan, however, when they put pressure on you to obtain information about our aviation, they made the mistake of exposing you and at that very moment we were waiting to pick you up! Don't be afraid, I am not bloodthirsty. Tell us the names of your accomplices in Armenia and Turkey, and you will get off with a light sentence.'

"When I asked him who the witnesses of my alleged nefarious crimes had been, he replied coldly, 'We still don't know who your bosses are, but you will certainly identify them for us.'

"Abak intervened periodically with his 'Iranian sausage.' According to Captain Abak, my parents personally had put Hitler in power, and as for me, I had been active since early childhood in the most fanatical Nazi movements."

"This is no laughing matter," the expert interjects, flabbergasted by the gravity of my case. On reflection, he reproaches himself for having taken me so seriously: "If you were a spy, you would already be dead in the morgue, and not in this cell with common criminals. Carry on."

"Nevertheless, Abak and Strel wanted to know about all the secret meetings I had had in Yerevan, on such a date, at such a time, in such and such a place. To give my head some peace, I would have admitted perhaps to meeting with suspects of their choice, but to invent, on my own, this street and this house, and the last name, first name, and patronymic of someone I had neither seen nor known, was frankly beyond my intellectual capacities."

"Perhaps they were aiming, through you, at bigger game. Did they ever talk about a third party, another suspect, or about a compromising acquaintance?"

"Yes, but he was an Armenian whom I had known without knowing him, and with whom I spoke without having a common language."

"Stop speaking in riddles. Tell me plainly what you mean."

"In Yerevan, Kola, the rest of the gang, and I used to frequent the Intourist restaurant where we occupied a table in the corner, isolated from the rest of the room by a large neoclassical column. There were only two other small tables there, one always empty, the other regularly occupied by a solitary, thoughtful young man who ate little and drank a lot of wine. A waiter told us he wasn't sitting there hoping to overhear us; he didn't understand Russian. Repatriated from France with thousands of other Armenians in 1938, he had apparently simply kept up the habit of drinking in a public place, as they do in Paris.

"When I heard this I immediately felt a keen empathy with this loner who had come from the West. And since my brother Boris had been a student in France, I felt sure that we would have lots to tell each other. In what language, though, since he didn't speak Russian, or I French?

"One evening I approached his table, saying simply, 'La Grande Illusion,' the title of the last French film I had seen in Poland. The Armenian hesitated, fixed his melancholy gaze on me, then guessed my intention. 'Jean Renoir,' he replied. I continued: 'Pierre Fresnay, Erich von Stroheim,' picturing these actors once again in my mind's eye during their last dialogue in the fortress. The Armenian visualized them at the same time as I did. 'Jean Gabin, Jean Carette,' he said, thus indicating the following scene to me, and I concluded with 'Dita Parlo,' the German woman who helped the two fugitives to escape. It was a marvelous discovery; we had found a means of communicating.

"He invited me to his table, ordered some wine, and passed on to another film. The rule of our dialogue was simple: We had to cite the names of the protagonists in each film in the order of their appearance on the screen, and mentally accompany them from one scene to the next. Since he had been brought up in France, it was inevitable that he would know French movies better than I did, and at the end of our first bottle of wine, I was having problems following him. And so, by an unspoken agreement, we turned toward Hollywood. There we could go on ransacking the archives forever. I said 'Al Jolson,' and the Armenian mimed his response. He kicked off with *The Champ*. He clearly seemed to rate this film, starring Wallace Beery and James Cagney, very highly. 'Bang, bang,' what do you say to westerns? 'Randolph Scott,' he replied, while making clear from a torrent of names that he preferred the great romantics, Clark Gable and obviously Gary Cooper. Then, with a single voice, we pronounced the same words: 'Paul Muni' and *'I am a Fugitive from a Chain Gang.'* What a coincidence! Perhaps because both of us in our different ways felt that we were 'fugitives,' that these movies, these stars belonged only to our world, and not to that of the Soviet Union.

"After the second bottle of strong Armenian wine, we summoned up the international stars, the magnificent women who succeeded in making all of the men in the West dream about them—Marlene Dietrich or Greta Garbo, the Blue Angel or Queen Christina. My Armenian friend gestured with great ardor, as if to say, 'I refuse to choose between them. I want them both.' And the blonde vamp Carole Lombard? At the mention of this name, he began to speak seriously and rapidly in French. Was he in love with Carole Lombard? Did he find it disagreeable to talk about her in this prosaic Intourist restaurant in Yerevan?

"My friends began to call for me; I had to leave. But, not wishing to leave on a note of misunderstanding, I repeated to him the first film that had allowed us to communicate, but in reverse. I said 'Dita Parlo,' and he, at the end, said to me by way of farewell: 'Ah! *La Grande Illusion!*'

"My 'conversation' with the Armenian undoubtedly provided Strel and Abak a pretext to harass me; according to their informer we had occasionally spoken in German (this was true to the extent that we had cited German movies and their stars), and the Armenian had called me by my name. (Perhaps this was how his mentioning Carole Lombard had been interpreted.)

"During the final interrogation sessions, I felt that Strel no longer believed in his initial accusation. He simply claimed that he no longer had time to devote to my case, and regretted my obstinacy in keeping to myself a secret that was going to poison my entire life."

"Let's walk a few paces to stretch our legs," says the expert. His bodyguards immediately clear a path, moving people to one side and warning them to be quiet. "My friends in your cell have asked me to give you some advice, because I know by heart the criminal codes of the former Republic of Transcaucasia, of the Republic of Armenia, founded in 1936, and of the USSR," my host explains, as though to let me understand that he could have been a Minister of Justice and thereby enjoyed altogether more significant perquisites than that of being the only prisoner to have the use of a double bed. "Unfortunately, your case leaves me perplexed. It's hard to know by which end to take hold of it, because it constitutes a *dyelo nye-oformlyen-noye* [a nonformalized matter, one that has no set form]. In our codes of criminal law, whether old or new, there are no articles relating to people found in possession of a thousand rubles who have made a partially erroneous declaration of identity. Perhaps in administrative law there is something on the subject of these trifles, but I'm not sure. In other words, legally speaking, you don't exist, you have no juridical identity. Ah, my dear student-raconteur, had your objective, in planting yourself in Yerevan, been to rob a state bank, I could have given you some advice. But you are merely a *frayer* who has succeeded in arousing the enmity, for no good reason at all, of the most important security services of our republic. I have never met a *frayer* like you; you are here but your head is elsewhere, in a world about which we Soviets know nothing.

"What should you do? If you were Armenian and a little bit wilier, less *frayer* in sum, I would have advised you to complain to the Armenian public prosecutor about wrongful detention. Since, however, you are from neither here nor there, you would perhaps do better not to make too much of a protest. Sooner or later they will have to put your case in proper form."

He concludes by asking me to see him for a further consultation as soon as I have a presentable "juridical identity."

Some days later, a typical prison uproar puts the future *pozharnik* in a state of alert. The grating sounds of the old iron locks draw closer and closer. Some of the prisoners are being led off, but which ones, and to where? He is one of them! He's given orders: quickly, shower, disinfection. Is it a good sign? Do they want him to be clean for his release? Under the shower, the future *pozharnik* questions his neighbor, an Armenian who is neither happy nor sad, a young detainee with a dreary air. "We are going to work," he says.

The journey by truck lasts less than an hour. Thirty prisoners, the future *pozharnik* among them, are taken to the nearest labor camp. They are to be used to replace exhausted *zeki* working to build a bridge across the Zanga River.

In his infirmary bed in the Volgalag, the *pozharnik* remembers that on the day of his transfer to the construction site, instead of being rebelliously inclined, he was really rather pleased about it, almost happy. To leave behind the vermin-ridden prison that was as dark as a tunnel, and to find himself beneath a springtime sun, on the banks of a sparkling river, was not a change of luck to be disdained. From the outside, his living quarters, situated in a gully near the river, hardly made you think of a penal work camp. There was only one watchtower and little barbed wire. The citizens of Yerevan strolling along the cliffs above the *zeki* below, taking advantage of the fine weather, wouldn't have suspected the presence of a labor camp. In the USSR at the time there were plenty of construction sites, both military and civilian, that were protected for security reasons. From the clifftops, it would have seemed as if only free men were working below, specialists in concrete work, who belonged to some Armenian construction company. Its concrete mixers poured out a concrete mix that had to be spread rapidly on the piers of the future bridge. Fast

work was essential, since the poor-quality concrete hardened immediately.

What month was it? April, or maybe May—it is of no importance
anyway. It was an awful month, less because of the heat than because
of the infernal rhythm of work: *shute, shute, shutarek*—faster, faster,
faster still. The concrete mix flowed without pause while we pushed
our wheelbarrows: an endless marathon. Even to go for a piss, permission was necessary. The supervisory personnel spoke only Armenian, and discriminated against those who didn't.

In the evenings, after the marathon, the future *pozharnik* collapsed
with fatigue. He wasn't yet as skeletal a figure as some of the women
he was to meet in the red-brick barracks, but he was already behaving like them, scarcely able to take advantage of his free time to walk
in the evening air or to talk to his companions in misfortune. He
dreamed not of herrings, but only of concrete mixers breaking down.

The overseer, at the beginning, had favored him when it came to
food servings, probably in tribute to his skills as a storyteller in
prison. Each morning before work, the overseer gave him an extra
mess tin of soup without explanation. One day, though, one of the
small fry came and told him an improbable story about his forthcoming escape. He claimed that he needed the future *pozharnik*'s shoes to
organize it properly. Why? Because they were better, more solid than
his. In Yerevan prison another would-be escapee had taken one of his
sweaters under the same pretext (he had later been obliged to return
it, on the orders from the "permanent delinquency"), but you don't
catch a fish twice with the same bait. After this refusal, however, the
overseer stopped dispensing favors to him and remained deaf to his
entreaties and explanations. As it happened, this reduction in his
food supply coincided exactly with an acceleration in the concrete
mixers' output. And so it came about that the future *pozharnik* began
to lose his red blood corpuscles.

One evening, when he was on the night shift, he had seen, on the
cliffs, behind the floodlights trained on the bridge platform, the silhouettes of four pilots on either side of a young woman dressed in
white. Blinded by the light, he hadn't been able to recognize their

faces, but their silhouettes corresponded exactly to those of Kola, Vassya, Volodya, and Kostya. And Svetlana always wore white.

It must have been his friends, then, the last friends he had made. The future *pozharnik* had been moved to tears and comforted simply at having caught a glimpse of them and at the thought that they were talking about him. Throughout his interrogation, Strel and Abak had never questioned him about them, as if unaware of their existence. It was obviously strange, for their informers must have told them all about the links between the Myechotka Musketeers and their friend from Poland. But this silence didn't prove that they had been left in peace; the reasoning of the NKVD was too complex to allow such a simple deduction.

For Svetlana the problem was different; Strel and Abak slyly used her as a kind of indirect witness, but without ever quoting her: "Instead of attending the hospital at such and such a time, you went with the student S. to the museum," and so on. Had they questioned her? Had she suffered because of his "unsavory company"? And, yet, it seemed that Svetlana was free. Kola and the others also were safe and sound, and looked on from afar as the future *pozharnik* shifted concrete mix onto the pier of the future new bridge on the Zanga.

From the height of the cliffs, his friends no doubt knew that they were watching a man obliged to do an exacting job, but they surely didn't guess that the slavery to which he had been reduced was transforming him completely, from the composition of his blood to the content of his brain. He was already no longer the same man; he was merely clinging to life as a drowning person clings to the first driftwood that comes along.

My good, dear Kola, on the mountain paths of Balkaria you explained to me all the stages of the evolution of humanity, from the remote epoch when tribes killed their prisoners who were of no use to them, to the stage of slavery when, on the contrary, prisoners were squeezed like lemons to build pyramids for their captors. But isn't the bridge on the Zanga, which will one day be the pride of Armenia, a modern pyramid? Except that neither you nor other free citizens suspect anything. And in the USSR, how many other bridges, factories, and towns have been built in the same manner, by men and women who were sacrificed, squeezed like lemons?

But the Pyramids of Egypt are also a mystery. Who, in that distant and forgotten epoch, could have built them, and how? One day the same question will be asked about those who built the bridge across the Zanga—and similar works—but it will be too late once again. There will no longer be any witnesses, and the future will hear only the official version of those with the whip hand. Of course, the official textbooks will mention in passing some regrettable errors inflicted on the victims, while pretending at the same time that these unfortunates ought to have exercised their right to due process of law, that of the Socialist Code of Criminal Procedure, the most advanced in the world, just as the Constitution of the USSR is the most democratic.

The *pozharnik* laughs aloud in his nice warm bed in the luxurious infirmary, which was intended for NKVD officers, the authors of the books of the future about the incomparable harmony of socialist legality.

"Get up, you are to get properly dressed for the road."

"But why? What road? Nothing has been decided yet."

"Yes, it has. You have been resting for four days, and now the commandant will explain things to you."

The *pozharnik* would prefer his own trousers and his padded jacket, which are certainly inelegant but very warm and well suited to the Russian winter. "No," the commandant's deputy retorts. "You are to dress like a free man from now on, and not in rags like a *zek*." He has brought back for him nevertheless his spare set of old clothes from the red-brick barracks, and a note from Nadia: "Dear *Pozharnik*, I am very happy for you. In ten years' time, if I am still alive, call at my former address in Moscow, which I give below."

The camp commandant approves of the *pozharnik*'s new outfit, undoubtedly inherited from a deceased *zek*—and informs him of the results of his consultation with the public prosecutor. As the *pozharnik* ought never to have been "taken away" from the Red Army, his dossier will show uninterrupted military service, and, so as not to complicate matters, even the six months' leave granted him in

Yerevan will be erased. On the other hand, to spare him long journeys and distressing reunions with his former friends, he will go first
to Saratov, where he will be given his new assignment at the Commissariat of Military Affairs. He will have to go there on foot, but it is
only a matter of a few dozen kilometers—a fine promenade on the
Volga, in fact, a pleasure rather than a hardship.

"I have assigned you dry rations for three days," the mustachioed
colonel continues amiably, "and I arranged to have added to them
several of the herrings that you like so much. But I am certain that
you will not take three days to get to Saratov, for there are quite a few
trucks that run along the Volga, and you will surely find one to take
you to your destination. Finally, given the solution suggested by the
public prosecutor, it isn't necessary for you to sign a discharge form
for the penitentiary administration. You have been in the armed
forces without interruption since September 1941; you know nothing
whatever about the camps. If, through carelessness or inadvertence,
you do speak about them, you run the risk of being charged with anti-
Soviet propaganda, under Article 58 of the Code of Criminal Procedure, paragraphs five and six. But you are a reasonable man, and
cultured as well. You have made an excellent impression on me, and
I am sure that you have already forgotten this whole embarrassing
affair. I wish you a safe journey."

Free now, and already half-transformed back into a soldier, thanks
to a long, rough sheepskin jacket, worn inside out, of the sort that one
sees in the army and civilian life alike, the *pozharnik* begins by
sitting down upon a tree trunk on the edge of the Volga and eating one
kilo and two hundred grams of bread plus his three herrings. This is
his three days' rations: Instead of kasha, he has been given extra
bread and a double portion of herrings. The commandant was generous in word only, but it is too late to protest. Besides, had there been
one herring more, the *pozharnik* would have swallowed it up like the
three others. Unless a truck picks him up, he has the prospect of a
long walk along the Volga on a soon-to-be-empty stomach.

He is not in a hurry to get under way, however. He is haunted by a
strange memory: He pictures his neighbor in Lvov once again, that

night on which he was deported to join the mosquitoes of Siberia, the neighbor who asked the NKVD men, "Why are you insisting on throwing this youngster overboard from society?" At the time, this question imprinted itself on his memory because it was so bizarre, for society was not a boat, nor was Lvov in the middle of the sea.

But now he understands everything and he says to himself, "Here I am, then, thrown overboard on the Volga, but fortunately it is frozen over, and I am in no danger of drowning." And then he bursts out laughing, because to go for a walk on the Volga is not an experience that happens every day, nor to just anyone.

The Volga is unique. The Vistula is only a stream, while the Bug is, well, so insignificant that it hardly seems worth mentioning. The Volga is so wide that you can barely make out the white trees on the other bank. It exudes a taste and feel of Russia more pronounced than elsewhere—much more, certainly, than on the banks of the Don, the river of the Cossacks, which is far narrower than the Volga.

The beauty of the Volga, frozen and covered over with snow, consists in its comforting tranquility, which no traffic disturbs. No doubt, trucks pass over it from time to time—the tracks of the wheels in the snow are there to see—but whoever was stubborn enough to wait for one would be in danger of freezing. The *pozharnik* doesn't walk for long on the Volga, therefore, to admire the landscape. His practical sense prevails; he climbs the banks and takes to the paths that link the villages, hoping to be fed by the local inhabitants.

This unavoidable choice—he would never make it to Saratov without eating—is risky. Russian peasants, who are renowned for their hospitality, are also very mistrustful; reluctant in normal times to open their doors to strangers, they are always ready to lay the blame for thefts or accidents in their village on them. During these years of war and hunger, women predominate in the region: widows, mothers, wives or sisters of soldiers—and often too, of *zeki*. In his latest guise, most of these women have no difficulty in seeing a resemblance between their dear ones and the *pozharnik*—half-soldier, half-*zek*. They are able to read the misery of the camps in his eyes, but also that of the labor battalions, and of the poorly fed soldiers at the front.

The welcome is not the same everywhere: Certain *izby* the stranger is not allowed to enter, while in others he is given only a piece of bread, like a beggar. Sometimes he is offered some hot soup, a little meat, some dried fish, and is allowed to rest in the warmth. Although it has been spared the ravages of bombs, the region around Saratov is not exactly opulent.

In the villages, which are often very near to one another, social distinctions are easily spotted. After three or four experiences, the *pozharnik* concludes that it is the middle peasant who represents his best hope: Those who are too poor have nothing to offer him, while the rich ones are quite capable of setting their dogs on him, so concerned are they with protecting their property. As to the middle peasants, who are the most generous with their food, unfortunately they don't offer—despite the departure of conscripted men—a habitable space to shelter a stranger. During the summer, he could have slept in a stable or a barn, but in January it is much too cold.

In one village a kindly old peasant woman advises the *pozharnik* to seek shelter in the local *kolkhoz* administrative center, which is well heated and isn't closed at night. Is it allowed? "As long as you leave early, before the office workers arrive," the old woman replies with a peasant's good sense. The next morning, however, in another village ten kilometers farther down the river, the *pozharnik* is stopped by some *kolkhozniki*. They question him about a man in rags, dressed in a half-torn jacket, whom they are looking for. A theft was apparently committed the night before in exactly the same building in which he spent the night. But there was no one else in the center, and the *pozharnik* hadn't even dreamed of stealing anything. Had the old woman sought to pin on him a crime committed by a member of her own family? To be sure, she had given a false description of his clothes, a precaution perhaps in case he had been seen with her—or maybe out of Christian charity? The *pozharnik* quickly learns that peasant hospitality has another side to it, and that the life of a traveler in the Volga region involves unforeseeable danger.

Such problems, among which is his personal enemy, the bitter wind from the Lower Volga (as it was called in the villages), preoccupy him so much that his sense of time begins to desert him. He is expected in Saratov, at the Commissariat of Military Affairs, on Thursday, January 20, but this date has already gone by and the city is not in sight. And then, a miracle, a truck finally stops for him; better still, it is going to bring him straight to the commissariat.

This will be one of the *pozharnik*'s last evenings, the most unexpected, the one in the course of which his *zek*'s obsessions and complexes almost destroy him. Ten days—four in the infirmary and six on the road—have gone by since his release from the camp, so that he presents himself at the Commissariat of Military Affairs in Saratov on a Sunday. There is only a sergeant on desk duty, but after taking the *pozharnik*'s papers, all that he can do is grant him leave to spend the night in the waiting room. Tomorrow those qualified to do so will deal with him, and he will then be able to take advantage of the military canteen.

Some hours later, however, the *pozharnik* smells the appetizing odor of cabbage soup—a great regional speciality, not to be confused with borscht—and, noting that the sergeant is sleeping behind his desk, he advances into the corridor, letting himself be guided by his sense of smell. A light behind a door suggests the route to the kitchen, and he enters without knocking. A colonel as bald as Taras Bulba or Yul Brynner knits his eyebrows in anger or surprise.

The *pozharnik* apologizes profusely for his intrusion, his late arrival in Saratov, his very existence. The colonel says nothing, but his expression still seems threatening. In a desperate effort to appease him, the *pozharnik* mumbles something about being hungry, but immediately proposes to clear off and return to the waiting room. "No," the bald colonel orders him severely, "sit down there and don't move." And he hurries off without even closing the files on his worktable.

For the *pozharnik*, this hasty departure indicates punitive intentions. Superiors who go off in this fashion, without even a single bellow, are the most dangerous; in the Gulag this is well known. "Why should I wait here for the worst to happen, rather than try my luck on the outside?" the *pozharnik* asks himself. To be sure, he no longer has his papers, as the desk sergeant held on to them, but he has just been on the road for six days, without ever having to show them. An inner voice within continues: "Go on, take courage, run. Don't let yourself be sent down for another thirteen months by these bastards. It will be a fine consolation when they announce to you a second time that you have done nothing and that the public prosecutor doesn't accuse you of anything." The *pozharnik* steals a glance into the corridor; everything is still, the path is clear, he can escape.

Fine, but it's nighttime; it would be futile to look for an unguarded official building in the city. What about the train station? But there frequent checks are made of waiting passengers' papers. Had it been daylight, and in the countryside, the *pozharnik* would have fled, tempted by the subterranean, unpoliced world that exists within the fissures of Soviet society. Every *zek* has heard of those who have lived for a time without any fixed domicile, of those who belong to the "permanent delinquency." By listening to the latter's folklore, you learn that they have their regular *pyvnyie* (beer houses), hideouts, and complex system of communication. The *pozharnik*'s neighbor in the Volgalag, the chemistry teacher, had scientifically demonstrated to him that any society incapable of putting an end to criminality for social and economic reasons ends up by making a pact with it in the hope of controlling it and of minimizing the damage it causes. Why not try to join this other world? the *pozharnik* asks himself one last time. But it is too late. In the corridor he can hear a large number of energetic footsteps approaching; he closes his eyes, convinced that he is once again about to meet up with four NKVD men accompanied by a large dog.

In fact it is a group of male nurses with a stretcher and a woman doctor. The bald colonel shows them the *pozharnik* while explaining certain matters in medical jargon. Then he summons the desk sergeant and asks him some questions, so he can sign the papers for the *pozharnik*'s admission to the hospital. What an extraordinary country, the stupefied *pozharnik* thinks to himself; the mustachioed colonel had judged him fit to march one hundred kilometers on the Volga, while the bald colonel doesn't believe him capable of going even as far as the hospital on foot! Unless, of course, during these six days on the road he has lost the rest of his red blood corpuscles?

This question, although judged to be crucial in the camp, will apparently cease to be important at Hospital No. 1683 in Saratov; military medical science, unlike that in the Gulag, doesn't seem obsessed by the blood count of the wounded or the sick. Besides, the *pozharnik* has been lucky: This hospital is one of the three best in the Soviet Union, and has just been awarded the Order of the Red Flag for the notable results it has achieved in the struggle for socialism. Its doctors are genuinely competent.

During this transition period, our memories—the *pozharnik*'s and my own—intermingle, and they are doubly confused. Something persuaded both the bald colonel and the doctors that the *pozharnik*'s life hung only by a thread and that he needed urgent care. Had he been overtaken by a bout of fever as a result of exposure to the cold on the Volga, or had he grazed his face in a fall, or was he lame after a march that was beyond his strength? Frankly, I don't remember. His case must have been serious, though; the nurse in the communal ward, a believer, blessed herself each time she approached his bed.

The seriousness of his condition was indicated by the intensity of the treatment administered: transfusions and injections, intravenous ones that generated an agreeable warmth, and also intramuscular ones, which gave him a sore backside. The dietary regime was unexceptional in either its quality or quantity, and the *pozharnik* had to appeal more than once to the Christian feelings of his nurse to get a second helping of whatever was available. By chance, his neighbor in the first few days was an officer who had had his appendix removed and who, having no appetite himself, discreetly passed his food to the *pozharnik*. Apart from these fragmentary recollections, however, neither the *pozharnik* nor myself can say very much about this obscure post-Gulag malady that was fought so efficaciously by the doctors of Hospital No. 1683. Once I was cured and had become myself again, I left to spend a month in a sanatorium for officers, in Khvalynsk, on the Volga.

The town of Khvalynsk, situated on the banks of Russia's national river and surrounded by magnificent forests of birch, is a charming place, or so they say. In the month of March 1944, however, a fine, persistent drizzle prevents the sanatorium convalescents from setting foot outside. This sojourn, which has been prescribed for health reasons, will be useful for catching up with news from the front.

In the Gulag the war was followed with a detached, distant curiosity. Fortunately, convalescing Russian officers hold very firm opinions about the course of the war, and do not hesitate to argue endlessly about battles won and lost. My account of the battle of Nalchik is appreciated and even excites some flattering comments. According to one of the convalescent officers, by immobilizing the Germans in the Caucasus and by inflicting severe blows on the Romanians, the 37th Army in Nalchik greatly contributed to the triumph of Stalingrad. This extremely dialectical reasoning will delight Kola when he hears about it some weeks later, and he will enrich it with additions of his own. On the whole, however, the 37th Army is held in low esteem in Khvalynsk (it is a *slabaya armya*, a sickly army).

This month in Khvalynsk reminds me of my stay in Moscow in 1940. In both instances I learned or relearned to behave like a normal Soviet citizen: in Moscow by trying to forget my Polish habits, here by trying to forget the experiences of the Gulag. Of course, during this convalescence I don't know that I will be returning to Rostov. At the beginning of April, after a medical examination, I am to receive a military assignment to rejoin either my original unit or another unit of the Red Army. But the doctors in Khvalynsk don't seem convinced that I am entirely cured, and without inviting my opinion in the matter, they demobilize me for one year, arranging an appointment for me with the army in April 1945, a month before the final victory.

Two surprises await me: For lack of an air force uniform, I am given an infantry officer's dress uniform, with a handsome overcoat that is remarkably elegant even without the epaulettes, which a demobilized officer doesn't have the right to wear; and I am paid all of my salary dating back to December 10, 1942, amounting to several hundred rubles, a fortune almost as fabulous as the unfortunate war booty that the NKVD confiscated from me in Yerevan.

Miraculous meetings sometimes happen in real life just as they do in the movies. In Rostov, upon getting off the train from Saratov, I catch sight of a tall, slim pilot with a snub nose: it's Kola! He has been demobilized and is no longer wearing epaulettes. What is he doing here? He is asking himself the same question about me. Our voices are choking with emotion and we just about manage to both say, "You haven't changed at all." It isn't customary for men in uniform to show their emotions in public. So we behave with an outward restraint, as if, one and a half years earlier, we had arranged to meet in the time between the arrival of the train from Saratov and the departure of the train for Myechotka. A look, a smile, suffice to express our happiness; for the first time in a very long while I feel that I am no longer alone, even if I still don't know where to go or what to do with my life.

Kola knows, all right: We will go to Myechotka, after having invested some of my rubles in buying a load of herrings, which are relatively cheap in Rostov and expensive in his hometown. His Aunt Valia will be delighted to have the two of us for a day or two, and we certainly need this time to tell each other everything. I ask him why he was demobilized. "Stomach ulcer," he replies. A minor matter; you don't die from it; but the air force decided nevertheless to demobilize this valuable "ulcerous" pilot, since he had already flown in several air raids. Kola is not complaining. Now, since the war is almost over, all his thoughts turn to the future. "We will become public-works engineers. Everything has to be rebuilt from scratch in this country, starting with our own Rostov. This task will guarantee us a future without suffering."

Kola wants to travel on the roof to avoid the crowded carriages and indiscreet ears. Don't worry, he assures me, all you need to do is give the ticket collector a small tip—one herring will do, and not a very big one at that. It works, and he is as delighted as any youngster by it. "In Russia, the roof is the best place on the train," he says. I agree with him, although the wind is definitely too strong for my taste.

"Well then, begin!" Kola tugs his ear in anticipation and puts his arm on my shoulder. But I don't feel at ease on this curved roof—those of the *tyeplushki* are flat and therefore more comfortable—and anyway, the Gulag is not a fairy tale by the Brothers Grimm. So it is Kola who will talk most, but this time without embroidering his narrative; he doesn't know yet that Commissar Byelokonyenko has just been killed at Korsun-Shevchenkovski, and therefore avoids inventions that the latter might contradict on the occasion of a subsequent meeting. I listen with great interest as Kola recounts the reactions of my commissar and all the others during my year in the Gulag:

"The first reaction of Vassya, Volodya, Kostya, and I, after your arrest, was quite banal: it was fear. We were petrified at the thought of being interrogated, purged from the air force, and thrown into a hole somewhere. It appeared inevitable, first of all because of the principle of collective responsibility that operates in our country, which applies as much to a family or to a group of friends, and next because we were jointly guilty with you of the offenses with which we thought you would be charged. You represented the 'weakest link' in our chain, as Lenin would have put it, but we really didn't feel much more secure. Aren't we the sons of *lichentzy* [people who were deprived of civic rights up until 1936]? The air force hadn't taken this into account and had believed in us, but the NKVD is not so indulgent toward those who are guilty of 'original social sin.' Logically, therefore, we ought to have been arrested and we feared it would happen from one day to the next. Perhaps it would be for having, along with you, made off with a small war treasure, or for having made stupid remarks while drunk at the Intourist restaurant, within earshot of Armenian informers who perhaps hadn't even understood our Russian properly.

"At the end of a week, however, since nothing had come of our worst fears, we took courage and went to question the only witness to your arrest, the one-legged Oleg. Because he is such a suspicious character, we were obliged to put the fear of the devil in him in order to rule out the danger of being denounced in our turn. Vassya took him squarely by the collar and threatened to throw him out of the window. Suicides are commonplace among disabled ex-servicemen, Vassya explained, to convince him that we would have no hesitation whatever about arranging his 'suicide.' He ended up by agreeing to talk and, while swearing that he had had nothing to do with it, he told us that you had been picked up because of your false declaration of nationality. He claimed that this was what he heard during the search of your room by the NKVD. For us, this changed everything. On this point we were in the clear. As soon as we understood this we decided to act, first by asking Commissar Byelokonyenko's advice.

"Byelokonyenko was thunderstruck by the news. He wasn't play-acting, either; he really knew nothing of what had happened. How could someone be arrested for an offense with political implications, without even his former superior having been informed of it? It was obviously possible since it had already been done, he told us, but added that it wouldn't be left at that. We tried to fan the flame of his indignation, assuring him that you had been planning to return to the regiment on January 1, 1943, without waiting for your leave to expire. 'Enough's enough. I've had as much as I can take from them,' he shouted like a madman. 'I've told them a thousand times that he is *nach* [one of us].' It was clear then that 'they' had spoken to him about you, but had kept from him the news of your arrest, and this had challenged his authority and honor. Quite forgetting our presence, he telephoned Colonel Ganachek to express his indignation and to arrange an urgent meeting to discuss the matter. Perhaps, though, he did it on purpose, to let us know that he was going to intervene on your behalf in the name of the regiment.

"A week went by. Byelokonyenko had the four of us come to his office and dryly instructed us not to reply to any summons that might arrive from the NKVD. 'Tear them up or bring them to me, but ignore them. That's an order. Your only concern is aviation and nothing else. Is that understood?' Perfectly. We went back to our airplanes.

"After that he used to summon me alone, under the most diverse pretexts, but obviously we always ended up talking about you. In the course of these conversations I gradually gained the impression that he knew a great deal about us, including our Caucasian past. In my view, this proved that he was in touch with the NKVD—but also, unfortunately, that the secret police had forced you to talk. Frankly, I didn't hold it against you, since they are capable of making the dumb speak. No one resists them for long. Nevertheless, our legal situation became precarious, for to salvage a roll of cloth amounts to looting, and in the army they take a dim view of that. Vassya and Volodya became very pessimistic, while Kostya and I searched hopelessly for a means of contacting you to find out what you had told them. In Rostov we would surely have found a way somehow, but in Yerevan, without the right connections, there was nothing to be done.

"When Byelokonyenko summoned us all a third time, at the beginning of 1943, I expected the worst and hadn't prepared a defense. 'I know all about it and I don't care,' he said. 'But I would like you to help me find the Georgian who bought this stolen cloth from you in Tbilisi.' He said that he needed to find him for personal reasons, because he had made a bet with a friend, or something of the sort. Now that I know that these assholes had accused you of receiving money from the krauts, I realize that he simply wanted to find a witness who could confirm your story. At the time, though, to be honest, all four of us thought that he had gone mad. How else could such a foolish wager be explained? Volodya described to him the *tolkuchka* of Tbilisi, the greatest flea market in all of Transcaucasia, or maybe even in the whole of Russia. It is a place where you can buy or sell anything, even a Hero of the Soviet Union gold star medal, but where it is impossible, four months later, to track down an anonymous individual. He was so disappointed that he showed us the door without saying good-bye.

"Some days later, he invited me to accompany him on a walk from the barracks as far as Yerevan's center to again talk to me about the *tolkuchka* in Tbilisi. He was visibly shaken by Volodya's claim that you could acquire the title of Hero of the Soviet Union with banknotes bearing Lenin's likeness. But, bit by bit, while storming against corruption, he delivered a lengthy speech against indiscriminate repression, and in fact against the NKVD, with precise charges directed against its Yerevan branch.

"I offered him my help, which made him smile. 'In this matter I would need the help of four air marshals, not four trainee pilots,' he said. In his view, the only thing that we could do for him was to become the best pilots in our squadron, and not to furnish the slightest pretext for any criticism of our conduct. That, then, had been the object of our walk, to alert us to the fact that we were being watched. Vassya and Volodya, who are always inclined to pessimism, then pointed out to me that there were only *two* air marshals in the entire Red Army, and that if Byelokonyenko needed four of them to get you out of this mess, then you really were in trouble.

"At the beginning of February 1943, at the time of the victory at Stalingrad, there was a festival in the streets, both literally and figuratively. After hearing all the speeches possible and imaginable, we were given two days' leave to get as drunk as we liked. Returning home on foot after a party, the Elephant met Captain Pyetya Danilov, staggering but still capable of speech. Vassya willingly helped him home as he wanted to find out more about the captain's buddy, the commissar. Thanks to Vassya, we learned the following:

"Before the war, in Zaporozhye, Byelokonyenko had had a run-in with the NKVD over a fellow whom he knew to be innocent but who had been condemned to endless years of camp, and perhaps even killed. He had never ceased to reproach himself with not having saved this man, for he ended up convincing himself that he could have done it. As soon as he learned of your arrest he therefore raised a hue and cry. This time not only the 'eleventh' regiment, but also the command of the 18th Air Force, exasperated by the NKVD's interference in the armed forces, had given him a free hand to do so. However, the NKVD were not easily frightened, and claimed they could prove that you were a German spy, and that such an accusation should suffice to close the case. The commissar, who had already been 'had' in Zaporozhye, replied that they were bluffing and insisted on seeing the proof. This was a little suicidal on his part, for if they had proof, he himself would be in danger, accused of complicity with a German agent. On the other hand, according to Danilov, even if they were bluffing they would still send you far away, to hell's gates if need be, rather than admit a mistake. Luck came to Byelokonyenko's aid, for, just at this moment, several of his friends from Zaporozhye secured senior positions in the leadership of the political services of the armed forces, as well as in the Communist Party. He immediately enlisted their support in his local war against the Yerevan NKVD, and also in obtaining his transfer to the army, which was about to advance to the Ukraine.

"Danilov knew nothing more. The next day, however, we went to see him to ask for authorization to send you a parcel. I had thought of this as a way to establish at least indirect contact with you, taking advantage of Danilov's friendly attitude. He refused at first, claiming that it was too dangerous, but since he isn't such a bad sort, he finally consented on the condition that we didn't indicate the address of the sender. All of us put together a handsome parcel of five kilos and sent it off addressed to you in care of the NKVD in Yerevan. At the end of February, the parcel was returned to Danilov's shop with the hand-written inscription, 'Addressee unknown.' How strange! They were not supposed to know the sender—whom they found nonetheless—while they must have known the addressee. It was the world turned upside down, and it would have been funny had it not been so serious. We arranged to see Byelokonyenko, for we hadn't even noti-fied him of the parcel. But he was calm, and told us, 'Forward the package to Yerevan prison, and don't complicate life for them by concealing the names of the senders.' All four of us signed, but I confess to you that I understood nothing any longer, really nothing at all of the tactics of the commissar, or of your situation as the accused.

"The package was returned one month later, at the end of March, accompanied by a standard note saying that only close relatives may visit and help detainees. Svetlana, who had come to ask for news of you, had the idea of bringing it to the prison in person, and declaring that she was your fiancée and therefore a close relation. It didn't work, but as she is stubborn and a born fighter, she gave them something to chew over, threatening to lodge complaints with heaven only knows who. Thanks to her, the prison administration—it was April by this time—informed her that you had been transferred to the construction site on the Zanga bridge.

"We saw you there, one evening, hard at work, and it was awful. Svetlana couldn't stop crying. No one knew what to do; to all appearances there were only condemned men on this semicamouflaged construction site, but you hadn't even been tried. When I questioned him privately, Byelokonyenko only said, 'He hasn't been, nor will he be, tried or condemned.' Well, then? Nothing. He shrugged his shoulders. 'In Nalchik,' he asked, 'did you believe that four months later the Germans would be encircled in the steppes of the Don?' 'Not that precisely, but I knew that we were going to win,' I said, failing to understand the comparison. 'This time it's the same,' he replied. Take it or leave it; he didn't ask for our help in this particular war, simply for our patience. To be honest, though I don't want to offend you, I didn't believe you were capable of standing this regime of forced labor for very long, and I lapsed into the blackest pessimism, worse than when we were put to rout in the Caucasus.

"In the autumn of 1943, they started to send us to operational bases in Georgia, not all at once but in small groups. We took part, in turns, in bombing raids against Romania, on the far side of the Black Sea. It was a real war between Cossacks and Romanians; they had come to take our petrol, and now we were bombarding theirs. In November—or was it December by that time?—when I saw Byelokonyenko for the last time, he gave me a wink, then whispered, 'It's all fixed; you'll see him again soon. Come and see me, both of you, in Zaporozhye, after victory, or as soon as it's possible.' Now you can understand why I wasn't altogether surprised at meeting you in Rostov this morning, although your smart uniform took my breath away. And now, 'look and admire,' as Mayakovsky would have said, we are coming into Myechotka, in the department of Rostov on the Don!"

In other times I would have found this journey extraordinarily moving. For better or worse, the four Musketeers of Myechotka had become my best friends in Russia and had promoted me, as early as our time in Kislovodsk, to the rank of honorary citizen of their hometown. I feel that I know almost every house in Myechotka, having had its smallest details described to me. This large village, almost a small town, is altogether worthy of the stories I have been told about it, especially at this time of year, when its streets are clean and verdant, after the mud from the thaw has disappeared and before the summer dust from the steppe has invaded.

But I arrive as an ex-*zek* who, three months earlier, was forced to wander from one village to the next on the edge of the Volga. This all-too-vivid memory eclipses older ones for me and dulls my enthusiasm. While visiting my friends' school, and then the *raisoviet*, the municipal buildings that serve the region, I think of neither Vassya nor Volodya, but of my nights spent exposed to risk in similar premises on the road to Saratov. Here everyone is friendly toward me, but I wonder if they would have been as kind toward the *pozharnik*.

Remarking upon my sullen mood, Kola imagines it is because I am disappointed by the absence of visible signs of Cossack folklore, or disgruntled at the fact that the quiet Don doesn't flow through the middle of his village. Instead of joking and trying to relax, I reply abruptly that I am well versed in geography and especially in Soviet methods of handling whole populations. All that surprises me in Myechotka is that the entire Cossack population hasn't been lately deported, as happened with the Volga Germans, and that no "Myechotkalag" has been installed there. And anyway, how can Kola be sure that, a few kilometers away from here, hidden behind palisades, there isn't a camp of forced labor employed in agricultural work, and farther away still, in some inaccessible corner of the steppe, a red-brick barracks of women *zeki* and a small *pozharnik*'s hut? "You can't hide anything here because the steppe is so flat." Kola thus pirouettes his way out of a difficult situation, and while strolling through his hometown, he outlines his plans for our studies, our political careers, and our whole future. Before the start of the academic year, we ought to take advantage of the travel privileges granted to demobilized ex-servicemen to accumulate some money by buying and selling between Tbilisi and Rostov. Given the huge disparity of prices on the black market in these two metropolitan centers, we could make vast sums of money out of each return trip. Then, once assured of a solid material foundation, we can apply ourselves to becoming public-works engi-

neers. We will begin by earning the title of *otlichniki*, first in the
class, which will automatically open the doors of the Party to us.

"Haven't you understood anything of my thirteen months and three
days in the camp?" I ask, breaking the spell abruptly. It frightens me
too much even to consider these plans for lucrative trips between
Rostov and Tbilisi. "Kola, I have to concern myself with only one
thing: my departure for Poland. In a few months, maybe even sooner,
I will be able to leave, preferably by the first available train."

My desire to go home seems natural to him, but he is saddened that
I am so bitter, vindictive almost. How could I so easily forget our
good times together in Kislovodsk, in Tbilisi, and even in Yerevan?
He reminds me of the vow that we made in Tbilisi to return there for
our respective weddings. Why not take advantage of our situation as
demobilized servicemen to go back there? "I am not the same as
before, Kola, I have more recent memories than those of Tbilisi."

At this he becomes very gloomy. "Let's go home. We'll have it out
over dinner."

The *pozharnik* would certainly have classed Aunt Valia among the
rich peasants. Her house looks well-kept: It is surrounded by a rather
large vegetable garden, and all the windows are fitted with clean lace
curtains. But I haven't the vaguest idea of the source of this wealth.
Aunt Valia is in her forties, and has been living alone since her
husband and son left for the front—if we exclude her father, that is,
who is simply called *Dzyed*, Grandfather, and who is unable to help
her since he is almost totally deaf and too old to work in the fields. If
it weren't for the lack of men in Myechotka, you would think that
Aunt Valia had seduced some regional leader, or a *kolkhoz* president
at least, who lavished presents on her, including gifts of food. But
perhaps she isn't rich at all, and is simply making a ruinous effort to
give a fitting welcome to her favorite nephew, Nikolai—as she ceremoniously calls Kola—and me, whom she decrees straightaway to be
an "artillery man," praising this branch of the army to please me:
"Artillery is the god of war!" One thing is certain: On the black
market in Rostov the dinner we enjoy would cost a fortune.

The menu is both classic and original: borscht with meat, mutton stew with potatoes, then as many blinis as we can eat; they are Aunt Valia's speciality. Honey and fresh cream are set out in magical quantities. The *dzyed* plays the part of wine waiter as we are eating the main courses, but then leaves the vodka on the table and withdraws to a corner of the room. His daughter is too busy making blinis in the kitchen to join in our conversation. Here are Kola and I, then, served like princes, as happy as reunited brothers, but still somewhat tense and anxious. The vodka has something to do with it: I am no longer used to drinking, and he is no longer allowed to because of his ulcer. He is drinking only in honor of the exceptional occasion.

Like all *zeki*, I am convinced that Kola cannot imagine what a camp is like; those who haven't been there themselves are not capable of grasping the unspeakable atrocity of this singular universe. But I try, tactfully, to explain to him, recalling that his deported parents never came back from it, whereas I managed to leave it, in part thanks to him; I realized just how much he had spurred on Commissar Byelokonyenko on my behalf, as I listened to his account on the roof of the train. My thesis appears suspect to him, nevertheless, and he asks for examples that might show in what ways this lived experience is inexpressible, incommunicable. I try to give him one:

"Look at Aunt Valia's charming cat. See how nice and quiet it is, how it lets us eat without meowing, without bothering us. I once saw an almost identical cat enter the Volgalag by mistake. A pack of starving men immediately threw themselves upon it; the first three crushed its head with a stone, tore off its skin, and put the rest into a frying pan. All the others watching, myself included, envied their good luck and admired their cunning, singling out the most cruel as the most valorous."

"In our villages, in time of famine, they have always eaten cats."

"In a camp you wish for the death of your neighbor who has done nothing against you, simply in order to receive an extra ration for helping to dig his grave—half a herring, or a bowl of repulsive soup. I buried a man on the Zanga bridge construction site, and another after my arrival in the Volgalag. Others were eagerly awaiting my death, and didn't even try to hide their desire to collect the reward for my burial."

"That could also have happened in a free community struck by extreme famine. People hang on to anything to survive. In such circumstances instinct gets the better of dignity. It has been so since the dawn of time," he says, before helping himself to a large measure of vodka.

"In the camps, the famine is *organized*, Kola, not produced by any natural calamity. In the same way, work serves only to destroy the *zeki*; it is a simple instrument of death and not of production. You would have to see a brigade of men, no longer able to hold themselves upright, harried all day long, prodded with bayonets by convict guards of the NKVD, who could have performed the same work in an hour. No free community, or even any penal system, however irrational, organizes production in this way."

"Russian indolence, aggravated by the stupidity of a bureaucracy with a police mentality. You only have to read Lermontov and Mayakovsky to understand the aberrations that you're describing." Kola persists, but his eyes reveal a gloomy turn to his thoughts, and it isn't from the effects of the vodka. "Is it like that everywhere, or are there some camps that are a little more human?" he asks in a suffocated voice.

Aunt Valia's merry interruption with a new mountain of blinis saves me from having to answer. She senses, however, that something is wrong. Anxious, she begins to blame the poor quality of the flour, but I assure her that after I have left Russia I shall cherish a fond memory of her blinis all my life. The dish almost drops from her hands. Is Kola's friend drunk or is he making fun of her? How could the young artillery officer possibly leave Russia? Kola avoids her baffled, incredulous stare; he tells her gently to go back to the kitchen and to continue making blinis. He goes off to fetch another bottle, and to hell with the ulcer!

I try to change the subject, thinking that even if Kola hasn't understood exactly what it is to live in a camp, then at least he appreciates the reasons for my haste to quit the USSR. But Kola won't let me. He wants me to "unburden" myself of this subject entirely. But what more is there to say? My "burden" is the memory of a Gulag as large as the mountains of the Caucasus, and I know no way of making it lighter.

"That's not what I'm asking of you," Kola replies. "I know from experience that bitterness makes a poor counselor. Now it seems to me that it would be a pity to forget, out of spite, the scientific truths concerning the march of history. Certain people have tried hard to sabotage our war effort, but, despite them, we are on the way to winning the war. That goes also for the construction of our socialism and for the transition to communism. Victory will bring rewards. The material foundations of our society will be enlarged and people will be motivated, active, different from the way they were before. I still consider changes inevitable, whether it pleases you or not.

"By refusing to place your trust in the future, you simply become the pawn of these bastards who are trying to delay our victory. You know them well, having suffered because of them. They are the all-powerful who abuse their power, jackals of all kinds, who don't even realize the harm that they are doing. But tomorrow they will no longer have the opportunity to wreak such havoc, and later still, under communism, they will disappear; our children won't even be able to believe that such people ever existed. Look at my grandfather; under Czar Nicholas he was a soldier for life, and he struggled in this world like a fly that keeps on thumping against a windowpane without seeing it, without understanding anything about it. We are lucky to have studied the science of how societies develop; we have learned Marxism-Leninism and can predict the course of events, thanks to it. What good would it do you, as a result of bitterness, to become like Dzyed?"

Since these are mere platitudes, I give in finally to his thesis, rejoicing in anticipation of the withering away of suffering and injustice. But after we have drunk to our renewed concord, I declare my total disagreement with some of his future plans: "I will not be taking the shuttle back and forth between Rostov and Tbilisi, for fear of finding myself again in these unspeakable places. I have no intention of becoming a public-works engineer, since I have no aptitude for such a profession, however well paid. Finally, I have no wish to become a member of the Communist Party."

Kola, despite everything, is elated. It's all right if I don't want to become an engineer. We will examine possible alternatives in Rostov, and I might become a poet (they are very well paid) or a teacher—the range of possibilities is almost infinite, in his view. He also understands my reluctance to join the Party, but advises me to reapply for my Komsomol "ticket." Upon reflection, he decides it would be better if he undertook alone the responsibility to feed our common coffers. After all, he is a flight lieutenant and a candidate-member of the Communist Party.

The honey, spread plentifully over the blinis, contributes to our rediscovered harmony. Kola has been advised to eat a lot of it because it is thought to be good for ulcers, while according to Aunt Valia it is a source of eternal youth, especially for women, because it improves the skin. In my opinion, judging by the experience of this dinner, honey has the virtue of increasing one's appetite while at the same time mitigating the effects of the vodka. That is to say, if we had continued to devour blinis with honey and fresh cream, we could easily have spent the whole night eating and drinking without getting drunk. But it seems unfair to us to leave Aunt Valia in the kitchen the whole time, and thus to exclude her from our reunion celebrations. We invite her to come and join us, but she still has one more treat for us: a magnificent cheesecake.

With an audience now, the two ex-combatants lean more and more heavily on the bottle so as to relate their war stories with extra *brio*. To dazzle Aunt Valia, I recite the Khvalynsk officer's argument on the importance of our front in the Caucasus. Its effect had been to immobilize four hundred Wehrmacht tanks and to inflict a decisive blow to the morale of the Romanian troops. During the decisive phase of the Battle of Stalingrad, it was precisely these four hundred tanks—not one more, not one less—that made all the difference. If the Germans had had them at hand, they could have broken out of their encirclement. On the other hand, to cut off the encircled Wehrmacht from the rest of the German lines, our men had struck the Romanian sector, which collapsed easily because it had already been so severely tested.

Aunt Valia is lost for words at this account, but even Kola is pleasantly surprised. "There you are now, we are heroes of Stalingrad too," he says, cutting another slice of cheesecake with hands that are already becoming a little clumsy as a result of the vodka we drink to wash down every bite.

The old man at the far end of the room suddenly interrupts our strategic considerations. "I have seen four generations of Cossacks eat at this table," he says in the loud voice of the deaf, "but I have never seen so much eaten as you two have eaten this evening." Is this a reproach or a compliment? Kola staggers over to the old man, and shouts to make himself heard: "Your four generations of Cossacks, *Dzyed,* never did any good; they were just so many flies beating against windowpanes. We are different and have thoroughly deserved our meal, for we have won the greatest war in history!"

Aunt Valia thinks Kola is drunk and sends us all off to bed. Before I drift off to sleep, the haunting memory of the camps takes hold of me once again, and in a moment of lucidity I call out to Kola, "I am leaving for Poland."

"When?"

"On the first train."

Too drunk to discuss it, he replies with something quite unconnected: "I forgot to tell you that one of your school friends, the Cosachka Klava, often asks for news of you."

"What difference do you think that makes? She is a youngster, a nice kid."

"Well, then, you must have become very demanding, for this 'youngster' is more beautiful than Nievka, Lyuba, and Svetlana all put together."

At this, we fall asleep, half-undressed, half-unconscious.

I would leave for Poland in April 1946, two years to the day of this dinner in Myechotka—not on one of the first trains for those repatriated, but on one of the last. Klava had a great deal to do with this delay.

5

KLAVA

I was to fall fatally in love with Klava, and Kola's praise of her beauty had nothing to do with it. To be sure, my old classmate from School No. 44 had blossomed into a young woman with an irresistible smile, but she had kept her round cheeks and schoolgirl's ways. Extremely diligent and studious, Klava had the gift of being at once serious and playful, very stubborn and very gentle. She admitted to being one of the most accomplished liars in Rostov; she had cultivated this art to pull the wool over the eyes of her traditional Cossack parents, thereby imposing her will on them while pretending the whole time to be a dutiful daughter.

Our birthdays, in August 1944, fell almost on the same day and roughly coincided with the "registration of our marriage," as Russians used to say of the day two people decided to become a couple by declaring the fact before the civil authorities. She was twenty-one and I was twenty, we were in love and everything was going our way. Klava had just passed her entrance examinations for the Rostov Institute of Public Works Engineers, while I had obtained a post with a fancy title in a factory. The war front grew increasingly distant from Rostov, and we greeted the approach of victory with more and more frequent parties that brought together our best friends: Kola, Churik, and Zhorik, known as Zeus, three fellow veterans of Kislovodsk and Nalchik, and their wives, Fira, Galia, and Kathinka. What more could we have hoped for? "It's not so much a life as a raspberry," as

they say in Russia when someone is lucky, and we sang lightheart-
edly, "Onward, joyous band of Komsomols!"

After the war, we hoped for a world without any further national
discrimination, permanently exorcised of the old, hateful ideas that
had engendered Nazism. Now, at the approach of victory, our official
propaganda, while remaining resolutely antifascist, became more and
more Pan-Slavic, as though the better to fuel Russian national pride.
Cut off from the world in 1943 by my stay in the Gulag, I had only
learned rather late in the day that the Comintern—the general staff of
the World Revolution, Lenin's personal brainchild—had been dissolved. Later, the "Internationale" ceased to be the national anthem
of the USSR; in its stead came an anthem vaunting the merits of
"Greater Russia." What's more, our Red Army of Workers and Peasants was rebaptised quite simply as the Soviet Army. Even today,
foreign commentators persist in ignoring the fact that there hasn't
been a Red Army in the USSR since 1944; this name no longer
appears in any official publication.

I was the last person to want to see the former Red Army export the
Revolution and make a seventeenth Soviet republic out of Poland. All
of us hoped that the Great Alliance would be maintained whatever the
cost, so that the English and Americans, though capitalists, would
help the USSR raise itself from its ruins. The Pan-Russian propaganda therefore did not go against the grain of our proletarian lean-
ings, but it was responsible for an eruption of all the most retrograde
prejudices, including anti-Semitism, which found open, public expression and met with the indifference of the authorities.

Then, instead of dispelling these misunderstandings, Stalin added
his own "patriotic" two cents' worth: on June 24, 1945, during the
Victory Banquet in the Kremlin, he raised his glass and thanked "the
great Russian people" because it had trusted in its government even
during the period of defeats. "Another people would have taken
advantage of them to overthrow its rulers," Stalin added, as if socialism, which had been held to be irreversible, had survived only thanks
to the goodness of the Russian people. Churik, who was studying the
complete works of Marx at the time, claimed that Stalin had been
drunk on this occasion. Kola and I shared a regretful and respectful

KLAVA 219

sigh for our Ukrainian commissar. Didn't he—and so many other non-Russians killed during the war—deserve a little bit of gratitude from our Supreme Commander-in-Chief?

The ideological confusion was compounded by the collapse of the official economy. In theory, we were living in a society in which the interests of the individual merged with those of the collective. In practice, however, the collective evidently didn't care a fig about our individual interests and we repaid this lack of concern fully in kind, especially where "socialist property" was concerned, which was generally considered as not belonging to anyone. At the start of the war, Moussia's graft had shocked me; by the war's end, all of us had become her emulators, with even more sophisticated rackets to help us get by.

This style of operating didn't help to calm my anxieties as a former *zek*, and it tormented my friends, for they would have liked their actions to be more consonant with their professions of Komsomol faith. But reality seemed both to confirm and confound ideology. Each victory by our troops seemed to demonstrate that the USSR was very powerful in all the sectors of the economy—a lot more so than we would have believed or imagined possible. From the Black Sea to the Baltic, our army was marching triumphantly on Berlin, alone, with its own cannons, tanks, airplanes, and engines "made in the USSR." A single unanswered question remained: Who would be the first to plant the Red Flag on the highest building still standing in the capital of the Third Reich—Zhukov, Rokossovski, or Konev?

All of these facts clearly contradicted Soviet inferiority complexes; our society evidently harbored a potential that we had never suspected. Even before dazzling the rest of the world, victorious Russia had astounded its own citizens. It had concealed immense productive forces and it knew how to use them to the best effect. Doubt was no longer possible. Stalin had been right: "The possibilities of socialism are unlimited."

It is well known, however, that certain exceptionally gifted people are incapable of simple addition in arithmetic; Soviet society was like them. Peerless in matters of dizzying complexity, it was unable to distribute herrings in the Don region, or watermelons in Rostov. Such trivial matters failed to interest it because of their extreme simplicity. Certainly it was hoped that one day, when the accumulation of minor matters had attained gigantic proportions, it would resolve all the problems in one masterstroke. Meanwhile, workers had to line up to buy practically every basic necessity, and they suffered the consequences of an inflation that reduced their official salaries to a pittance. The black market imposed its laws upon victorious Russia even more thoroughly than it had during the grimmest phase of the war.

Klava and I had other, more personal problems. When our marriage was registered, I was questioned about my attitude toward the National Liberation Committee of Poland, recently set up in Lublin. It was explained to me that in the event of my return to Poland, Klava would not be allowed to follow me there. "Your marriage will be annulled at no extra cost," the authorities announced, as if it were a piece of good news. I was then offered the opportunity of remaining in Rostov and of opting for Soviet nationality, but if I did, I would, like all my fellow citizens, forfeit the right to go abroad, even to Poland.

Klava never thought of keeping me by her side. For one thing, she sensed that my mother was still alive. For another, she knew that I had been too badly scarred by the Gulag to remain in Russia. Once it had been accepted as inevitable, the prospect of our separation no longer seemed to frighten her.

We lived from day to day and didn't bother ourselves with the future. We succeeded so well in this that people said, "It's a pleasure to see a couple so much in love." But we knew that final victory would precipitate a separation that neither of us wanted.

I prolonged my stay in Rostov as long as possible, then left for Poland in April 1946.

In spite of the Cold War, Klava and I continued to write to each other, and this correspondence only came to an end in 1949, when I broke with "People's" Poland and with the Soviet bloc. In my memory our separation took place gradually, gently, in the least painful manner possible. But Klava's letters—which I reread once more when this chapter was almost completed—show that it wasn't quite like that. In them she frequently alludes to a rendezvous that we had apparently planned, to the hope of resuming a shared life together. She even offers me financial help, for, having completed her studies, she had found a well-paid post as an engineer in the Ukraine. So I have to accept that my memory misleads me, that we had always planned to meet once more.

At the time of our reunion in April 1944, I suddenly feel an extremely strong attraction for Klava, which doesn't seem to be reciprocated. I wonder how different my life would have been without the Gulag. On seeing my former classmate, I say to myself, "You imbecile, why didn't you show more interest in her in 1941? Why, instead of enlisting in the armed forces, didn't you go off with her to Central Asia to study, to work, and to fall in love?" But Klava quickly brings me back to earth; she is happy to see me again, that's all. Love? What love? There was never any question of it between us. Is there another man in her life? Her answer is evasive. "All girls have men who hang around them." Well, then, not to worry. I will soon outdistance these rivals; after all, at School No. 44 she didn't think too badly of me.

But wooing a Cossack girl in a half-destroyed town is not only a full-time job, it is also an obstacle race and an infinite torment. Using various pretexts, Klava obtains without difficulty permission from her parents to go out, but there is no question of inviting her suitor to her home. As for me, I live in the tiny apartment belonging to Churik's family, the same Churik who had been my messmate and who had had a leg amputated after his injuries in Nalchik. I can't decently be expected to put him outside, along with his father and his sister, in order to entertain Klava in their home! Worse still, as I enjoy a degree of hospitality that is as generous as it is undeserved—Churik tells everyone that I saved his life, which is frankly an exaggeration—I don't dare to disturb them beyond a certain time of night, and I prefer to hang out in Rostov until the morning and then return home discreetly.

The second obstacle is the sense of insecurity that prevails in the darkened, ruined streets. The times are propitious to criminals and to the drunkards who drown their war memories in vodka. With the exception of Gorky Park, where there is hot competition for unoccupied benches, lovers stroll after nightfall only at their peril. Where, then, can we shelter our potential love?

"In the Central Post Office," Klava suggests. She has discovered a small telephone and telegraph office that stays open all night. It is a godsend, for the people of Rostov seem to be unaware of the existence of this nighttime facility and rarely intrude upon our interminable conversations. The discreet post office clerks don't bother to ask us what urgent matter keeps us in their office for nights on end. We sit far enough from the counter to allow us to talk without fear of being overheard; we are better off here than we used to be sitting at our desks in School No. 44. But I hardly dare to take Klava in my arms, fearing her resistance as much as the look on the face of the clerk, who is generally sleepy but seems to nap with one eye open to put an end to any hint of hanky-panky.

The absence of a romantic setting didn't stop us from spending many happy evenings on our bench. Klava taught me a great deal about her life as a young woman in Rostov, which changed hands in 1941, 1942, and 1943. I had never thought of the war from this angle. A woman, in addition to the fear shared by everyone of shells and bombs, had to be wary of the "bad soldiers," including, alas, some of our own. Immediately after the entry of victorious troops, there is a period of uncertainty during which armed soldiers make their own law. In Rostov, except in 1942, these terrible periods had coincided with the periods of extreme cold, and Klava, hidden in a cellar, had endured fear, hunger, and cold. She went out only rarely, disguised as an old woman in rags, realizing anyway that her camouflage afforded her only scant protection. "Some of them even raped grandmothers," she says.

After the terrors of the interregnum and with the stabilization of power, certain women decided to take advantage of the times, and made of themselves a sorry spectacle of debauchery and venality. Once again, Klava had to hide in her cellar in order to avoid "voluntary work" in Germany, but she knew that among the women of Rostov, volunteers were not in short supply.

"The Ataman Krasnov came back to recruit a new Cossack White Army. Yes, yes, I had also believed he was dead, and yet, I swear to you, there he was parading in Novocherkassk, in Rostov, and in the Kuban. At that time a lot of people, thinking that Stalin had lost the war, believed they could achieve Cossack autonomy within the German Reich." She talks without enmity for "these foolish people," but for the women who have gone off to Germany, those "witless whores," she has no pity.

I listen to her in rapt attention. How has she managed to embellish her looks so much throughout these awful years? Is it suffering that has sharpened her features, adding to them this hint of glamour and seriousness that were absent from her pretty schoolgirl's face? Considered separately, her features really haven't changed. She still has the same beautiful green eyes, the same graceful oval face, a shapely figure with a slim waist; and yet, overall, something has changed. And she is well aware of it, because the men crane their necks much more as she goes by—too much for her taste. She also expresses herself differently, more confidently—she is no longer at a loss for words—and accompanies herself as she talks with a whole range of versatile facial expressions. Is it coquetry, or is it her new manner of speaking? Klava loves to surround herself with a slight air of mystery; she doesn't reveal herself totally, as though certain aspects of her life had to remain in shadow.

As I listen entranced, Klava's trust in me grows. She explains her conflict with her parents, her break with their values, their nostalgia for Cossack ways. She can no longer stand their traditions, which she considers "humbug." But Klava continues to live among a family of traditionalists, surrounded by friends who all remain attached to their specific identity as Cossacks. "They are not counterrevolutionaries," she adds, "and they haven't thought of enlisting under the flag of the Ataman Krasnov's collaborators." But they cling tenaciously to the old ideas. Klava loves her parents too much to confront them directly, so she lies instead.

Klava asks me to describe the Gulag; she says she will understand. I doubt it. Not even Kola, who is the son of deportees and who has suffered since his childhood, is able to grasp this unspeakable world. She insists and I talk to her at length about my nightmare journey across the archipelago of *zeki*. She listens with compassion as I tell her that the great problem is not merely hunger or physical exhaustion, but their consequences inside the *zek*'s head.

Certain aspects—the sadism of the convict-guards, the brutality among *zeki*, or the dead buried like animals—make her shiver with fright and she presses against me. "Let's change the subject, Klava," I suggest. "I don't want you to feel pity for me."

"No," she persists, "it isn't pity," and she wants us to talk about it even if it frightens her and even if she suffers as a result.

She swears that she will avenge me and settle accounts, starting with the traitor Oleg; since he is from Rostov, he will come back here sooner or later. This must be the influence of her Cossack roots, and I plead with her to forget any ideas about pursuing a vendetta; it could lead her straight to the red-brick barracks in the Volgalag. "We shall see. Who lives will see, the blind say," she replies with a mysterious smile.

Escorting Klava as far as her wooden maisonette, miraculously preserved near the train station, I have the right to a few kisses but nothing more, especially not to any promise; and yet, God knows, we haven't much time left before the war is over. It would be a pity if, after the school bench, our only shared memory remained the creaking bench in the Rostov Central Post Office.

It's a small world, this is well known, but this fact sometimes favors friendship between ex-servicemen like Zhorik, known as Zeus, and me. In Kislovodsk we hardly knew each other at all, for he belonged to the third squadron, housed at the other end of the barracks. To tell the truth, I still don't know why he was called Zeus, or who had been sufficiently learned in Greek mythology to give him this nickname. Having also suffered a concussion on the Nalchik hill, Zeus had passed through the hospital in Beslan before ending up "under observation" in Krasnovodsk; at the latter, a ferocious nurse had told him a lot of stories about the medical dossier of another fellow in his unit. It was the Siberian Lyuba, for who else would have had the nerve to slap the face of every patient she accused of having wandering hands, and would have known that one such, from the air force, was currently carrying around an "uncured concussion"? Having ascertained that it was indeed me, Zeus continually throws his protective arm over me either out of a sense of solidarity between the "brain-damaged," or else because he promised Lyuba that he would keep an eye on me. This tall, fair-haired lad, something of a dreamer, isn't lacking in resources, or at least in luck.

At first our relations were distorted by our respective reputations. I didn't greatly appreciate being considered a "head case" who hadn't been adequately treated, and I was convinced that Zeus remained a little cracked in the head. For he had me read his poems commemorating our battle on the Nalchik hill, poems with lame rhymes that described in detail the terrible damage we had done to the Germans.

Zeus had landed the job of canteen manager at the Rosa Luxemburg Tobacco Factory, and he often invited me to come along to discuss poetry. One day Kola joined us and decreed, after making a rapid inquiry, that our friend had the legal right to feed us every day, without food tickets or money. Zeus quickly understood the advantages of his job. He agreed to call Klava two or three times a week to replace a cashier who was often absent because of illness, and helped her to fix her till so that she made from it much more than her wages.

Some time later, Zeus gives us conclusive proof that he isn't at all crazy. He strikes an agreement with the factory management that allows all three of us—himself, Kola, and me—to make some extra cash. This factory, like all others, operates at a spasmodic rhythm, and when it has to speed up the production line to meet its quota, it finds itself with large stocks of cigarettes that it hasn't managed either to pack into cartons or to send off in time. For these busy periods it needs additional packers, who are neither planned for in the labor flow chart, nor easy to find in a town where workers—especially male workers—are in short supply. The three of us are ready to help, provided that we are not paid mere pin money. The simplest thing would be to pay us in cartons of cigarettes, but the law forbids it; moreover, tobacco is rationed, and all factory workers are searched on their way out. But Zeus devises a scheme that proves his common sense. After work, we will leave by the canteen exit, where there is no search, with cartons in trouser pockets cunningly designed for the purpose. In short, he obtains permission for us to make off discreetly with as many cigarettes as our pockets can hold. "It's not theft, we are authorized to take them," he insists, in order to dispel my fears as a timorous ex-*zek*. And so it is that I stuff the packets of "Belomor-kanal" into my trouser pockets, taking care not to crush any. The ironic touch here is that this very popular brand of cigarettes bears the name of a canal built in the far north by common-law prisoners who, if we are to believe a film made about them, were reformed by this forced but highly reeducative labor.

Kola isn't satisfied, however; he's more ambitious than we are. He argues that we have to take advantage of these few months' respite to create for ourselves a solid material foundation, because after the start of the academic year we will no longer have the time to work as warehouse packers, and still less to travel. Kola and I have a shared kitty, and this gives him the right to demand my help in carrying out the plan that he had previously sketched for me in Myechotka. Unfortunately, this plan involves numerous return journeys to Aunt Valia's home—with herrings on the outward journey and honey on the return—but I am reluctant to leave Rostov and to abandon Klava.

Kola, trying to win me over, lectures me endlessly on the laws of the market economy: "We need capital to invest in my expedition to Tbilisi. If I set off there with the pathetic five hundred rubles that we still have left between us, and if I spend half of it on the way, the profit will be insignificant." And to whom is he explaining these elementary matters? To me, the son of a former Rostov proprietor who, among his other properties, once owned the whole Central Post Office building! But I don't give a damn for this lost patrimony; I simply prefer my relatively risk-free routine as Zeus's helper to the roof of a train shuttling between Rostov and Myechotka. "Right," Kola declares threateningly, "if you insist upon dying of hunger in a few months' time, just so you can talk all night to a Cossack girl, I will be forced to look for another partner. But, you ought to listen to me. Cossack women are a curse; they have no independence, and nothing in their heads. They think only of keeping you under their eye, and they will stab you in the back at the slightest infidelity."

Thanks to a surprising reversal, Kola will be even more stubborn about ever leaving Rostov than I am. One evening in the middle of May 1944, he invites me to a show at the Theater of Musical Comedy. Someone has given him two tickets. Though I am no fan of operetta, I accept his invitation. I am enchanted; an intrigue unfolds onstage that stirs a responsive chord in me. Gentlemen of leisure, in evening suits, deplore in song the fact that they are never able to go to bed early because they are so attracted by the ladies' boudoirs—do they even know what a boudoir is in Rostov?—and by these beautiful courtesans for whom life is just a bowl of cherries. At the end of their song, irresistible temptresses come fluttering onstage, very scantily clad by Rostov standards. Smiling contentedly, they shake their lovely legs about, pirouetting underneath the noses of the idle gentlemen. I would never have believed that in Rostov there could be shows like this one. Kola wants me to pick out one of the dancers onstage: "No, not that one, the other one, the blonde, yes, that's the one, that's her, that's Fira, she's my girl."

"Your girl? What do you mean?"

"She's mine, all mine, and not just on a Central Post Office bench, either," he says proudly.

His boasting is understandable; he has won the girl with the loveliest legs in Rostov—Fira, nicknamed "the young widow," because of her role in *The Merry Widow* or perhaps because she really is a widow. And he would not have met this woman's match at the flea market in Tbilisi, or on the Transcaucasian.

After Fira's entry into Kola's life, there will no longer be any talk of journeys to Georgia, and a good-humored atmosphere envelops our little circle. Kola's blond-haired dancer doesn't simply have a pair of shapely legs that she often shows off, for her skirt has a spontaneous tendency to rise far above her knee; she has above all a heart of gold. Fira is always ready to help, to comfort or to distract a friend in distress. Once she guesses that I feel cramped in Churik's place, she

sets up a bed for me in her kitchen—which doubles as a bathroom—
and with a peculiarly Cossack energy, she dispels my fears about
being a nuisance. Kola has chosen a "pure-blooded" Cossack, a
native of Novocherkassk, capital of the atamans, and she speaks in
her region's broadest accent, full of harsh *O* sounds. Onstage she
pronounces perfectly the words "How do you do, Mr. Brown?" but
she really doesn't know how to say *Moskva* or *pozhar* with a short *O*,
like a Russian; it is beyond her.

Fira is a very independent woman. Her days are filled with exercises, rehearsals, and performances, and she cares little about
whether it suits Kola or not. She even has her own income, which is
just as well for us, and prefers to keep her savings out of our "crack-
pot schemes." Fira, as a performing artist, belongs to the privileged
sector of the official economy and receives two free tickets from her
theater each evening. Entrusted to a practiced scalper, these two
tickets earn her sixty rubles net.

The Theater of Musical Comedy considerably brightened up the
last two years of the war for us. Unlike the cinema, light opera is the
least important art to the Soviet regime, virtually unusable for propaganda purposes. It would have been incongruous and, to a certain
extent, indecent to take the Revolution, and even the history of the
Czars Ivan, Alexander, and Peter as the subjects for musicals. That is
why works such as *Princess Csardas*, *The Gypsy Baron*, *La Vie Pari-
sienne*, and *Mr. Brown and Lady Gil* remained popular. In this period
of alliance with the Anglo-Saxons, the management of the "Muscome-
dia" in Rostov revived a good twenty of these operettas, sometimes
giving their titles a proletarian twist (*Princess Csardas* suddenly became simply *Silva*), but without altering anything at all of the content
or decor: Austro-Hungarian castles and Parisian or London-style
luxury.

The operettas were a roaring success, and we never missed one of
them and even went to see some of them two or three times. While
fully realizing that this decadent art should not be taken seriously, we
gladly abandoned our war songs in favor of arias on the torments and
pleasures of love. After all, our women, even if modestly dressed,

also "set our hearts on fire" and inflicted incredible sufferings in return for some sublime moments.

The infatuation of the people of Rostov with light opera had inevitable economic consequences, since the law of supply and demand operated as implacably in the entertainment sector as in all the other sectors of the economy. To see a new film—even the worst of B-movies on the war—you had to pay fifteen rubles to the scalpers for a seat, which, at the ticket office—inaccessible to ordinary mortals—cost only five. It was perfectly normal, then, to pay forty or fifty for an operetta; the people in Rostov, in spite of their modest official wages of between three hundred and five hundred rubles a month, were clearly not short of money. Fira generally managed to obtain seats for us at official prices, but sometimes, so as not to create problems for her, we played the part of big spenders and bought our tickets from the scalpers. "They have to live as well," Kola used to say.

This phenomenon reached its peak when Alexandre Vertinsky came to Rostov. Vertinsky was a singer of great charm, an emigrant who had decided to return to his native country with an entire wagon-load of medical supplies. The prices on the black market for his performance went through the roof: three or four hundred rubles per seat. I couldn't possibly miss this performance because Vertinsky had been adored by my parents, and since my early childhood I had known his languorous songs exalting his love for Yvette (an uncommon name in Russia), and many others. So it was with a lump in my throat that I heard this elderly man, with a sad expression, sing again. But the others in the audience, who had never been able to buy even a single record by Vertinsky—how was it that they knew these great "smash hits" from the West by heart? They gave him an ovation such as I had never seen at any performance in Russia, calling out "Yvetta! Yvetta! Encore! Bravo!"

Klava and I are no longer restricted to the post office bench, for it is now the beginning of the summer of 1944, and the longer days make it possible to go for romantic strolls along the Don. As the circle of our friends grows larger, we go out together to the movies or the Musical Comedy, or else we play games at Churik's place.

One of Klava's friends, Kathinka, who sings in the Don Cossacks Performance Arts Ensemble, moves in with our friend Zeus barely one week after meeting him. And even Churik finds a soul mate in Galia, the assistant librarian and daughter of the deputy director of the Karl Marx Library. From her Jewish mother, Galia inherited a slightly Mediterranean look that contrasts sharply with the blondness of Kathinka or Fira. She is highly cultured, as is Churik, and together they are the most intellectual couple of our circle.

I ask Klava why, since we are both grown up, in a hurry to taste life and to make up for the lost war years, we must remain chaste. She has a good answer: "What good would it do us to become even closer to one another, since you are soon going to leave?" What she says is true; I ought to leave her in peace and let her find someone else. But my feelings for Klava are too deep; without her, life in Rostov simply wouldn't make any sense.

It is Fira who most encourages me to pursue this "serious love." She informs me that their bed is at our disposal when she is onstage in the evenings and Kola is off elsewhere. "You will be much better off than on your post office bench." Next she insists upon the fleeting character of love: "It is a magic moment that you have to grab hold of; think of nothing else, because it is possible that it will never happen to you again." Finally she suggests that I explain to Klava that Fira's own marriage to Kola neither brought him closer to her nor distanced him from her: "It cost us five rubles, no more than a cheap theater ticket. It won't break your bank."

Fortified by such advice, I arrange evenings with Klava on Fira's bed, which she accepts with a challenging look that says, "You don't scare me." Then, one July evening, she turns up for our date dressed as though for a party: white bodice in very fine linen, a dark made-to-measure skirt, and high-heeled shoes. She casually announces: "I've decided to get married." So as to be clear in my mind about it before strangling her, I ask her who the lucky fellow is. "You," she says, and our marriage is consummated there and then. Was it Fira who had prompted her miraculous decision? "As early as our schooldays, I knew that it would come to this," she replies. "Sooner or later I had to catch you, my dear little bird from afar." It is flattering, but it doesn't correspond to my experiences of these past four months. "I had to put you to the test, because otherwise you would have taken advantage of me and then left me. And if you think that I owe you apologies for having made you be patient, you've got another think coming."

I don't have time to answer. A noise on the stairway persuades her that either Fira or Kola is about to come in. Dressed with speed, she has just enough time to tell me: "Tomorrow, at ten o'clock in the morning, you will meet with Papa Emilyan, who will give you my hand. I have already prepared the way. But whatever happens, don't neglect to tell him that you have killed ten Germans, and I mean ten; eight killed and five seriously wounded won't do at all. And if you can manage it you might also slip in a kind word on the Ataman Skoropatski. It will increase the size of my dowry."

Fira arrives first and congratulates me. "You will see, this bed brings happiness, you will be very happy."

"But I haven't killed ten Germans, Fira, and I haven't the vaguest idea who the Ataman Skoropatski is."

"What of that?" she asks, surprised. "Wait for Kola, he will tell you all you need to know. Kola is capable of wrapping all the Cossacks on earth around his little finger. After all, he succeeded with me, even me!"

A middle-ranking inspector in the government department of agriculture, Papa Emilyan is not a very senior public servant, but neither is he a nobody. He spends most of his time sorting out different reports, but he fills his role with more efficacy than his Gogolian predecessor. You sense it as soon as you set foot in the family-owned maisonette, the furniture of which suggests comfortable ease: a large clock in perfect working order under a glass cover; an opulent settee; a magnificent rustic table for mealtimes, and another smaller one for the samovar. We sit down on the settee, facing a portrait of Marshal Budenny, and the conversation is very cordial because he remembers me from before the war, when I helped "little Klava" to do her homework.

This man of about fifty, rather short, with white hair parted in the middle, is the very picture of the tranquil father, and I hesitate before telling him the bloody tale about the ten Germans skewered by my bayonet. But it is he who eggs me on through this episode, which is supposed to raise my prestige as a prospective son-in-law.

He tells me that during the occupation of Rostov a German officer who was billeted in the end room of the house used to walk stark naked to the toilet. Had the officer tried to rape Papa Emilyan's wife and daughter, as often happens in wartime, Klava's father would have defended them to the death. But, without such a pretext, he couldn't attack this shameless brute who attached no more importance to the gaze of a Russian woman than to that of a dog. Wounded by this affront to his Cossack honor, Papa Emilyan had informed his three sons in writing that unless each of them killed at least ten Germans, they would no longer be welcome under his roof. As I narrate my Nalchik saga, Papa Emilyan punctuates each mortal blow of my imaginary bayonet with nods of approval.

The second and more redoubtable obtacle—for Kola hadn't known who the Ataman Skoropatski was, either—is surmounted even more easily. Papa Emilyan brings in from the next room a photograph taken in 1915 in Novocherkassk, showing the ataman presenting Papa Emilyan with a sword on the occasion of his twenty-first birthday. "What a coincidence!" I say. "My parents were hosts to the Ataman Skoropatski that very same year, and preserve a splendid memory of him." The success of this revelation is stunning, but double-edged: Papa Emilyan is going to introduce me to all of his acquaintances as the "son of some of the ataman's Polish friends, who had later gone abroad." A fine detail—and one that would doubtless have interested Captain Strel!

Before bringing out another souvenir, he delivers a very tactful speech about his respect for the Poles. What the devil is he leading up to? Papa Emilyan slowly unfolds on the table, with the kind of care usually reserved for works of art, a large old poster in which a Red

Cavalry soldier on horseback soars high above a town. WARCHAWA
NACHA!—"Warsaw is ours!"—proclaims the caption in black letters.
Klava hadn't told me that her father, after having been a White, came
within an ace of conquering Warsaw with the Red Army. Nearly at a
loss for words, I mutter some banal remarks on the reputed rivalry
between Budenny and Tukachevsky, which is supposed to have allowed the Poles to attack their troops separately and to win the battle.
He sweeps this thesis aside: "God didn't wish us to have the victory,"
he says, as though he could see Abbot Skorupka making the sign of
the cross in a corner of his own poster.

Klava is right: Her father's head is full of nonsense, otherwise he
wouldn't have been able to admire Budenny and Skoropatski simultaneously. During the Civil War he changed sides four times before
ending up, "by God's grace," on that of the victors. He congratulates
himself and reminds me that the Whites, after the fall of the Crimea,
were reduced to exile and became "folk dancers who live from their
tips." Papa Emilyan's sincerity prompts me to a certain indulgence
with regard to him. All right, I decide, he is attached to the memory
of Ataman Skoropatski because he is the most important man he ever
met—the one who, at the time, was master over the Don region. The
fact that the younger generation, beginning with Fira and Kola,
doesn't even know his name proves that he wasn't one of the worst
atamans, and that he didn't try, like Krasnov, to capture St. Petersburg in order to hang Lenin and all the Bolsheviks.

Unlike her father's, Klava's ideas are clear-cut, but three-quarters
of the things she has told him about our love, about my family (of
Polish noble stock), and about me are pure fabrication. I am obliged
to confirm them all, even if, in their details, they are ludicrously
improbable—for example, that we maintained a lovers' correspondence throughout these three years of war, without ever losing contact. In my heart of hearts, I wonder if Klava hasn't pushed her taste
for invention too far. Why deceive her father, who, judging by my
impressions, wouldn't object to our getting married? The answer will
be given some weeks later.

On the matter of the dowry there isn't a lot to discuss; the most beautiful girl in the world can only give what she has, and that goes too for a father attached to his only daughter. Since his only material wealth is his wooden maisonette, he offers us a large share of it, proposing to extend Klava's room to include that of her three brothers. He has already arranged for some carpenters to come and take down the partition wall. "You will have twenty-eight square meters of habitable space, which is not to be sneezed at," he explains, adding that the reconstruction plan for the area around the train station unfortunately requires the demolition of the maisonette. But the implementation of this plan will take years, and then the authorities will have to relocate us in an equivalent space. For the moment, he notes, laughing at the incongruities of bureaucracy, our house has as its address "apartment number 22" of the building next door, destroyed by German bombs.

It's amusing, I agree, but the real problem is knowing where Klava's three brothers, who still have a chance of killing ten Germans apiece and demanding their place under the parental roof, will be housed. Papa Emilyan's answer seems evasive—"They are all stout lads"—but clearly he can only deal with one problem at a time. Later the Soviet Army will extricate him from his embarrassment by sending his sons, after victory in the West, to go for a double in the Far East.

From the Bug to the Vistula the Nazis destroyed half or three-quarters of the houses in an area whose population was already poorly housed before the war. Our twenty-eight square meters represent, for Rostov, the equivalent of a suite at the Hilton, a luxury that is better hidden from outsiders. With our close friends it is different. Our parties nearly always take place in our home, around a table that is very long and narrow. Ten can sit at it comfortably, but there is no room to place the serving dishes in between the guests' plates. No matter; Rostov is not Myechotka, our meals will not be banquets, and Klava doesn't aspire to match Aunt Valia in producing an endless supply of honey-filled blinis.

In the evenings, four of us can be found studying around the long table: Klava and Kola at one end, Churik and I at the other. They struggle with the sciences, we with history; in the middle, a lamp gives out meager light—in Russia they manufacture only low-wattage light bulbs. Each couple speaks softly so as not to disturb the other one, which gives a vaguely conspiratorial atmosphere to our long evenings of study. Suddenly, Fira makes a flamboyant entry; she is here to fetch Kola after the show, but, asked to wait awhile, she falls asleep on our bed as quickly as a tired child.

Why do we study with so much determination? It is because the war isn't over and all sectors of education are under a military-style regime. This almost Prussian discipline is especially pervasive at the Institute of Public Works—Kola foresaw as much—which offers an advance salary and not merely a grant to its students, who are assured of rewarding careers, but it is the institute itself that finds them their jobs. So those students who fall behind are in danger, first, of being relegated to an establishment of lesser prestige, and, second, of being sent upon completion of their studies to regions far from Rostov.

Kola, of course, is less threatened than the others. He has fought in the war, and all authorities must take this into account: A demobilized officer won't let himself be intimidated by some teacher who has spent most of the war hidden somewhere in Asia. Not that Kola has any need of preferential treatment; in the air force academy he has already studied the basic sciences on the institute's syllabus. He is predestined to be *otlichnik*, the most brilliant of his year's class. Nevertheless, he comes to our study sessions to help Klava keep on top of things.

Churik and I are more relaxed. We are enrolled at the University of Rostov, which, like all old institutions, is more accommodating in matters of discipline. Churik studies full-time and therefore receives a maintenance grant, while I study by correspondence and without a grant since I receive a good salary as supply foreman at the Savelit factory. But I have overestimated my capacities and my resources of energy in wanting both to work full-time and to study. In the evenings, after leaving the factory, I am too exhausted—physically and mentally—to go to the library or to a class that is specially arranged for students in correspondence courses. Without Churik's help I would not have been able to pass any examination, except in Latin, which I had already studied in Lodz.

Churik is very gifted, and he teaches me with great patience. Having read Marx and other classic socialist theorists, he maintains that the teaching in our faculty is a load of rubbish and that Stalin's dialectic, in the fourth chapter of the *History of the CPSU (Bolsheviks)* is less than accurate. These things reawaken the *pozharnik* buried in me and instantly conjure up the faces of Captains Strel and Abak. Churik, though, is not afraid of anything; he too has fought in the war and thinks that everything is permitted to him, just as I used to think in Yerevan. The number of these "invulnerable characters" has increased prodigiously, and those who are still on active service generally share their frame of mind. My friends Vassya and Volodya, on the line of the Bug, and Kostya on that of the Dniester, reveal in their letters military information to me—which I have no desire to know about—as if censorship no longer existed in Russia. When I beg Churik not to indulge in attacks on Stalin, he answers with the old adage about the mouse that is convinced that the cat is the most fearsome animal in the world, exactly like my cousin Stepan in Moscow in 1940, when making fun of my fear of the Wehrmacht. Be careful, I say to Churik, remember that the German cat came close to devouring us, and in your place I wouldn't underestimate the NKVD cat.

It was a waste of time; the Russians know—or think they know—how to read the secret intentions of their rulers by observing the shifting expressions of their eyebrows, which announce either a hardening of attitude or a greater tolerance. In this period they are convinced that these barely perceptible signs presage a thaw. Let us not forget that at the same time a certain Captain Solzhenitsyn, himself a native of Rostov, wrote to another captain at the front, without troubling to conceal it, that Stalin was neither a worthy heir of Lenin nor a good Supreme Commander-in-Chief. For that he would get ten years in the Gulag.

Do I really know what I'm doing? I have enrolled at a university in which it takes four years to get a degree—a lot longer than I plan to stay in the USSR. Also, I put considerable effort into studying subjects that, after I leave, will surely never be of any use to me— including the extremely tedious history of primitive communist societies. In fact, what most interests me is Churik's Marxism, but I am too scarred by the camps to pay it much attention. The sole thing about which I'm sure is that Klava is pleased to see me there at the other end of the long table, and that she would think less of me if I didn't study. She often tells me that the value of a man is measured by his cultural progress. If I weren't making an effort at my studies, Klava and I would certainly get on less well together.

From Turgenev's *Fathers and Sons* to Zoshchenko's *The Joyful Life* there is a tradition in Russian literature that describes the conflict of the generations and the difficulty, even after the Revolution, of their cohabiting in communal apartments. Our life perfectly illustrates this conflict. Klava and I haven't even a sink of our own and cannot avoid the other generation. We also must share a kitchen. It is the lot of many people in Rostov, where an apartment like Fira's, which is small but self-contained, is a rarity.

At first the Cossack tradition of leaving the young couple in peace works in our favor. Klava's parents disappear nearly every evening to join their friends and only reappear to serve us in one way or another. Klava's mother, Maria, even though she goes out to work, is used to taking care of most of the domestic tasks. She heaps praise on me when I help her hang up her washing in the kitchen, as if no man had ever done it for her before. Convinced that my émigré parents still have a score to settle with the Republic of Soviets, she whispers to me by way of thanks, "The Revolution didn't bring much good to my family, either. But that's between you and me. Don't breathe a word of it to Klava." This prematurely gray-haired woman regrets not having seen her daughter dressed in white for her wedding party, but she doesn't hold me responsible. The times are ugly, and have made people lose the taste for fine ceremonies and pretty dresses.

With Papa Emilyan my conversations are more complex and are

usually about the war. I try to avoid politics, which I have promised Klava I would never discuss with her father. I will break my promise, however, when, during the second half of July 1944, the Red Army liberates Majdanek, the first Nazi extermination camp discovered by the Allies. It is total horror, with oven crematoria and an industrial apparatus of human destruction—something that not even the man from Sablinsk could have imagined, much less I, who hadn't believed him when he said that the Germans were killing all the Jews. The shock of Majdanek is felt very keenly, even though the Russians themselves had already been victims of sustained massacres and destruction during the German occupation, more so than any other people in the world. But with Nazi barbarity, reality transcends anything in fiction. Everything is organized so as to end in death; it is even worse than in the "kingdom of darkness" that we denounced in our war songs.

On the same day that the revelations on Majdanek appear in the press, two German POW carpenters have come to knock down the partition separating our room from that of Klava's brothers and, while they're about it, to repair a plank that is warping the whole house. Skilled craftsmen, working with efficiency unknown to Soviet workers, they finish the job in less than a day. On my return from the factory, I find them seated on the settee, admiring with Papa Emilyan their respective photos. The one of the Ataman Skoropatski impresses the carpenters—"Schön, sehr schön!" "Kosaken gut, sehr gut!"— but their own photos also please Papa Emilyan. He asks me to tell them in German that their wives are pretty and their children so lovely that he wouldn't mind having them for his grandchildren. But I don't speak German and, especially, I don't talk with any Germans on the same day as I hear the news about Majdanek.

"Come and see how nicely they are dressed," Papa Emilyan insists, and he will not let me leave until I have looked at these two nice German families.

"It was Russian deportees, women like Klava, who made them those pretty clothes," I say, to break this ambience of fraternization. Before being taken prisoner, these carpenters had perhaps built barracks in a camp similar to Majdanek. Later I shall reproach myself for having criticized Papa Emilyan. He would like his sons to create orphans in thirty German families, but he feels no hostility toward these German prisoners who no longer bark out orders and who are learning to speak once again like normal people. Perhaps he is right after all.

Rostov is built rather high up on a bank of the River Don. This bank climbs in a gentle slope as far as the Sadovaya, the longest and widest avenue in the city. On the opposite bank is a plain that, in spring, becomes an immense lake. In the summer when it is hot, you only have to cross the river and go off a little way to find spots that are ideal for picnics and bathing (although the grayish water of the Don looks rather suspect). Swimsuits are impossible to find in both the shops and on the black market. The demand for them is so small that no one imports them from the bathing resorts of Georgia. But our underwear is perfectly suited to these summer outings: Men's underpants look like the Bermuda shorts that will be in fashion a quarter of a century later in the West, while women's underwear is neither see-through nor tantalizing. Still, when a young woman who is picnicking not far away from us comes over, undressed like this, to ask us for some salt, it excites us a little because we aren't used to it. When they emerge from the Don, our two blond Venuses, Fira and Kathinka, offer an even more daring spectacle, but of short duration, for the sun quickly dries their cotton underclothes. Neither Klava nor I go bathing; we don't know how to swim. The fresh air and the relaxed atmosphere of the green beaches of the Don are enough of a pleasure, the more so since proper holidays, like swimsuits, do not exist in Rostov.

On the last Sunday of August 1944, two or three days before the start of the exhausting academic rat race, we would surely have gone to relax at the beach, but the conflict of generations in apartment number 22 broke out. The rain was the cause of everything, including our sullen moods, and presaged an awful day from the start.

Klava and I confine ourselves to our room, and it is only in the

afternoon, on hearing the agreeable, sonorous sounds of Gypsy music—one of Papa Emilyan's great passions—that I venture out to pay
the folks a visit.

Things are fine. Mama Maria makes room for me on the settee and
her husband puts the very lively "Gypsy Caravan" on the gramophone. Hardly has the record stopped than he heaves a sigh of regret:
"Idiot Hitler, why does he kill the Gypsies, who sing so well? He
would have done better to slit the throats of a few more Yids." He
says this with conviction, as if he were stating the obvious. Then he
cranks the gramophone in order to play the next record. He is not
expecting an answer.

Well, he's mistaken. I'll show him what I'm made of. Enough is
enough; the anti-Semitic cracks in the barracks in Kislovodsk were
not an incitement to murder such as Papa Emilyan's, and the world
was not reeling from the shock of Majdanek. Unfortunately, confronted by such a grotesque remark, I'm torn by contradictory im-
pulses. The first is to refuse to accept the evidence of my senses (just
as in Yerevan I hadn't wanted to believe that Strel was really accusing
me of espionage); the next prompts me to assault him physically,
while the third suggests irony: I consider explaining to him that,
according to his daughter, Utyossov, a Jew from Odessa, is a far
better singer than all the Gypsies put together, and that if Hitler were
to slit Utyossov's throat, Klava would be inconsolable.

But I have to think of Klava, for whose sake I have sworn not to
discuss politics with her father. While I am trying to figure out how to
react, the second record finishes and Papa Emilyan says again, "Idiot
Hitler, why is he killing all the Gypsies?" I leave without waiting for
the finish.

Klava is standing in the middle of our room, leaning against the
long table; two tears are running down her face. She has guessed
everything. The look in her sad green eyes invites me to wait patiently
without making a scene. However, I feel that her method of handling
her parents is not the right one, that "you should talk with the older
generation in order to drill a bit of sense into their heads."

She shakes her head and says, "No, no, no."

I insist: "You ought to have told them the truth, because I don't want to hide my origins the way they had to do under the German occupation."

All that she can do is shake her head.

The monologue is a difficult genre; into mine I pack considerations on the utility of giving Papa Emilyan at the very least a kick in the ass, and a lecture on the deep-seated reasons for his fraternization with the German carpenters.

Klava finally recovers the use of her tongue to contradict me.

After a long silence, she says, "Along the Don they threatened a penalty of five years of camp for anyone who uttered the word 'Yid,' and that sanction still applies. Well, then, your method hasn't much more hope of succeeding. My parents' prejudices have to do with a particular culture—or lack of culture—among the Cossacks, their nostalgia for a lost paradise. They believe the Cossacks were a nation privileged by fate or by God. They received as their heritage land so fertile that women could cultivate it without difficulty, which enabled the men to charge around the world on horseback and to slit the throats, here and there, of Jews and other infidels."

Perhaps she's right, but it doesn't resolve our problems. "Let me think it over for a day or two," Klava continues. "I will find a means of preventing him from talking so badly of others."

In my view, to prevaricate with Klava's parents isn't the right method, but she argues that it is the only one that can avoid creating trouble. "You take a condescending view of your father by claiming that he is incapable of understanding the horror of Majdanek," I tell her.

"No, I don't," she replies. "I simply know him well, that's all. He and his friends are a lost generation, poisoned by religion and the myths of the past. Majdanek, Majdanek . . . Don't think that they only use the newspapers for rolling cigarettes with their *makhorka*; they also read them."

"Let's not talk any more about it now. We could go to the movies— that would take our minds off it." I make this conciliatory suggestion knowing that I lose my temper easily and because, deep down, I don't care about Papa Emilyan—while Klava, torn between her attachment to her "old folks" and her frustration with their "old ideas," really suffers because of them. To my astonishment, she prefers to go instead to the Central Post Office. It is a strange idea, but having laid on her shoulders all the weight of the conflict between the generations, I can't refuse her this choice.

Here we are once again on the rickety bench in the post office waiting room. The clerks seem delighted to see us back again, and must imagine that we have just made up after a lovers' quarrel.

"I ought to have spoken to you from the beginning about Cossack anti-Semitism," Klava says. "They drink this poison along with their mother's milk. In the days of the atamans, Jews were forbidden to live in the 'special region of the army of the Don.' Why? The only possible explanation, outside of the Cossacks' cultural primitivism, is that they were more pious than other Russians, more faithful to the Orthodox Holy Church."

I object that not all Christians are automatically anti-Semitic, but in her view, the overwhelming majority—in the region of the Don, at least—have always been anti-Semitic, because Jews are accused of having killed Christ. "When I was small, my parents told me about it too, because they wanted me to become a Christian even if I didn't go to church."

Later, at school, she always had Jewish friends, and it was thanks to them that she understood the insanity of the "traditions" of the older generation in general and of her parents in particular. "Because if it was hard for me to verify for myself their legend about the fertile land that yielded its fruit with a minimum of labor, this wasn't at all the case where Jews were concerned, since I rubbed shoulders with them every day, and they didn't correspond at all to the description given to me. Then, in my adolescent head, the idea took root that the Cossacks' lost paradise was as grotesque a lie as that about the 'Yids.' I was fifteen or sixteen years old at the time, and I turned my rebellion against my parents, who couldn't get over it and gave way a little. As I failed to get my brothers' support, however, I realized at a certain point that open and direct argument was going to poison all

our lives—theirs and mine. I thought I could perceive in my parents'
eyes the unstated fear that I might denounce them to the NKVD; at
the time this was commonplace. For another thing, they accepted
without protest my entry into the Komsomol, and suggested the basis
of a truce: Let us eliminate politics from our discussions and love
each other as befits a 'healthy family'—an expression used by our
government. It was obviously more easily said than done, for you
can't get away from politics, but ever since then I have made do with
lies or simple omissions. My Jewish friends Liza and Arkady, to name
only two, have always been well received by my father and mother,
who fortunately never said the word 'Yid' in front of them. If, however, you insist that I break the truce, I will, although we then run the
risk of complicating our lives enormously."

Since the ball is now in my court, I consider a practical solution
and ask her about the feasibility of fitting a sink in our room to reduce
our contacts with her parents. Otherwise, I tell her to act as she sees
fit, without worrying on my account.

"I will devise something," she affirms, and on the way back home,
having recovered her enthusiasm, she talks to me about the "new
culture" that will banish prejudice, ignorance, hatred, and make
people better and happy. *Kultura, kulturnyi, kulturnoye, kulturich,
nye-kulturnoye*—Klava's vocabulary abounds in expressions devoted
to learning, which alone is capable of changing the attitudes of the
people of today and tomorrow. But not those of the past, of yesterday;
her parents, for example—whom she loves, even preferring her ec-
centric father to her overly self-effacing mother.

Two days later, she puts on a record to please Papa Emilyan. He
lets himself be charmed by the Gypsy music, and when the record is
over, he sighs and comments again about "idiot Hitler." Klava is
ready, smiling: "In fact, Papa, just what harm have these Jews done
to you?"

"To me?" he replies, amazed. "But I have never met a single one of
them, God forbid that I ever should," and he makes the sign of the
cross.

"It is just as well that, thanks be to God, you haven't had to suffer personally at the hands of the Jews. The Germans, on the other hand, have brought down much misery on you, your family, and your country. Isn't that so?"

"Of course, my little Klavochka."

"Well, then, since the Jews have done nothing to harm you, and since the Germans have overwhelmed you with woes, shouldn't you logically wish for the Jews to kill the Germans, and not the other way round?"

"Logically speaking, you're right, but in reality things are different, because the Jews engage in commerce and not in warfare."

Here she affects an astonished air: "Papa! You surprise me! We have Jewish marshals, generals, colonels, combatants of every rank, and their chests are covered with medals. You let that slip out, but you don't really believe it, do you? You're a reasonable man; you wouldn't go as far as to deny the evidence. You know perfectly well that not only do the Jews fight very courageously in the present war, but that they also did so in biblical times. For what is your Holy Bible, Papa, if not the history of the wars waged by the Jews? When I was still a youngster, your friend Stepanovich once said, in this very room, that the Old Testament is an epic song to the glory of the Cossacks of Jerusalem."

Seeing her father run short of arguments, Klava presses on: "Hitler only slits the throats of defenseless Jews, those who have already been disarmed, just as he came close to slitting our own throats, in this very house. But you cannot describe someone who has committed such monstrosities against innocent people, including women and children, simply as an idiot, or encourage him to slit the throats of even more defenseless people. Papa, Hitler is a *dzikiy zvier* [ferocious animal], and we have to put him down—nothing else will do."

At this, she leaves the room, casting at her discomfited father a glance that has more sympathy than anger in it. "How did I do?" she asks me.

"Brilliantly, but I didn't realize that you were so well versed in the Bible."

"You always have to listen to what the adversary says in order to turn his own arguments against him. I have also looked into the

possibility of acquiring a sink. We can do it through the black market." Klava is like that. All that she needs is a day or two to think
things over and then she fixes everything. From now on my contacts
with the older generation will be greatly reduced.

"It is by setting out from small things that one arrives at a better
understanding of the larger matters in life," Joseph Stalin teaches us,
and with good reason. Take, for example, the sink. Why do we attach
so much importance to having one while the idea of having a separate
kitchen installed never crosses our minds? Because even in a period
of penury we wash every day, while we cook very little. We limit
ourselves to boiling some water for tea now and then. We take our
main meals in our respective canteens. The student cafeteria at
Klava's institute, intended for the future scientific and technical *nomenklatura*, is one of the best in town and even serves two meals, one
at midday and one at five o'clock in the afternoon. My factory canteen, however, is poor, and since I have a rather flexible work schedule, I am terribly attracted by the gastronomic delights of the *kolkhoz*
market, the very one in which Moussia sells her borscht. In this
marvelous place you can find, for a price, the most varied dishes,
cooked by the most welcoming of *baby*. Have I the right to spend
entirely on myself my illicit income while ignoring the fact that we are
short of many household goods? Is it reasonable to let the money
vanish into the steam rising from a bowl of borscht or from a *somm*, a
fish from the Don that is fried in its own fat? In this *crise de conscience*, my stomach more often than not gets the better of me, from
which I deduce that it is particularly demanding—having thirteen
months of the Gulag to make up for—or else that the others, having
more character, resign themselves more readily to living a life of
semi-starvation. One thing is certain: People in Rostov think of food
above everything else and, because they are unable to satisfy their
needs, are often ill-tempered without reason, as though a good fight
could free them from their obsession about food. One of these incidents, which erupts over nothing, makes a particularly strong impression upon me.

One day the four of us—we four ex-members of the air force—are out for a stroll along the Sadovaya, dressed up in our uniforms. At the time, the section of the main avenue between the Voroshilov and Budenny Prospekts was, in the evenings, the favorite spot for those trying to pick up sexual partners in Rostov. But just now we are walking without such thoughts, on a Sunday at lunchtime, exclusively for a breath of air.

At the corner of Vorshilov Prospekt, at the busiest intersection in the city, we encounter a disabled man on crutches and reeking of vodka. He greets us with quite a harangue: "You there, Russian officers, why aren't you doing something about these Jews who are leading our country to rack and ruin?" It is a classic anti-Semitic speech: Jews and Communists are in command, while the Christians, reduced to simple servants, carry out their orders. You don't need a diploma in political science to know what he is leading up to. While listening to him, I feel myself go back in time five years, for his speech resembles that of a particular Polish rightist group that fought against "Judeo-Communism."

Gaping onlookers of all ages gather around. The militiaman who is directing traffic doesn't intervene; he isn't concerned with what happens on the sidewalks. The plainclothes police—of which there must be some among the small crowd—don't come forward either. As for the honest citizens, they listen with a most benign air to the anti-Semite.

Zeus reacts by saying, "Pathetic wretch, who has filled your head with so much crap?" But Churik dissuades him from further insulting and provoking a drunkard. Kola has an idea: He will whisper discreetly to him that *Dzhugashvili*, the real name of our Supreme Commander-in-Chief, really means "son of a Jew" in Georgian; then, when the drunk begins to pick upon Stalin personally, the militiaman and the plainclothes police will have to drag him away. But this stratagem, suggested by a rumor that was once widely current among the Cossacks, only makes us laugh, and Kola himself isn't serious. We continue on our way, therefore, discussing anti-Semitism.

"It's simply a phenomenon of the superstructure," Kola says. "It will disappear when the material base of society has been broadened."

Churik, our resident Marxist scholar, immediately reproaches him for being so simplistic: "You don't understand anything of the relations between infrastructure and superstructure; things are a lot more complex than you suggest."

Absorbed in our controversy, we don't pay a great deal of attention to the appearance of Klava, Galia, and Kathinka, who pretend not to recognize us. Decked out in their Sunday best, in flowered dresses, they flutter around us to make fun of our "silly habit" of putting on our uniforms from time to time (which they themselves have ironed). "My, my! Would you look at that? What pretty little soldiers. And we are so lonely. Please take us with you when you go to war."

We don't take the bait. Kathinka takes it a bit too far; she pouts sexily at Zeus and then takes him by the arm, saying, "Officer, I think I really like you. Show me some attention; I'm terribly lonely." A passerby about forty years of age, outraged by these provocative gestures, calls her a "virgin in heat," and she bursts out laughing. "Virgin, did you say? Come and look a little closer!"

Zeus doesn't find any of this amusing, and driven on by jealousy— the great problem with this couple—he lays into the prudish passerby, calling him a sex maniac and a bum—"nye voyeval"—one of those who haven't fought in the war. The other man bares his fists and Kathinka has to separate the two of them. A large crowd gathers, even more numerous than at the intersection where the drunkard had been holding forth, and infinitely more interested.

A debate quickly spreads from the particular to the general. Some use the "bum" as an example of all the deadbeats in Russia, who make poor patriots and are known to rape young girls. Others rail against the arrogance of demobilized soldiers who, because they have fought in the war, believe that they can get away with anything, for on this occasion, according to this group, the airman had violently tugged the girl by the arm, seriously hurting her. Kathinka's age diminishes as these exchanges progress, and we hear in the background the raised voice of a woman passerby outraged by the behavior of the men—in a city like Rostov, where there are so many single adult women, too!—who can shamelessly attack a young girl of fifteen years of age, a "virgin" who will be scarred for the rest of her life. A brawl finally erupts that will later be reported to have produced two knife-wound victims, one of whom was taken to the hospital in serious condition.

I say "reported to" advisedly, for I heard this snippet through the agency of "OBG"—*odna baba govorit* (a *baba* speaks)—which is not one hundred percent trustworthy. Nevertheless, as far as local news is concerned, and more particularly news about topical trivia, it is the only agency that functions; Tass only mentions Rostov in order to inform the country of the reopening of Rosselmach, our large factory for agricultural machinery (which is producing, according to the OBG, Stalin tanks, the best in all of Russia). To know what is going on in town—why, for example, following an inexplicable breakdown, the tramway doesn't work for three whole days—you must visit the *kolkhoz* market. That suits me fine; I have a perfect alibi when I go there to stuff myself selfishly with borscht and fried fish. Unless I am actually caught in the act, neither Klava nor anyone else can contest the purely information-seeking character of my visits to the *baby* of the OBG.

Largely preoccupied with the chronicle of local affairs, the OBG doesn't give out any international news unless it has implications for the town market. Such was the case in 1946, two months before I left Rostov, when Churchill's speech at Fulton, Missouri, gave rise to a very pessimistic OBG interpretation, precipitating a run on the shops the like of which I had never seen before. I remember that on this occasion Mama Maria, forgetting all our conventions, came in to admonish us. "My little Klavochka, the Grand Alliance is finished. Run out quickly and buy some salt and sugar so we won't be caught without them if a new war should break out." We told her that there wasn't going to be another war, but this stubborn woman didn't believe us and ran from one line to another, until the food shops ran out of stock.

"A factory is like a woman; to get along well with it you need to know it thoroughly, intimately even." A Cuban, Regino Boti, was to explain that to me about twenty years after my departure from Russia.

KLAVA

But to begin a relationship with someone, there has to be a measure of
mutual attraction in the first place. In Rostov I have never liked the
Savelit factory where I work. It is dirty, noisy, and located in the
poorest part of town. In July 1944, the regional Bureau for Aid to the
War-Disabled—set up by Stalin's personal decree—assigned me to
the post of stock manager (*zavyeduichchy,* or *zav* for short) in this
factory, which belonged to the People's Commissariat of "Black Metallurgy," a branch of heavy metallurgy. At first I was pleased, but
Kola somewhat dampened my enthusiasm by citing an old proverb:
"Those who churn butter never run short of it; but those who make
needles have only needles." My factory produced heavy-duty thermal
insulators, *savelit*—hence the factory's name—which were totally
nonnegotiable on the black market and were therefore worth even less
than needles. What I didn't yet know was that Kola's folk wisdom no
longer obtained in the age of the black market and a centralized,
planned economy.

My first meeting with my factory manager misfires. Ivan Petrovich,
a man of about forty with a paunch and a square-shaped head, can
think of nothing better by way of welcome than to ask me if my brain
is working more or less normally after my injury. He was not embarrassed about not having fought in the war, having been kept in the
factory by the Moscow authorities, who deemed his presence indispensable to the smooth running of the economy. I try in vain to make
him understand that the Bureau for Aid to the War-Disabled looks
after all of the demobilized, including Kola, who suffers from a mere
stomach ulcer. From the moment of our first meeting, this unpleasant
man's arrogant behavior will continue to feed my aversion for his
factory, even when he feigns to be well disposed toward me.

What upsets me most, however, is a visit to the workshops, bor-
dered by railway tracks on one side and by a strip of wasteland on the
other. At Savelit, as in the whole of Soviet industry, women came to
work as replacements for their husbands or brothers who were at the
front. The production of *savelit* requires much hard physical effort.
Our factory makes white sheets of metal as large as a mattress, each
one weighing a good fifty kilos, by smelting yellowish ore imported

from the Donbass region, in furnaces fired by coal from Shakhty. Everything in the factory is covered with a film of dust that clings to the faces of the workers, both the few men and the numerous women, the latter protecting their hair with peasant-style head scarves. These noisy and overheated surroundings make one think at first of a forced-labor camp. The comparison, though, doesn't bear close scrutiny. These women haven't the sadly resigned eyes of the *zeki*; they leave their workshops freely and decide many things on their own initiative. Some of them bring their kids to the factory; they play on the waste ground, and their mothers join them when breakdowns in the plant occur, or during breaks. Unlike women *zeki,* they don't tremble in front of a man, however aggressive his manner, and often rebuke him sharply, joking about it, as though in these times of role-reversal he were only a timid slip of a girl. Still, if Savelit has none of the characteristics of a camp, neither is it the sort of place that you go to with a carefree step.

My assistant is a woman, Vera Pavlovna. She is an accountant, efficient and little given to daydreaming. She is in her thirties, fair-haired and careful of her appearance, rather stiff and reserved. She insists on keeping her distance from the other women workers, and won't allow her ten-year-old son to play with their children. From the time he leaves school at two o'clock until his mother leaves work at six, he waits patiently in our office without making any noise, busy reading books by Chukovski, creator of the famous "Doctor Aybolit," who is adored by Russian children. According to Kuzmich, the truckdriver who is often put at my disposal, Vera Pavlovna once had an affair with our antipathetic manager, whom she calls with a touch of irony "Caesar Imperator." I haven't noticed, though, that he shows her any special consideration; on the contrary, he barks at her over even the smallest mistake that she occasionally makes in the calculation of wages.

Employees' earnings are determined according to a rigorous scale, and everyone earns a different amount. Some work at piece rate and earn bonuses for exceeding fixed norms; others are paid by the hour—between 1.67 and 1.89 rubles—but the rate for the standard two hours of overtime (the factory operates a ten-hour day shift) is higher and varies from one category of worker to another. I also qualify for a supplement of about fifty rubles a month, which is added to my basic salary of four hundred rubles, although I never work ten hours a day. The women workers in my factory could have found less physically demanding work in Rostov, but they have chosen to work here because it entitles them to a first- or second-category food ration card, that is to say eight hundred or six hundred grams of bread. I do not underestimate the importance of the ration of six hundred grams of bread that comes with my job. Klava, like all other students, receives only four hundred.

For other foods, the situation is more complex; their low prices have remained stable since the start of the war, but they are considered to be interchangeable, and the shops sell only what they have in stock. So, instead of two kilos of meat per month, you might be given some fish, a few eggs, and also some canned food or honey, without ever being able to understand the mysterious law that governs these substitutions. At any rate, the lion's share of the coupons for meat, wheat, bread, dairy products, and sugar, is used up by the canteens. Since the beginning of the war, salaries have increased in Russia—particularly as the working day is longer—while opportunities for spending them have been drastically reduced. For our canteen meals and other fixed expenses, Klava and I pay out at most three hundred rubles, or the equivalent of her monthly maintenance grant as a first-year student. In the Kremlin they are so well aware of this disequilibrium in the private citizen's budget that we are obliged once a year to subscribe one month's salary to a state loan, as though, during this month, out of patriotism, we were supposed to live without spending a kopek.

Unfortunately, on the black market, money has very little purchasing power. It is almost as if, in switching from one market to another, we were entering another world where everything has increased in value a hundredfold. With her monthly three hundred rubles Klava could buy only three kilos of bread on the black market, and I could afford on my salary only four and a half kilos. Our two incomes combined wouldn't even be enough to purchase 750 grams of butter (a kilo is worth more than a thousand rubles). What is the sense in offering material incentives to encourage productivity in such circumstances? The promise of a bonus of twenty rubles—half the price of a bowl of borscht from Moussia's stall—isn't enough to prompt anyone to work harder. My factory manager imagines that his managerial authority rests on his right to hand out these meaningless bonuses to the "best workers" and to penalize the "slackers." Nevertheless, some people do slave away for reasons I don't understand.

My job brings me more headaches than I had imagined would be the case. At first sight, you don't have to be a genius to do it, and my predecessor, before returning to his native Ukraine, taught me the job in less than a day. As the economy is centrally planned, I have to carry out orders contained in a very detailed document—the *raznariadka*—countersigned by I. F. Tevossyan, the People's Commissar of "Black Metallurgy." Everything in it is minutely calculated: the quantities of raw material that will be delivered to us on such and such a date, and the schedule of delivery dates for our factory. My job is to remind our suppliers of their obligations toward us and to encourage our chief engineer to ensure that our deliveries are on time. For the smooth running of this ingenious system, all that it takes is for everyone punctually to carry out the elements of the centralized plan.

In practice, it operates altogether differently. One day, only a few weeks after starting work in 1944, armed with duly stamped requisition papers, I arrive in a truck at the supply depot of *Neftsbyt*, a gasoline distributor, to pick up a ton of gasoline. On the way there, Kuzmich, my driver, had confessed his skepticism about our prospects of success, and had advised me to settle for a half-ton or even less. But the supply manager at the depot is not at all inclined to haggle. He claims to have no gasoline at all, and declares that this has been the case for so long that he has even forgotten the smell of it. "What fuel there is goes to the front," he informs me, and he offers me in friendly fashion a hundred grams of vodka and half a salted cucumber as compensation. Convinced that he is acting in good faith, I don't insist; tomorrow, or perhaps in a week's time, the gasoline will arrive and Kuzmich and I will come back to get it.

At the factory, Caesar Imperator doesn't view things in this light. *"Davai benzine!"* ("Bring me that gasoline!") he screams, as if I had a tank of it at home. In fact, I have so little that in order to light my cigarettes, instead of a cigarette lighter I use two flint stones and a wick. Overtures made to the powerful Industry Committee of the Rostov Communist Party yield nothing, as gasoline is temporarily scarce throughout the city. My boss refuses to understand and pesters me without respite. Ten or twenty times a day, he puts his head around the half-open door of my office and hurls at me, *"Davai benzine!"* Growing tired of it, I return with Kuzmich to the *Neftsbyt* depot to try to appeal to the sense of solidarity of its foreman. He sympathizes, and promises to phone me himself as soon as he receives any gasoline.

Two days later the telephone hanging on the wall behind my desk rings. It is a *zamzav*, the assistant manager of the Port of Rostov, who claims to have met me earlier in the year, in May, during the ceremony for the award of bronze medals "for the defense of the Caucasus." His name doesn't mean anything to me, and in any case, I have no business with the Port of Rostov. He thinks otherwise; he is going to put some business my way that should turn out to be "mutually profitable":

"There are five freight cars on their way to your factory, loaded with Donbass ore. Give them to me for forty-eight hours."

"What? But I have to load them with *savelit* in accordance with the plan. How can I lend them to you?"

"Your *savelit* are not perishable goods; my fish from the River Don are, especially in this heat." He informs me that the catch of fish this year is nothing short of miraculous, because all the armies that have passed through Rostov have been throwing their food reserves into the river so as not to leave them for the enemy. "The fish have taken advantage of it to fatten up and to multiply, but I need a means of transport to distribute them to the different towns in the Rostov region. Lend me your five freight cars and I promise you that you won't regret it."

Why doesn't he approach the management of the railways directly, particularly since "my" freight cars, which are very dirty, appear to be so unsuited to his needs? He has an answer for everything; railway workers are notoriously uncooperative and nearly impossible to deal with. Also, refrigerated cars are so rare that they have almost become collectors' items; fish are transported now in ordinary *tyeplushki*, packed with lots of ice. I agree to keep my part of the bargain, but I want to be sure of recovering "my" freight cars. "In forty-eight hours they'll be back. You don't imagine, do you, that in this heat I could take my fish any farther than Salsk to the south and Novocherkassk to the north?" While I'm thinking this over, he begins to make the oddest suggestions. He is ready to deliver one hundred kilos of fish to my factory's canteen. But the canteen is not under my control. "Don't worry about that," says my friend on the phone. "I can deliver to any address you care to give me." The deal is becoming clearer now, and seems a lot more worth my while. I promise to give him an answer in an hour or two, and I leave in a hurry in Kuzmich's truck to look for Kola; he will come up with a solution, and should it prove necessary, he will know how to get rid of this heaven-sent merchandise.

But the truck can't leave the factory grounds without a reason, and I indicate as our destination the *Neftsbyt* supply depot, which means that the truck logbook will have to be stamped there. I use the occasion to ask the *zav* who has forgotten the smell of gasoline if a large amount of fish would tease his sense of smell back to life and allow me to obtain my order more rapidly. "Why didn't you tell me in the first place that you had such a treasure?" He seems almost angry, and doesn't ask any questions about the origins of this miraculous catch. Having decided against consulting Kola, I telephone my new friend at the port: "You will deliver your fish to this address."

We set off again, Kuzmich and I, with a ton of gasoline in our truck. When it comes to private deals, the supply managers of Rostov conduct business boldly, relying on the spoken word, as on Wall Street.

In 1944, according to the official figures, the USSR allotted 27 percent of available foodstuffs to canteens in which about 40 million meals a day were sold. Yet it never occurred to anyone to install a self-service system, which would have made life easier for consumers while simultaneously saving labor. Khrushchev would finally discover this principle in 1959 on a visit to the IBM plant in San Clemente, California, where he was carried away with admiration not for the most modern laboratories in the world, but for the self-service cafeteria. Also in 1944, in order to compete with the *kolkhoz* market, the Soviet government created its own network of shops and restaurants designated as "commercial," which, for exorbitant prices that bore no relation to the workers' official incomes, offered practically everything, as well as à la carte food. This innovation, which was said to be temporary, would mark Soviet society in an enduring way by accentuating its inequalities and by fueling the race for money. But in Rostov I didn't understand the deeper significance of this development.

On this day in September 1944, I go back home relieved at having gotten rid of these fish so quickly, rather as if they had been burning my fingers. But Kola soon arrives and, in front of an impassive Klava, launches into a fierce ethical attack on me. Just as it is better to go to bed a thousand times with one woman than to go to bed only once with a thousand different women, he argues, so too is it preferable to earn a pile of rubles at a single stroke rather than to circumvent the law repeatedly by multiplying petty schemes day after day. A kilo of fish costs at least seven hundred rubles in Rostov—and more than a thousand in Myechotka—so my hundred kilos would have allowed us to live honestly and studiously for many months. Besides, if I had insisted, the port *zamzav* would have delivered to us not just one hundred but probably two or three hundred kilos.

I don't share his views, for I still recall the interrogation sessions that dealt with our "war treasure." I have no desire to become a "millionaire in the land of Soviets," and it is perhaps the instinct of self-preservation that has driven me to allow these fish from the heavens to slip through my fingers. Kola answers angrily that I was put away in a camp not because of my ostentatious expenditures in Yerevan, but because I gave myself the superior airs of a Polish gentleman who had contempt for proletarian Russia. And what does

Klava say to all this? Nothing. She leads Kola toward her end of the table to study math.

It is only a quarrel between friends, but it badly upsets me. For the first time since falling in love with Klava, I feel an overwhelming desire to flee from Rostov. I want nothing to do with the dilemma that Kola poses: Is it better to risk everything once or to risk a little bit every day? Anyway, I am the only one among us to know what the word "risk" really means in this context. But an ugly thought slips into my mind: I want to leave so that Klava will miss me, to punish her for not having come to my defense against Kola. "I'll make you mope around the banks of the Don and long for my airs of a Polish gentleman." And anyway, what do the two of them know about their own country, never having known the Gulag?

Kola doesn't even realize that he has hurt me, and after a brief silence he continues, "We can still salvage something. Tomorrow I will offer our help to the port *zamzav* for the work to be done loading your freight cars; that will allow us to make at least a few thousand rubles from this lost opportunity."

The *zamzav* gladly accepts Kola's offer: To accelerate the dispatching of the fish, he needs an additional crew for Saturday night, and he gives Kola the go-ahead to recruit it himself. The pay is two hundred rubles officially, and authorization to leave the port twice during the shift without being searched. According to the *zamzav*, it will take ten of us ten hours to load one freight car, but he doesn't object to a smaller crew willing to work twelve hours.

But where are we quickly to find eight or ten likely men? I can bring only Kuzmich, a solid old worker. Zeus gets hold of an Armenian who he says is as robust as Joe Louis. Kola finds two male dancers who work with Fira. "Among the seven of us, we'll manage," Kola declares, and he runs off to deposit the list of names at the port. Klava meanwhile finishes sewing immense pockets onto the insides of our greatcoats, veritable sacks capable of holding four or five kilos of fish. A final detail of our expedition: Two *baby*, fish wholesalers, are going to spend the night near the port exit to buy whatever fish we bring out to them.

The good mood in which we set out begins to evaporate from the moment we assemble at eight o'clock in the evening. Each of us has exaggerated the strength of his recruits: We discover that the dancers are rather puny; that the Armenian is as frail as a delicate tropical flower; and that Kuzmich is too old to play a longshoreman. The layout of the site presents us with a second disagreeable surprise: Between the fishing boat and the freight car, the slope to be scaled is by no means gradual. To cover this distance carrying large baskets loaded with fish is no picnic. After an hour or so, my legs feel like lead weights and I choose a less exacting job, transporting the ice from a container that is stationed at the same level as the freight car. The dancers have the same idea, though, so the quantity of ice in the freight car increases a lot more quickly than that of the fish. Kola calls me to order and I return sheepishly to the steep slope, where we form a human chain and pass the baskets from hand to hand. Eventually we decide to take our first break, nowhere near the halfway stage, as we had planned.

Our collective exit goes off smoothly; the guards pretend not to notice that our greatcoats, wholly unnecessary at this time of year, literally flutter about on our backs, as the fish that are still alive try to leap out of our pockets. Then comes the third disappointment: The two *baba* wholesalers behave just like a cartel and arbitrarily fix the price of our fish at two hundred and fifty rubles per kilo, a third of the market retail price. They reproach us for not having selected larger and fatter fish, and in a remarkable display of bad faith, each *baba* reiterates that the other one knows what she is talking about. There you have perfect evidence that social being determines consciousness, and proof that a good Soviet citizen who gives herself to commerce behaves no differently from a bourgeois profiteer of the worst kind. We have no choice and are obliged to sell these goods for a pittance—goods that we have really earned by the sweat of our brows. Each of us comes away, nevertheless, with the sum of one thousand rubles—less than we counted upon, but enough, despite everything, to give fresh vigor to our efforts.

The second phase of the work is the hardest, and arguments inevitably break out among us. The dancers, both of whom have decided never again to set foot inside a port, would like to stuff the freight car full of ice only. Kola rebuffs such plans, and is supported by Kuzmich, who reminds us of the principle of the job well done, and also of a well-known proverb: "Never spit on the plate that you may want to use a second time." Zeus wants to know if our second exit has to be at the very end of the shift. Since no principle is at stake, we decide to check this clause of the agreement without further ado. The guards let us pass through once again, with no questions asked. And the second thousand rubles each of us is paid renews our efforts.

The port controller arrives at the appointed hour. After examining the load aboard the freight car, and after seeing the state of our faces, which must arouse pity, he says, "That will do." The hold of the boat is far from empty, but, he tells us, by packing too many fish in the freight car one runs the risk of crushing them, and in any case, on Monday there will be another car to be loaded. I get the impression that he wants to justify himself in his own eyes for allowing us to leave because we are so clearly exhausted. The controller then gives each of us, over and above the terms agreed, a large fish for his personal consumption.

Throughout the vast territory that separates Leningrad from Rostov there are probably no other two women as resolutely anti-alcohol as Nievka and Klava, and a strange fate willed me into the arms of first one and then the other. But vodka acts as an excellent remedy for aches and pains, and Sunday evening, during our party to celebrate our "miraculous catch," we need plenty of it. While we go off to clean ourselves up and get rid of the tenacious smell of fish, Fira and her friends decide to organize a culinary competition to see who can prepare the fresh fish in the most delectable manner. Galia wins hands down with her stuffed carp prepared in the Jewish manner, a dish also widely appreciated in Poland, where it used to delight even the most rabid anti-Semites.

Churik contributes to the party's success with a sumptuous present of five liters of vodka. His father, a high-ranking figure in the government supply department, receives plenty of presents, but he won this particular jackpot at cards, for he is an ace at "preference," a Russian variety of bridge. The abundance of vodka provides an opportunity to make up with Kola. He takes back his phrase about the "disdainful Polish gentleman" and assures me that by giving myself airs, I gain both in charm and authority. For my part, I commit myself publicly, under oath, to make better use of the next load of fish that falls into my lap. Klava shows her approval of us both, but appeals for moderation with respect to the vodka. She drinks only small quantities herself, to keep us company. Her favorite tactic consists of replacing her vodka with water on the sly. With me it is just the opposite. I swallow vodka as easily as I do water; it doesn't burn my stomach or make my eyes water. If there is none around, I can easily go without; otherwise, I drink to quench my thirst, especially when, as now, it makes my aches and pains disappear.

In addition to its curative power, the national Russian drink causes a certain amount of drowsiness beyond a certain dose. The women seem to be more vulnerable. Fira, for instance, after drinking two hundred grams of it, curls up on the bed and falls asleep, displaying her dancer's legs in all their beauty. Possibly as a result of my imprisonment in the Gulag, I am more prone to sleep than the others. Seated on the bed, I slide imperceptibly on my back as if under the pressure of an invisible force, although I want to follow the fascinating discussion taking place around the narrow table. I contribute very little, not because I have drunk too much but because I don't wish to side with Galia and Churik, the critical intellectuals, against the camp of the optimists, led by Kola and Klava. Zeus's position is as changeable as the mood of poets, while Kathinka only raises her lovely voice to plead occasionally for a little order and to let each person speak his or her piece.

It is the Soviet coal miner, Afonyev, who is the cause of a great debate. Along with the vodka, Churik has brought with him a clipping from *Pravda* that states that this exemplary worker has earned over ten thousand rubles a month since the beginning of 1944. Nor does he owe this astronomical sum to the circumstance of being paid in coal, which he then sells on the black market, as we have just done with our fish; not at all. He receives his ten thousand rubles at the pay counter, alongside the other workers, some of whom are apparently content to receive as little as 250 or 300 rubles a month. Afonyev is probably even more productive than Alexei Stakhanov, the record holder of 1935, but he is unlucky with the newspaper coverage of his feats: The liberation of Bucharest and Sofia takes up more space in *Pravda* than does the chronicle of his exploits in a coal mine. For Churik it is significant, however, that the press talks only about Afonyev's earnings and doesn't mention his rate of coal extraction. "It's on account of the war," Kola quips. "You don't reveal your levels of productivity to the enemy."

Galia and Churik consider that we no longer have the right to joke about such matters, for our "new society" is in danger of absorbing into its system some of the most retrograde aspects of capitalism. They garnish their critique with apt quotations from Marx, Engels, and even Lenin. This is the opportunity they have been waiting for. Kola and Klava try to play the devil's advocate by arguing that the egalitarian leveling-down effect—resulting from the absolute impoverishment of the workers—is one of the characteristics of capitalism condemned by Marx, and that our sacrosanct principle "To each according to his labor . . ." also derives from his writings. They have read it somewhere in an old speech of Stalin's on Marx's "Critique of the Gotha Program." But they are no match for Galia and Churik, who are familiar with the original text in its entirety and not merely with an interpretation of it.

"Just because a society cannot become egalitarian overnight," Churik says, raising his voice, "is no reason for it to aggravate existing inequalities between workers." Then he adds, for Klava's benefit, "And as for these stupid references to capitalist ultra-egalitarianism, they are completely untrue."

I ought to defend Klava, but I know that Churik is telling the truth. There is no egalitarianism under capitalism, "ultra" or otherwise. After all, I have lived in a capitalist country and I was able to observe that equality is the least of their concerns. Kola takes up Klava's

defense and talks instead about the priority given to the development
of the productive forces. He knows this subject well and expresses
himself with great clarity, even after half a liter of vodka.

Tempers rise. Galia and Churik retort that socialism is not simply a
technique for broadening society's material foundations, that it is a
phase in the transition to communism, in the course of which social
hierarchies and inequalities will be systematically abolished. "Right,
I agree," Klava says, "but these things will only be possible when
people are better educated, *kulturnyie*, fully developed, and have
gotten rid of their egoistic individualism."

"Well, then, is Afonyev in your view *kulturnyi* and fully developed?" Galia adds sneakily but gently. "My dear Klavochka," she
continues, still more tenderly, "we shall be truly fully developed
when there is no more social division of labor and no more difference
between town and countryside. Our full development will not come
about simply from studying a large number of books."

"Yet it's what you do yourself," Klava replies swiftly.

"She studies in order to understand why things are going wrong and
how new social stratifications are crystalizing in our society," answers
Churik, who is in no mood to allow Galia to be teased.

Lying back with my eyes fixed on the ceiling, I suddenly feel
transported to Lodz, several years before, to the time when my mother
used to debate on all these subjects with her friends. You might say
that this evening a new generation, with similar cultural and political
ideas, is continuing their legacy. But if so, it is doing it under strange
conditions. For how can we forget that our discussion takes place
after we have enjoyed stolen fish in a world in which you cannot even
live on your salary unless you happen to be Afonyev? No, Klavochka,
I haven't drunk too much; it is our absurd, paradoxical society that
renders me speechless.

The growing bitterness of the exchanges between Churik and Kola
obliges me to intervene. I propose a toast to friendship. By suddenly
jerking the bed, however, I awaken Fira, who, invigorated by a nap,
lashes out against the "thoroughly corrupt nature of the artistic
world." It is no longer a party but a critique of Soviet society on the

eve of victory. And who would have thought that Fira was scandalized to such an extent by the "star system," by the privileges and corruption of the entertainment world? And that she finds it intolerable that our airplanes bear the names of those who designed them, just as in the West they carry the names of their owners? "Mikoyan and Gurvich give us 'MiG,' while 'T' comes from Tupolev, and 'Yak' from Yakovlyev. It's ridiculous!" she maintains. After Klava, Fira is my favorite. But she gets carried away quickly and when she declares that our heaviest tank shouldn't be carrying the name of Josef Stalin, I stop her from continuing: "Right! That's enough discussion for this evening. Kathinka, give us a song instead."

Kathinka doesn't need to be begged; she knows a new song that has been translated from the English: *"Put Dalokiy do Tipperary"* ("It's a Long Way to Tipperary"). I seem to know this song, yes, of course, I remember now, the English prisoners sang it in *La Grande Illusion.* And Kathinka lowers her pretty blond head close to mine, as though she were dedicating her song to me: "Good-bye Piccadilly, farewell Leicester Square," and I feel that there is a hidden meaning in this unexpected evocation of the faraway home of my brother Genya. That's it, I shall soon be going to see him in London. It is the only possible significance of the message.

While waiting for my journey to London, I have to leave on November 30, 1944, to spend a day in Moscow, where I no longer have any family. Letters addressed to Aunt Lisa are returned to me officially stamped "addressee unknown," and I have never had the addresses of any of her sons. But going to Moscow is something of an event in itself, even with the prospect of spending the night in a hostel. The renown of this city grows endlessly; capital of the Proletarian Revolution, it has become the capital of victory as well, because it was in the suburbs of Moscow that the Wehrmacht suffered in 1941 its first great defeat. It is also in the large squares of Moscow, beginning in August 1943, that the *salyuts* are organized—sumptuous fireworks displays and artillery salutes—to celebrate each significant advance made by our army. To be sure, Nievka used to argue that Moscow's glory was stolen and that the history of modern Russia and of the Bolshevik Revolution was in reality inseparable from that of Leningrad, the site of the Winter Palace. Moscow, though, is incontestably more prestigious. As a fugitive from Western Siberia, I had arrived there in 1940 overcome with emotion at the prospect of seeing the white walls of the Kremlin, Red Square, and all the other monuments. Since that time our poets have added a verse to Lermontov's "Borodino," so that his famous poem pays homage to those who "one hundred thirty years later, on the same battlefield, kept their oath to Stalin: 'We shall not abandon Moscow!' "

Moscow is the best-supplied city in the USSR, doubtless because of the presence of numerous foreigners, diplomats and journalists. Though "commercial" shops have been opened throughout the country to compete with the black market, there is still no doubt that you will find in those of Moscow consumer goods that are impossible to find in the provinces, items as rare as swimsuits in Rostov. Everyone knows that even a short stay in the capital offers the opportunity to combine business with pleasure. It can even be a lucrative experience.

Obtaining a seat on the Moscow train is a notoriously difficult undertaking that requires patience. I didn't choose to leave on November 30, but this date, decided by chance, is a good omen: It is the fifth anniversary of my arrival in Russia, and the fourth anniversary of what Klava and I consider the beginning of our engagement: a performance of *Anna Karenina* we attended together at the theater in Rostov when we were still classmates at School No. 44. Without these two events we wouldn't be together, that's clear, and although neither of us is that superstitious, we think that November 30 is a lucky day for us.

Our entire group applies itself to organizing the trip properly. My friends know how fragile I feel, how often I am prey to persecution obsessions, which, on certain days, totally confuse me. I sometimes run away when a passerby approaches me from behind to ask for information, or I make Kuzmich take detours around the streets of Rostov to shake off a truck that I suspect is tailing us. Thanks to

Klava and her soothing reassurances, I recover my equilibrium quickly enough, but we don't know exactly what provokes my crises.

The solicitude of my friends on the eve of my departure in no way upsets me, and I too prefer that what I have to do in Moscow should be carefully arranged in advance.

This isn't possible with respect to every detail; Klava and Fira would like me to spend my Moscow evening at the Bolshoi in order to see Galina Ulanova, Russia's pride and joy, but the big shots of the entertainment black market in Rostov don't have any contacts among the ticket scalpers in Moscow and are unable to reserve me a seat. Luckily this is not the case with the food market wholesalers and the employees of the state commercial sector.

To make it in Moscow, you need only have the magic formula, and the rest becomes easy. This is the *kommandirovka*, a document certifying that its bearer is traveling on urgent state business. It is impossible to enter the capital without it, as identity controls have become very rigorous. But I have a *kommandirovka* from my factory: I have to go to the People's Commissariat of "Black Metallurgy" to collect my *raznariadka*, my planning schedule for the first six months of 1945. This dossier could, of course, have been sent by mail—which, all things considered, isn't working too badly. Tradition has it, though, that the supply and factory managers go periodically to the capital, which allows them to fatten their wallets and to help distribute durable foods around the different cities of Russia.

Nevertheless, my *kommandirovka* doesn't come under "normal administration procedures" as they say in Russia, and it lands on me from out of the blue, or rather from the office of Caesar Imperator. To understand how this came about, I must digress a little on what Fira calls the "eternal feminine" and the "eternal masculine" in Rostov. In October, Kathinka comes to look for me at the factory, to ask me for a favor requiring urgent attention: One of her friends is willing to pay well for a little drive somewhere in a truck, a delicate matter, since it concerns the transport of sheets of glass. It is perfectly feasible, for I am in a position to obtain an exit permit from Kuzmich, but we talk it over in the corridor so that Vera Pavlovna shouldn't hear us. It is here that Caesar Imperator surprises us and, from that very moment, falls off his imperial throne, his heart having been shattered in a thousand pieces by the "magnificent *blondinka*." Certainly Kathinka has a bewitching voice, but during this brief instant she had just had the time to introduce herself—"Ekaterina Nikolayevna"—and if these two words were sufficient to enchant this fat, arrogant factory manager (who is a misogynist to boot, for he treats his women workers really badly), then it is conclusive proof that love at first sight doesn't occur only in operettas.

These are the facts: The attitude of Caesar Imperator toward me changes miraculously. He calls me to his office ten times a day, not to bawl out *"Davai blondinku!"* but to throw himself at my feet: "Please help me, my friend, I am dying!" His amorous behavior is as exaggerated as his managerial conduct is dictatorial, as if he wished to demonstrate to me all of the outrageousness of the Russian "eternal masculine." How can I help him? Simple. I have to tell him everything I know about this "dream creature," and of course I have to give him her address. Cornered, unable to deny that I know Kathinka, I end up talking a little bit about her to him, and also giving him her address.

The sequel to this affair would always remain a mystery to me. Klava would claim that I had nothing to be sorry for, first of all because the manager could have obtained Kathinka's address at the Rostov City Information Bureau, and secondly because, in any case, he didn't stand a chance with this *blondinka*. And to dispel any of my remaining apprehensions, she reveals—swearing me to secrecy—that her friend, following a traumatic abortion at the age of seventeen, is very reticent in the matter of sexual relations and frankly avoids making love as much as possible. According to Klava, "Zeus gets jealous whenever Kathinka shies away from it; for men generally believe that if you aren't sleeping with them, then you must be sleeping with someone else."

Despite this persuasive interpretation, I am obliged to note that Caesar Imperator is henceforth familiar with the movements of both Kathinka and the Don Cossacks Performance Arts Ensemble, and if he doesn't openly boast of having won her, neither does he wear the hangdog look of a rejected lover. With me he is extremely affable in a way that I wouldn't have believed possible before, and he continues to address me politely, as though to repay a debt. According to Klava, none of this means anything, and she refuses to talk about it with Kathinka.

So be it. My Moscow trip is the fruit of this new "friendship," and I wonder if Kathinka has suggested it to allow our circle of friends to improve its material situation, or whether Caesar Imperator has offered it himself to please her and to obtain what he wants of her. Obviously I haven't any proof, merely suspicions, but the very thought that our fate can hinge upon such a barter, between such an ill-matched couple and at the expense of the unfortunate Zeus, thoroughly disgusts me.

This shadow looms over my trip and it will also influence my behavior in Moscow, it seems to me. Otherwise the whole thing works out beautifully. The passengers in the train have a few hours to spare, and spend the time playing cards, chatting, and picnicking as though they were on board a cruiser. In my compartment an enormous wooden chest serves as a table on which we play preference; this chest is mine and contains a large sack of sunflower seeds that I am carrying with me to present to the workers' supply section of our sister factory in Moscow. In fact, a wholesaler will come to collect it at the station, and this time we have taken every precaution against being conned as we were by the *baba* fishmongers. Sunflower seeds are obviously a bulky commodity, but we decided upon them because they yield a very high profit: the contents of my chest cost us 6,500 rubles and will be resold for 26,000, which is a good deal by any standard.

On the return journey, with the profits from the sunflower seeds, I will bring back a smaller suitcase filled with an assortment of underwear, rolls of cloth, and clothes selected by the manager of a "commercial" shop. He is a friend of Churik's father, who asked him to make up a large range of items, first of all because of the lack of textiles in Rostov, and secondly so that no inspector should suspect me of indulging in speculation. I am only the go-between in this operation, but I set out with merchandise worth 6,500 rubles and I will bring back goods worth about 50,000. No Afonyev, with all his records for coal extraction, ever comes close to rivaling our exploit, achieved in forty-eight hours (or seventy-two, counting the time for the round trip). We are all associates and beneficiaries, including Galia and Churik; I don't pretend either to claim all the credit or to shoulder the entire moral responsibility for the coup, which simultaneously fills us with joy and yet causes us genuine anguish. If we are capable of analyzing the disastrous effects of the growing inequalities among workers, we realize perfectly well that privileges in Russia produce a far greater yield than any honest work, and we ourselves join in the rush to take advantage of them.

Such doubts nag at my conscience until the moment of my arrival in Moscow, where the Muscovites' lack of courtesy aggravates my morose mood. The people I have to see at the People's Commissariat of "Black Metallurgy" force me to waste an extravagant amount of time to settle a matter that could have been concluded in an hour. Even Moscow no longer pleases me very much beneath this gray, rather dirty snow; it really isn't an attractive city, and nothing indicates that it is the "capital of Victory."

But the evening is even more of a letdown. To force me to amuse and "culturally enrich" myself, Klava has given me one hundred rubles from her personal savings, saying, "That ought to be enough for a black-market seat at the Bolshoi, or at the Art Theater, and you can tell me what you think of Ulanova or of Tarassova." It would indeed have been enough, but rather than go to a show, I feel the need to see my Aunt Lisa's house again, even if she is no longer there. Everything appears so different to me from the Moscow of 1940 that I end up doubting whether I really was in this same city during the last summer of peacetime. Or is it just I who have changed? Once I reach the Arbat district, I want to resolve the mystery of the stamp "addressee unknown" concerning Aunt Lisa, for I find this bureaucratic formula revolting. My aunt lived in this building for at least fifty years and her daughter Maria was probably born here; but when I ring the doorbell, the tenants who live in their former apartment send me on my way with scant ceremony—"The old lady died in 1941 and her daughter left"—as if they had something to hide or as if I represented a threat to their "habitable space." On the first floor, people scarcely more helpful declare that they never knew my aunt or her family. What exactly can this mean?

After this failure, I decide to look up the address that Nadia, the woman *zek* who showed such kindness, gave to me, the one at which I was to call to see her in ten years' time "if she were still alive." Hardly a year has elapsed since I left the Volgalag, and barring a miracle, Nadia cannot have returned home. What's more, it is not very prudent to stroll about with 25,000 rubles in the suburbs of a large city in which you don't know your way around. But I must go to Nadia's home; this impulse is stronger than my fears. One thing is certain: Reaching her address is no mean feat, for the street signs in Moscow are scandalously inadequate.

A dark-haired woman of about thirty shows me into a room in which two children are getting ready for bed. She is very mistrustful, and asks me to wait. We can only talk in a *pivnaya*, a bar, not far from here; in communal apartments the walls have ears.

The *pivnaya* is "commercial," and therefore recently opened; it is expensive and already very dirty, and it reeks of beer and crayfish. It is as if the terrible smells were an indispensable part of Soviet gastronomic establishments. The dark-haired woman is also called Nadia; she is the cousin of the one I knew, and not the sister as I had thought at first. Two beers and a dozen crayfish cost one hundred rubles, as much as a theater ticket, or one-third of the legal minimum wage of the ordinary worker. "That's a bit steep," I say, and the dark-haired Nadia agrees with me, a typical conversation between people who have nothing to say to one another. Suddenly the dark-haired Nadia becomes animated and says, as if the sentences had been on the tip of her tongue, "The kids up there are the children of *your* Nadia, and she suffers a martyr's torment from not being able to see them. You must have known about them, since you were friends with her."

What am I to say? It seems simple in Moscow, but in a camp

nothing happens the way it does in normal life. Should I explain the Gulag to this mistrustful woman? I simply reply with another question: "And do the kids miss their mother badly?"

"They were very small when she left, it's five years now."

The calculations become muddled in my head: "She has been in the camp for five years and has to stay there for another nine?"

"Seven," she corrects me, "since she was condemned to a dozen years."

"Men killed each other for her and she got twelve years?"

"She told you that?" More shadow-boxing. I give up, because a wall of suspicion separates us.

In the darkened staircase in front of her apartment, I withdraw one thousand rubles from my pocket and give them to her "for the children." She hesitates, uncertain as to whether she should take them. "You can write to Nadia that it is a little something from the *pozharnik*—she will understand."

"It would be better not to write," she replies. She takes the money and murmurs a few words of thanks. "Are you thinking of coming back to Moscow?"

"I have no idea, but if I do, I will come back to see you."

"Not here. Come and look for me instead at the exit to the bread factory where I work." Agreed. I leave in an ambivalent frame of mind, now reproaching myself for having come, now for not having left a larger amount.

On the train back to Rostov, a good half of the passengers are old acquaintances, my friends on the outward journey. Moscow is a big city only in appearance; one of them saw me with Nadia in the *pivnaya*. He doesn't ask any questions but instead congratulates me on having "picked her up." The others, not to be outdone, start to tell stories of their own sexual exploits, each of them having found a Muscovite to his taste and spent the night performing incredible feats, far more interesting than anything they ever got to do with their lawful spouses. If boastfulness weren't such an important part of the Russian man's character, you would have to conclude that Moscow was the capital of debauchery and not victory.

The account of my trip disappoints Klava, but she doesn't reproach me for having neglected my cultural duty. The fate of Nadia's children, deprived of their mother, saddens her most: "It is inhuman, they shouldn't have done that, whatever crime she committed." Then, so as not to add her own melancholy to mine, she changes the subject and makes fun of the erotic delirium of my travel companions, most of whom are obviously cuckolds, she thinks, and tell each other these stories to forget their own inadequacies.

The trip to Moscow brings to a close my dabblings in the black market. According to my rough estimate, our joint expenses (Klava's and mine) rose to three thousand rubles a month, even without my illicit gastronomic purchases at the market. We were probably better dressed than the average person—thanks to the clothes I brought back from Moscow—but otherwise we lived very meagerly, like our friends and most other people. I find it hard to believe that anyone could have survived this period on official earnings alone. There were perhaps citizens in Rostov who made do with their official incomes. But for whom, in that case, did the state create a "commercial" network in which two beers and a dozen crayfish cost one hundred rubles? These were questions that would remain unanswered for me in Rostov, but which, later, would help me to reflect upon the nature of the USSR and upon the societies that regarded it as a model.

6

NYEZNAKOMKA

Spending half the night of V-E Day dressed only in underpants, on a park bench, alone in the middle of a crowd gone wild with joy, will be for Solik one of the last episodes of his stay in Rostov, and, to tell the truth, one of the best. Even before I was given this nickname, I had dreamed secretly of a surprise attack by the USSR against Hitler, and of the collapse of the Third Reich under simultaneous blows of the British and the Soviets. (In 1940, of course, the United States had still not entered the war.) But neither then nor later had I ever imagined that the Nazis' unconditional surrender would be a nocturnal event. Here was Rostov, an early-to-bed town, pulled from its slumber by an exuberant party.

The next day, May 9, Stalin, in an address to the Soviet people, explained that "knowing full well the perfidious nature of the German leaders and having no confidence in their word," he hadn't been able to acknowledge the Wehrmacht's surrender formally until the moment when "the German troops actually began to surrender their weapons and to give themselves up en masse"—that is, at 11:05 P.M., Moscow time. Certainly he was a man who was notoriously mistrustful, but not to the point of fearing in 1945, after the capture of Berlin, the treachery of the surviving German generals. He surely preferred to announce this great news in the middle of the night to make a greater impact in his own country. This time it was not a matter of just one more celebration, but of Victory with a capital *V*, bringing this tragic and glorious chapter in the history of the USSR and of Europe to a close.

It had already come to an end, of course, on May 7, when, in Reims, the Germans signed the provisional act of surrender—which is why all the other victorious countries celebrated V-E Day twenty-four hours before the Soviets. But Stalin needed time to prepare the entire nation. Time was needed in Rostov, for example, to install along the Sadovaya, in Gorky Park, and along several other main arteries immense searchlights borrowed from the antiaircraft defense forces, and to assemble military bands and civilian orchestras for the occasion. Thus, when Stalin gave the go-ahead the city was illuminated, and triumphal marching tunes blared out. No daytime ceremony would have generated such an emotional spectacle. Had Klava and I been less busy, we might have noticed that searchlights were being set up on the Sadovaya and we would have guessed their purpose. However, we were taken by surprise, and wanted to find our friends immediately, so that we could celebrate together.

That was why I left the house in a hurry, without even pulling my pants on. Halfway to Kola's place, we met, embraced, and began to weep. "Now we really are going to be happy," Kola said again and again, between sobs. His voice was drowned out by the cries of an agitated young girl: "Wherever Stalin is, that's where victory is!"

We decided there was nothing indecent, on that night at least, about walking around half-naked in Gorky Park, amid the noisiest and best illuminated part of the celebrations. Sooner or later all of Rostov would pass through the park and in this way we would meet up again with Klava, Fira, and the others; meanwhile we would watch the people dancing around us. Shortly after we arrived, upon being asked by a pretty schoolgirl of about seventeen with long blond pigtails, Kola decreed that at the moment of victory it was also permissible to dance in your underwear. After the first waltz he returned, but only to excuse himself, looking rather embarrassed about abandoning me for a schoolkid: "You understand; adultery, like the economy, has to be planned a long time in advance."

And so it was that I found myself alone on a bench. Almost all of those dancing close to my bench were women. Since my return to Rostov I had learned a great deal about the misery of women during this final phase of the war. I remembered vividly women workers at my factory breaking down over notifications of the deaths of their loved ones, fallen somewhere in Germany or the Balkans. Yet these women continued to come to work as usual; their grief was keenly felt by the entire workshop.

That night I thought a great deal about the worldwide swing to the left that was likely to follow the defeat of fascism. That expectation rekindled my desire to renew the fight for socialism. It might seem paradoxical to leave the "socialist Fatherland" the better to struggle for socialism, but I had remained faithful to Solik's early ideas. Long before crossing the River Bug in November 1939, I knew, thanks to my mother, that Soviet political culture was based upon the Stalinist interpretation of the history of the workers' movement. I had discovered for myself how it was applied without the slightest effort being made to arouse people's interest, let alone their participation, in political life. This country, with its widespread reputation for skillful "indoctrination," simply kept on repeating the tired themes of a single book, the *History of the CPSU (Bolsheviks)*. It didn't care one iota about spreading socialist ideas. Under the colonels' regime in Lodz, I had known more friends who read Marx and the classics of socialist literature than I ever did in Rostov, where my earliest protector, the mathematician Motya, advised me to concern myself only with the natural sciences. Besides, hadn't I been made a member of the Komsomol without having been asked even a single question about my opinions or my readings?

But it is difficult to hold to any certainties on the future of this Soviet Russia. Suppose it became more bearable to live in after victory? Perhaps it would learn to govern itself differently, allowing its citizens to decide their own affairs and to discuss matters openly. Kola hoped for a Russia without suffering, Klava for a society in which everyone was well educated, Churik and Galia for a USSR less dependent on hierarchy, more egalitarian.

All of these aspirations seemed to me to be legitimate, but while not altogether rejecting the possibility that their desires had some chance of becoming reality, I couldn't wait to see what would happen. I couldn't afford to hang on the words of the Supreme Commander-in-Chief cloistered in the Kremlin, and deal indefinitely with the fear of the unpredictable NKVD. In Rostov I was in danger of becoming a permanent burden on Klava. In Poland and the West I would be able to contribute my building block to the construction of a freer and more just society. Suddenly Klava arrived, breathless, carrying a pullover and a pair of pants for me. "Get dressed quickly, and come see Fira dance."

At the end, like a fireworks display crowning a spectacular Fourth of July, there was Fira's furious, unbridled dancing. Accompanied by a fiddler and by the rhythmic clapping of hands, she alternated between the Cossack *hopak* and modern ballet, inventing extraordinary figures of movement. She had removed her skirt, but there was nothing at all immodest in this gesture, simply an artist's need to have all her freedom of movement. Never before had she improvised so successfully as she did on this occasion. While living in her kitchen for three months, I had watched her practice her exercises and her dancing innumerable times, but this evening she surpassed herself with her art, her suppleness, her fantasies, as though victory had increased her stamina and the agility of her legs tenfold. She was divinely inspired. When finally she had danced herself to a standstill, she came over to lean on me. "I will miss you very badly," I said to her, and even though she couldn't understand the reason for my regrets, she presented me with a sweet kiss on the lips to celebrate our great night of victory.

Living in the Soviet manner among Soviet people, sharing their joys and sorrows, doesn't help one much in getting to know the intentions of the Kremlin, for the Soviet people are the last to know what those intentions are. Thus it was that in Rostov neither Klava nor I nor any of our friends had guessed that at Yalta, three months before the end of the war, Stalin had agreed with Roosevelt and Churchill to divide Europe into zones of influence. Although we discussed politics endlessly and considered a thousand future scenarios, we never imagined the one that shaped the political map of postwar Europe: an Iron Curtain at its heart, and Cold War between erstwhile allies. Was it simply for lack of information, a traditional flaw of Russian life?

Today, looking back, I believe our mistake also resulted from a flaw in method: We examined Stalin's speeches with his own bible— the *History of the CPSU (Bolsheviks)*—either to criticize them (Churik and Galia especially did this) or to draw optimistic conclusions from them (Kola and, to a lesser degree, Klava) without realizing that this doctrine restricted our vision. Everything combined to deepen our belief in its hoary theses—from our university syllabus to the films we saw. What we didn't fully understand was that our Supreme Commander-in-Chief was above all a pragmatist, guided by his concept of Russian national interest; he didn't give a damn about socialist principles or for the opinion of mere citizens.

We were victims of an enormous deception. We took at face value Stalin's assurances that he would never covet any territory or interfere in the affairs of neighboring states. But Stalin was even then clearing the way for the expansion of his empire. The old Russian nationalists were unerringly accurate about his determination to make other peoples pay dearly for the aid of the USSR against the German invaders. We believed naïvely that the Soviet Union would be satisfied with these countries' grateful acknowledgment of Soviet aid, and that it would rapidly demobilize its large army. Didn't it need the return of its men to continue with the work of socialist reconstruction?

We imagined that all the POWs or civilian deportees in Germany would soon return to their homes, covered with glory and honor for the sufferings they had endured. In one of Stalin's statements of May 24, 1945—"Our government has made a rather large number of mistakes"—we even thought we could detect a hint of self-criticism. Was he regretting his pact with the treacherous Hitler? All of us knew the negative effect that the pact had had on the political consciousness and morale of the Komsomols. But neither Stalin nor, later, his critic Khrushchev, nor any other Soviet leader, ever expressed the slightest regret at this major operation of realpolitik in 1939, which never troubled their communist consciences for a moment.

The morale of Klava and my friends in Rostov must have been

badly shaken when, shortly after my departure in 1946, the great deportation of ex-POWs to the Gulag began, and when, two years later, Stalin decreed that all the countries liberated by the Soviet Army now belonged to the "socialist bloc"—a concept unknown in my time. Neither then nor later had my friends the slightest opportunity to influence the course of events, but I am certain that they retain nostalgic memories of the few idealistic months that followed the great victory festival, during which we dreamed together of the advent of a fraternal and more just world.

Having already absorbed a certain political culture in Poland, I would not have found it possible to love Klava, or to feel so attached to my friends, had they shown any attachment to the values of a Greater Pan-Slavic Russia. But they too believed in equality and freedom, in the incessant quest of men and women for the right to determine their own lives and fate. That is why we got along well with each other, and why we also knew that my departure, however painful, was inevitable.

It is no simple matter to repatriate to Poland almost two million of its former citizens who are dispersed to the far corners of the USSR; still more difficult does it seem when one remembers that at the same time, through the Yalta accords, Poland has lost its eastern provinces, inhabited chiefly by Ukrainians and Byelorussians, and recovered by way of compensation vast tracts of Silesia and Pomerania that were historically Polish but had been in German hands for hundreds of years. To carry out such a transfer of population successfully in a war-ravaged country would require an effective administration that the Soviet Union clearly didn't possess, and a political consensus that also was lacking. Nevertheless, the Kremlin, which still refuses to allow any of its citizens to travel freely abroad, punctiliously checks all the dossiers of applicants for repatriation to Poland, a measure guaranteed to delay departure still further. There are no problems where I'm concerned: The dossier compiled on me by Captains Strel and Abak in Yerevan was theoretically destroyed, but sufficient documents remain to prove that I am not Soviet "in origin." Even better, immediately after May 9, the Rostov authorities offer in friendly fashion to allow me to leave on my own, without delay, suggesting that "People's Poland" probably needs an ex-combatant of the Red Army. I decline this offer on the pretext that I want to complete my year at the university and my year's experience as a planner at the factory. (The real reason is, of course, Klava.) We decide by mutual agreement that I should await the arrival in Rostov of a Polish mission, which will be organizing a convoy for all those to be repatriated from South Russia. But no one knows the date of departure.

Until then, Klava and I live in a state of uncertainty. We begin to worry about what will become of us after our separation.

Since I have committed myself to completing the first year of my studies, I take six exams—and pass—with an ease that astonishes me. It is no mystery to anyone, however, that at the university preference is shown to students who have fought in the war, and that they are given an easy ride by their examiners. At the same time, Klava has to face a panel of hostile examiners who have probably been ordered to fail the majority of women students. She acquits herself rather well, but she has to retake two subjects in September. As soon as examinations are over, full-time students like Klava are sent off to the countryside to help the *kolkhozniki*, or else are incorporated into brigades working on urban reconstruction. Klava's brigade in Rostov isn't one of the worst, but it doesn't leave her much time to study, especially since we hope to spend the evenings together, alone or in the company of friends.

Overall, things are going rather well for me. At the Savelit factory I still enjoy an easy ride; in addition, I have the agreeable surprise of seeing my pilot friends once more—they are the first servicemen to return home on leave to Rostov. Klava is happy to get to know them and goes to some trouble to ensure that they will keep fond memories of our reunion parties, but at the same time I sense that she is a little irritated, and is concealing a mounting bad temper, which she finds hard to control behind a smiling façade.

Fira has none of Klava's reserve. She is weeping uncontrollably

beside me in the omnibus-*tropheinyi*, Rostov's most remarkable war
trophy and the pride of its citizens. We are sitting in the midst of 150
passengers, all of whom are undoubtedly convinced that I have mis-
treated or been unfaithful to her. It isn't I, however, who am making
her unhappy, or even Kola. She has invited me to go for a ride in this
incredibly long red bus—the biggest I have ever seen, brought back
from East Prussia—in order to tell me about the big new love in her
life, a theater producer. She is crying because she "cannot do without
him." Love is far stronger than she is; it is a kind of sickness and she
must succumb to it. It obsesses her day and night, from the top of her
head to the tips of her toes. Fira wants me, as Kola's best friend, to
help persuade him to let her go. She is really upset, incapable of
controlling herself, alternately laughing and sobbing. She is neither a
cheated wife nor an abandoned lover, but simply a woman distraught
with her happy passion. Perhaps if I had read Freud or Adler in Lodz,
I would have been able to speak sensibly with her. But what can I
say? Besides, what would I do if Klava were suddenly to declare that
she had fallen victim to a lovesickness for someone else? Am I in
danger of contracting it myself? Behind my grave expression Fira
thinks she glimpses my approval. "I'm really grateful to you," she
says between tears.

We have reached the end of the line. We get off after having
traveled the length of the Sadovaya, and now the German giant tries
to turn around in Karl Marx Square. The omnibus is three times too
long for our town, however, and the driver has to perform an infinite
number of maneuvers before the eyes of the more than one hundred
passengers waiting to get on. A small crowd of onlookers races to the
scene to gape at the spectacle. The most expert shout out their
advice: "Turn to the right!" "No, no, more to the left!" I add my own
cries to the medley—confident from my experience as a truck driver
in the Caucasus.

Finally, the driver completes the turn and opens the door. Fira and
I board to continue our talk. But once again, after a calm start, she
begins to sob. And, again, the new batch of passengers stares reprov-
ingly at me. Not knowing what to do, I suggest that we get off; the

weather is fine, we might enjoy strolling. "No, let's not," she replies firmly. "We are perfectly comfortable in this monster taken from the krauts. Besides, it reminds me of our victory." Nothing I say seems to help. Fira is disconsolate. Even with the aid of the greatest psychologists, I would not have succeeded in calming her. She merely declares that "I am an independent woman." And, with this, she is off, for though love causes all the fibers of her inner being to tremble, it is no excuse for missing even a single one of her indispensable dance rehearsals.

The uniform of flight captain fits my friend Vassya as if it had been tailored expressly for him. In the outfit of a trainee pilot he cut quite a figure, but with his silver-braided epaulettes and his three stars he looks quite magnificent. You only have to hear him to measure the enormous distance that separates his generation of officers of Cossack origin from that of the former "army of the Don." Vassya is a highly qualified pilot who knows how to observe and understand everything that is going on around him. He is capable of recalling the war's closing stages and of commenting upon it with a skill worthy of the Mikhail Frunzé Military Academy, the Soviet West Point.

According to an old Russian saying, "From the height of the Kremlin tower you can see things that are outside the field of vision of ordinary mortals." Logically, then, from the height of a heavy bomber this field of vision becomes immeasurably wider, and Vassya was well placed logistically to follow operations during the final stages of the war. Vassya says he is certain that our Supreme Commander-in-Chief couldn't see "from the height of the Kremlin tower" certain operational opportunities because his subordinates didn't inform him about them. Apart from me, no one wishes to believe him, and Kola, to reassert his shaken authority, openly makes fun of Vassya: "Of course, I suppose if you had been our Supreme Commander-in-Chief, we would have won the war three months sooner and taken Hitler alive!"

At this point our dinner party becomes agitated. The Elephant discloses certain details that greatly interest me: On January 19,

1945, for example, his squadron came within an ace of bombing Lodz, but the order was rescinded at the last moment because the town had fallen without any resistance from the Germans. Having corroborated his impressions with those of other pilots, Vassya maintains that by the beginning of February, when our forces arrived on the Oder, the Germans no longer had the means left to defend Berlin, and that a swift attack would have allowed us to take the capital of the Third Reich with many fewer losses than in May 1945.

"Whose fault is it, then?" asks Zeus. Vassya replies obliquely; he knows those who are blameless—Stalin and Marshal Golovanov, the commander of the 18th Air Force—but not who is to be blamed. In his view, our generals tend to be one war behind and in this war they underestimated the capacity of heavy aircraft to protect our troops heading toward Berlin.

About twenty years later I would be furnished with the formal proof that Vassya had thoroughly grasped a real problem. During the period of de-Stalinization, Marshal Vasily Chuikov, who commanded the defense of Stalingrad, published his contribution to the criticism of Stalin's "errors." Stalin assigned Chuikov the command of one of the armies engaged in the winter offensive of 1944–45, so that the man who had barred the way to Hitler on the Volga would be one of the first to enter the German capital. At the beginning of February 1945, Chuikov found himself, a lot sooner than planned, some eighty kilometers from Berlin, ready to swoop down on it without delay. He told how, in the course of a meeting with all the senior officers, he had already obtained the green light from Zhukov, when suddenly the latter received a telephone call from Stalin. Although Chuikov hadn't heard Stalin with his own ears or even taken notes, he summed up in his testimony the gist of this conversation, which resulted in the cancellation of the attack on Berlin.

Chuikov's study provoked a prompt and energetic retort from Zhukov, who flatly denied ever having taken part in the meeting and cited documentary proof of his claim. On the date cited by Chuikov, February 4, 1945, he was in a totally different sector of the front, in Pomerania. But in the second part of his refutation—this is the only public controversy to erupt in the USSR between two such high-ranking military officers—Zhukov resorts to unconvincing historical analogies, claiming that a premature attack on Berlin would have resulted in a failure comparable to the one that the Red Army had suffered in 1920 on the outskirts of Warsaw. Now even I know that the balance of forces in 1945 was not the same as at the time of the "miracle on the Vistula." Although he was only a twenty-three-year-old captain, Vassya had a strong strategic sense, a speculative mind, and analytical gifts on a par with those of the marshals on the spot.

Changing the subject, I ask him, "What do you think of Germany? What should be done with it?" He launches into a description of East Prussia, which has impressed him with its roads and especially with its fantastic number of gasoline service stations. Rather more doubtful considerations follow on the weakening of Germany that will result from its loss of East Prussia, the cradle of German militarism. Next he talks about his forthcoming transfer to the Berlin region, and slips with all his considerable machismo into the spirit of the barracks: "I am waiting impatiently for that day to settle accounts with the krauts and to lay their women."

He has really put his foot in his mouth—the government supports neither individual vendettas nor the rape of German women—but his statement doesn't provoke a general protest from those present, and Vassya must get the impression that we rather envy him his future orgies.

What he doesn't suspect is that the four women present are lying in wait for him from this moment on; these are the three usual women—Kathinka, Galia, and Klava—and Assia, a famished fair-haired student who has been invited to join us.

Their stratagem consists of a series of questions formulated with exaggerated kindness by the two *blondinki*, Kathinka and Assia. They pretend to be conducting an interview for a sort of "Kinsey Report" on the sexuality of Russian male pilots.

"No doubt you have been terribly deprived of women during all these years of military life," Kathinka sighs, with a compassion that would lead one to believe she is ready to relieve his misery.

"Not at all," the Elephant replies as he takes out of his pocket a photo of his PPG ("mobile field wife"), an attractive woman in military uniform who satisfied his sexual desires perfectly well.

"But if you aren't sex-starved," Assia pursues, "where then does your appetite for German girls come from?"

In answer, Vassya cites his theory of "love revenge," based on the conviction of Russian soldiers that the sexual act represents a victory for the man and a defeat for the woman.

These are clearly not the kinds of remarks to air in front of representatives of the fair sex, but none of the men present moves to howl Vassya down, and he sinks slowly and surely as he develops his arguments on the dominant role of the male, determined by his very nature: The man normally makes love from a position on top of the woman. "It isn't up to me to change nature, any more than it is my job to change the regulations of the Soviet Army," he declares, pleased with himself. His blond interlocutors don't even bat an eyelash; they want to establish with scientific precision what happens if the roles are reversed—for example, if the woman is in the position above the man. Are the gains the same or are they diminished? Thus do they attempt to calculate the rate of losses suffered by his future German partners. "If you rape them all, your masculine gains will certainly increase and your vengeance will be complete," the scrawny Assia suggests perfidiously, and the heavyweight Vassya walks right into the trap: "Some of them love being raped, but I won't give them the pleasure of it."

Klava calmly poses some technical questions on the nature of the defeat that women experience during the sexual act, then she gets up and goes out to the kitchen. The other women follow her, which is unusual, but since none of them has slammed the door, we are not immediately aware that it amounts to an incident. Besides, their collective exit might be explained by their concern for discretion; Vassya must have plenty of things to tell us about our pilot friends whom they don't even know and couldn't care less about.

But the first thing that Klava will say to me when we are alone is that she was "green with anger" and that at the very least I should have asked her why she was so upset. And she adds, "At what rate do you calculate your masculine gains since we have been living together? Do you keep an exact count of them so as to boast about it in front of all the pilots of the 18th Air Force?"

I don't appreciate this sort of sarcasm, I tell her; I am not a career serviceman like Vassya, and my silence at dinner was an obligation deriving from my duties as a host.

At this she explodes, "Run off to Poland, then! I have had enough of your gains. I won't lose anything by staying on my own."

It is the most wounding thing she's ever said to me. I don't understand her behavior, or that of her friends. Why didn't they criticize Vassya openly and ask everyone to state his views? Klava refuses to reason with me, and even reproaches me for not having smashed Vassya the Elephant in the face. That says everything!

As soon as he returns to East Prussia, Vassya sends us an enormous chest filled with war booty. As soon as it arrives, we round up some friends. The scene resembles one in *La Grande Illusion*, although in reverse: We are the victors who are to enjoy the fruits of victory. Is it wholly in conformity with our socialist principles? The Soviet Union, according to its dogma, has always been opposed to territorial annexation and to war reparations as practiced by the rapacious imperialists. Nevertheless, Stalin has just annexed East Prussia. Here we are with a chest containing war plunder. The discrepancy between our ideological discussions on the world's future and this treasure suggests that reality diverges more and more from theory. When one is very poor, however, the here-and-now counts above everything and we think more about the contents of the trunk than about its suspect origins.

Kuzmich finally manages to break open the lid of the chest, and a thick pile of sky-blue velvet cloth appears. What is it? A bolt of cloth? "Stand back, please, we have to get it all out," Klava says. Only when all of it is unpacked do we realize that it is an immense curtain. Devil take them! Does this mean that they have such high, wide windows in East Prussia, or did Vassya get it from a theater? "It comes from a castle," decrees Kola with great certainty. While the velvet is being unfolded, a rectangular casket of polished wood falls to the floor and the entire gathering exclaims, "That's the real treasure!"

The wily Vassya has used the curtain to protect the casket during the journey and probably also to ensure that it would escape detection. The opening of the casket makes us tremble with impatience. It contains a brand-new microscope, a Zeiss Ikon with a three-lens turret, all its accessories attractively set into the casket.

It is very handsome, a worthy example of German precision engineering. But what can it fetch on the Rostov black market? "Really, the simplest thing to do is to sell it to our Institute of Public Works, whose laboratories are very poorly equipped," Kola suggests, and the men among us discuss the price to ask for it. The women examine the curtain. Klava points out that there are two layers back to back, and that once the two lengths are separated there is enough cloth to make several winter dresses. Klava can sew, Kathinka too; already they are taking orders and sketching patterns for Galia and three other girlfriends. And the price for the microscope? "Ask for 100,000 rubles," Klava replies with an expert's assurance. She also asks me to find a dyeing company that will clean and dye her curtain without damaging it: "You often do business with people from the chemical industry at Savelit."

A battle on two fronts commences. Kola is unsuccessful at the Institute, since the latter doesn't pay cash for its equipment, which it receives through government allocations. Churik and I try our luck at the university, which does have the necessary funds at its disposal and would like to acquire our microscope, but only on the condition that we give a series of guarantees about its origin. The negotiations illustrate very well the Russian bureaucracy: It invents pointless obstacles for each problem it seeks to resolve, and then finds that it can't surmount them. Tiring of the protracted discussions and having nothing to hide, I ask for an interview with the dean of the faculty of sciences, who turns out to be the worst of the lot. Mistrustful, he even inspects my university record, as though he suspects me of having stolen this little marvel. Then he blathers on about the difficulties and risks of such a transaction.

Since nothing comes of it, I leave Kola to make the rounds of different laboratories—he has more time than I have—but in the end, he concludes that we are stuck with an extremely valuable but nonnegotiable object. An exasperated Klava decrees that "We'll keep the microscope for ourselves, on the shelf, as an ornament." Of course, we could have made a present of it to these blockheads at the university, but I share her antibureaucratic anger and agree with her decision; this Zeiss Ikon is far more handsome than Papa Emilyan's old samovar.

Some time later it will be stolen from us. In Rostov everything is stolen, from private homes as well as state enterprises. It is a traditional problem in Soviet Russia, deliciously satirized by Zoshchenko in a short story set well before the war. In it he describes a crowd of people who give chase to a monkey, not to return it to the zoo but in the hope of selling it on the black market. One of Papa Emilyan's guests must have noticed the microscope and made off with it. What consoles me is that the thief will have a lot more trouble finding a buyer than the fellow who caught the monkey in Zoshchenko's short story.

On the second front, that of the velvet cloth, we have more success, but I wonder if it's worth the bother. To have a dress cleaned in Rostov means a wait of several months, and for a curtain probably one of several years. Thanks, though, to Savelit, I find a dyeing factory in Salsk, which, for an inflated under-the-table fee, agrees to quickly clean and dye our velvet, half black, half dark blue. It amounts to a ruinous investment that absorbs all our savings. Still, after Klava and the others have sewn some beautiful dresses, we largely recover our costs by selling the rest of the curtain. What saves us is that the price of cloth has risen rapidly since the end of the war. We even manage to keep a little nest egg of three or four thousand rubles for the 1946 New Year celebrations.

These various operations greatly preoccupy me. I don't talk about it with Klava for fear of upsetting her, but I have the feeling that the mental habits, the ways and customs of Soviet society, will not improve after this victory, which enriches it only in appearance.

It is winter already, a sad season, and every morning on my way to the factory, I see the driver of the bus seized from the Germans make superhuman efforts to turn his large vehicle around on narrow ice-covered roads. There are no onlookers to cry out their advice; it is too cold. The people prefer their old trams or trolley buses, which at least work in these harsh conditions, even if they don't commemorate the joy of victory. The giant of the German *Autobahn* is useless in Rostov.

It won't concern me for much longer. The representatives of the Polish Office for Repatriation (PUR) have arrived in town and I will soon be leaving. Since I am privileged to be able to travel and to try my luck elsewhere, I experience, if not remorse, at least a measure of anxiety in thinking of those who remain behind. Most of the disadvantages of their lives result from flaws that are inherent in their society and are not the consequences of wartime. I still sincerely wish, for the sake of Klava and our friends, that their hopes for the future are realized, but as the euphoria of victory begins to evaporate, skepticism overtakes me.

Stretched out flat on her belly with all her concentration focused on a textbook placed on a cushion in front of her, Klava is studying for her midwinter exams. I have no more tests to take since I have abandoned the idea of adding one subject more to my university record. Our study group of the previous year has therefore dissolved. Churik no longer comes to help me, nor Kola to help Klava. She manages now on her own, and I spend my time watching her while pretending to read Maupassant. I find it moving to observe her obstinate struggle with science, and I know that she has chosen the correct path. My friend Motya had advised me a thousand times to opt for a scientific career. Yet it is only now, six years later and on the eve of my departure, that I finally understand all his reasons. Professional specialization in the USSR is a safe path for those who want to do something useful without being ground under by the *nomenklatura*. I imagine Klava surrounded by other engineers, discussing their projects together, as Motya used to do with his learned friends during our nighttime walks in prewar Rostov. For Klava's sake, I would like to see her become a woman of science who enjoys her work and has the leisure as a result of it to cultivate her mind through reading Alexander Blok and listening to classical music, as Motya did.

She will succeed in any case, though, I am sure. It isn't simply a certainty that I have forged for myself in order to leave with a good conscience. Kola also tells me that after a difficult start last year, Klava now does better and better and is even more diligent and conscientious than he is. Of course, she has to pay a price for it and takes less and less interest in the international news given to me by the people from PUR. Of what use could it be to her, anyway? I had paid only cursory attention myself, the previous year, to the changes of government in King Michael's Romania, because the names of the new ministers meant nothing to me, no more than those of the outgoing group, and because the overall picture resembled a jigsaw puzzle. The differences dividing Poles are no more comprehensible to Klava, and I have no desire to distract her from mathematics in order to guide her through the labyrinth of Polish politics, which at this moment is the most complicated maze in all of Europe.

Although I am pretending to read, she knows that I am looking at her, and it probably gives her pleasure since, from time to time, when she changes the position of the book on her cushion, she flashes that smile of our happiest days together; I know how to recognize it among the range of her engaging expressions, and this one means, "I'm very happy, and you mustn't worry on my account." Even her favorite remark, "I am a bird of the Don, and my nest must remain on this side of the river," is perhaps not meant simply to console me after the refusal by the authorities to allow her to leave with me. She is right to want to complete her studies and to become an engineer, after equipping herself with this "baggage of learning." If the opportunity to go with me doesn't arise, she will always have a very different "nest" from that of her parents, for she is in the process of laying the foundations of a fuller life that can someday give her all that she could wish for. The act of concentration makes her even more lovely, and it is also one of the reasons why I am looking at her, bent over her books, slowly stretching a leg to remove the stiffness, with a grace that only she possesses.

She doesn't like for me to call her "my pretty Cosachka," though. "Pretty is fine, it's always a pleasure to hear, although it doesn't amount to anything. I am not an exotic bird; I didn't choose my origins." For the others, however, she is still "Cosachka Klava," and that doesn't upset her. Anyway, two and a half years later she will be "engineer Klava." And what will have become of my friends by that time?

Kola will graduate the same year, but I don't think that he will be satisfied with specialization, even enhanced by music and highbrow reading. We often see each other because he presses me to pull off one last coup in order not to leave Klava without a "strategic reserve" in rubles. Kola has an unrivaled eye for the main chance. It would be unfair, though, to present him solely as a schemer. He is a leader of men. He has a political temperament, and in other countries he would not have wasted his time studying to become an engineer. It was only with some difficulty, and after an exceptionally long wait, that he was eventually admitted to membership of the Communist Party in Rostov. Kola is well aware of the reasons for this delay and of the handicap he will still have to live down: He is the son of resolutely White Cossacks who were deported to an unknown destination— perhaps even shot—in 1926, when he was four years old. A lot has happened since then, certainly; and he didn't choose his origins any more than Klava chose hers, but it is recorded in his dossier and it cannot be erased, even if he were to spend days on end denouncing all the harmful characteristics that he attributes to the Cossacks, and especially to the Whites.

He assures me stubbornly that this sorry page of Soviet history will soon be turned and that he must position himself well in the race for posts of responsibility. "It is the only means available, in our country, to carry on the struggle against suffering," he says. I wonder, though, what his chances are of making his way in life while remaining faithful to himself and avoiding compromises. For the moment he is only a candidate-member of the Communist Party, enjoying no particular privileges. While he doesn't give himself any airs, neither does he relinquish his efforts to broaden his own material base, or to help me do the same for Klava's benefit. In fact, he is even more of a "Don bird" than she is, because, neither obsessed by the sciences nor very interested in the outside world, he dreams of utopias only for his native region: "If they leave it to me, we will transform this region into a flourishing garden." This sums up his relationship with socialism.

As for dear Fira, only twenty-four and already widowed twice by the war before she met and married Kola, she will indeed seek a divorce after falling head over heels in love with her forty-year-old theatrical producer. "Kola has style, but he didn't know how to keep the flame alive," she will confide to me. Kola, however, will resist granting her a divorce for a time, not because he wants to hold on to her but through fear of the Communist Party. As a candidate for membership he is supposed to set a moral example. Fira will drop out of our circle, and we will no longer see her except from our seats at the Theater of Musical Comedy, where she will continue to dance on her long and supple legs. After Fira's departure, Kola will change partners each week, apparently unconcerned that such behavior is even more likely to spoil his chances of being admitted to the Communist Party.

Churik, the most cultivated of our friends, has a weakness for Kola, even though he wasn't among the Musketeers in Kislovodsk. Of course, that doesn't prevent him from often calling Kola a political ignoramus, even in public. But he doesn't think of Kola as a lost cause. "He has unquestionable merit; moreover, since early childhood he has experienced hardships such as we have never known," Churik says, thereby implying that we two, from families of intellectuals, have benefited from the patrimony of our parents, which is not the case with Kola, or for that matter with Klava.

In the matter of hardships, however, it is Churik who has been hardest hit. I stop by his place occasionally during the day because he is often unwell, and each time I see him hop on his single leg, holding on to the furniture for support in order to open the door for me, I understand the extent to which this mutilation is an ordeal for him. He has a sharp mind and is very polemical, and his reading has made him an impeccable analyst of texts, which he knows how to dissect in detail and explain better than all the teachers in Rostov. In my view, in different circumstances he would have made an excellent satirical essayist, but in the USSR I don't see an easy career open to him. Not that he is against the regime; on the contrary, he makes demands on it that derive from the original ideals of the October Revolution, as if he were enjoining it to remain perfectly faithful to them. Conscious that during the twenty-eight years that separate us from 1917, all too many things have occurred that were unforeseen or were inconsistent with the aims of the Revolution, Churik doesn't attempt, nevertheless, to put the entire experience in the dock, but he does hope that after the war Stalin will give a new impulse to Soviet socialism and take it in another direction, more in the spirit of Lenin's *State and Revolution* or Marx's *Critique of the Gotha Program.* I don't entirely understand him, and I know that he is unrealistic because the impetus for a socialist democracy would have to come from the grassroots and not from the peaks of power, but in particular I am afraid for him when I think of the chemistry professor I met in the Volgalag who had been condemned to fifteen years of the Gulag for far less subversive ideas.

A great deal will depend on Galia. I knew a different Churik when I stayed at his home in 1944, before he met Galia. At the time he didn't have an artificial limb and used to say that he would never succeed in getting used to his disability, or in interesting himself in other problems. Then Galia took him in hand and gradually reawakened his taste for reading, discussing, and studying. Since she herself is not one of the disabled veterans, some of whom wrongly imagine that they are immune to criticism, Galia has a shrewder appreciation of the point beyond which it is unsafe to go in the USSR. Her mother is well connected in academic circles and will help her to temper Churik's exacting idealism. In time he will become a good history teacher who will teach the official syllabus and consign his private thoughts to the desk drawers of his study.

And Zeus? He is still dozing on his Olympus, for he only wants to study in a "technicum" for aircraft technicians, and such an institute doesn't yet exist. In the meantime he works as manager of his canteen and composes poems for our ears only. Remaining neutral throughout our discussions, he shows a great concern for objectivity, but he always appears to be floating somewhat in the clouds. His lack of ambition is obvious, and Kola sometimes invites him to shake himself. "No, thanks," he replies, pointing to his head. "I have already been shaken sufficiently."

His case is really bizarre. Zeus is not crazy, and his behavior cannot be explained by the concussion he suffered in Nalchik. He simply prefers to listen, and talks very little about himself.

Throughout the celebration on the night of victory, Zeus remained at home on the pretext of composing an ode to Stalin, which he never read to any of us. The visits from Vassya and others on leave don't make him particularly happy, since he didn't belong to our squadron in Kislovodsk. You can always rely on him never to miss a rendezvous and never to arrive anywhere empty-handed, but something prevents him from enjoying himself like the others. What could it be? He never complains about anything, he eats his fill, he has a little money put aside. It seems likely that he just belongs to the category of persons who let life pass them by, day by day, without ever undertaking anything. Perhaps, despite everything, he will end up deciding to study or to become a proper poet, but it is too early to predict what life has in store for him.

That leaves Kathinka, a sort of little sister to Klava, her childhood friend, who feels perfectly at home in our twenty-eight square meters. She sings and dances, but never reveals what she is really up to. I think she is leading a double life, with Zeus and Caesar Imperator. Klava tells me that I have an overheated imagination and that in any event it is none of our business. She is perfectly right, except that I am soon going to leave and therefore risk never finding out the truth, which bothers me. Despite Klava's admonition, I eventually ask our favorite *blondinka* an indiscreet question, but she simply confuses me further: "That's it, you've guessed. I'm Caesar Imperator's mistress, but I find you interesting. Unfortunately, apart from Klava, you had eyes only for Fira, and you never noticed any of my hints." Perhaps I don't understand women well enough to guess what goes on in Kathinka's head, or to imagine what she hopes to achieve by playing around this way with the men in her life.

Nevertheless, Klava and I are among the first to benefit from it, as we did when I went to Moscow the previous year. Shortly before my departure for Poland, Caesar Imperator gives me a kind of courteous talking-to by way of farewell, and chides me for having replied so readily to his clients, "*Savelit? What savelit?* I don't even remember what they smell like," adding, as though he knew through Kathinka about our caper with the gasoline and the fish, that *savelit,* unlike gasoline, haven't any smell. Next he hands me a requisition voucher for a hundred pairs of men's rubber-heeled shoes, asking me to solve this mystery if I still have the time, because we don't even have one hundred male workers, and haven't any need of rubber-heeled shoes. It is a gift from Providence. Kola and I race off to Kharkov and manage to sell the entire stock on the spot to a wholesaler. The latter barely examines them, so accustomed is he to poor quality, and throws them on top of an impressive pile of similar pairs, as though this shoe factory kept producing just for him. Even Kola, who is usually capable of finding something positive in the most wretched situation, says simply on this occasion, "What a total shambles, our industry. . . ." But we bring back a respectable sum with us to Rostov, all of it for Klava, because Kola relinquished in advance his share of our last joint coup.

The last phase of my sojourn in the Soviet Union unfolds at an accelerated pace, like a succession of snapshots. In February 1946 the elections to the Supreme Soviet take place. It is an astonishing spectacle of self-mystification. Had I not witnessed it, I wouldn't believe that fortunes are spent in this country on an electoral campaign, as though the single list of "Bolsheviks of the Party and of those without party" could fail to be elected. Nothing is spared to entice the voters—meetings, of course, but also free entertainment, buffets at competitive prices, and plentiful meat rations.

It is Kola's baptism of fire as a Communist Party member. He has been entrusted with the role of "agitator" in our area of the city, and he obtains the best seats at a very good nonpolitical concert in the Theater of Musical Comedy. During the intermission, a buffet table groans under the weight of exquisite *piroshki*. Then, at the end, comes the cold shower: the speech delivered by someone named Boris Ponomarev, head of the electoral list in Rostov, who appears to me to be even more stupid than the average Russian *apparatchik*. On the way out I warn Kola, "I've no intention of voting for that guy."

It doesn't bother him in the least; he says, "You have only to strike out his name in the polling booth." Kola's duty is to make sure that all the voters go to the polling station, preferably early. Whoever does best in this socialist competition among "agitators" will earn special praise in his dossier.

Churik can't stop laughing, and keeps saying, "We need Japanese-style elections." It is a favorite joke in the history faculty. A lecturer who was denouncing electoral corruption, but who couldn't criticize the democracies of our British and American allies, had told his students that in Japan, on the occasion of some election, the bosses paid cash for each vote. The students, who are always broke, privately think "Japanese-style elections" a good idea, declaring their readiness to sell their votes in order to make ends meet. According to Churik, everyone in Rostov would prefer to receive an envelope with a few rubles instead of posters and leaflets. Nevertheless, he will vote, and at eight o'clock in the morning in order to please Kola. Considering myself to be only half-Soviet—my convoy is scheduled to leave on March 15—I grumble a little. There is no good reason for getting up so early on Sunday morning. Klava, though, thinks it will be a mere formality lasting only a few minutes, after which we will be able to go back to bed. Fat chance! The line in front of the polling station is like that in front of a food store. Each "agitator" has dragged his flock out of bed at sunrise, and everyone waits before depositing his ballot—which most people don't even bother to read.

There are at least six of us who go into the booth determined to strike out Ponomarev's name; Klava has invented this stratagem to avoid my gesture's being noticed. She has persuaded her parents to imitate me, and also Kathinka and Zeus. According to the next day's *Molot*, 99.9 percent of the electors at our polling station voted for Ponomarev, and not a single voting slip had been canceled. Kola refuses all responsibility; he had no part in the count and had nothing to do with this fraud. He swears that he himself struck out Ponomarev's name in a gesture of solidarity with us, and because he didn't like the look of the candidate. We could well have refused to take part in the rite, but it would have been dangerous, and what have we lost by it? One or two hours of Sunday rest. On the other hand, Kola will perhaps derive some benefit from it to help him make his way within the Communist Party.

Flight Lieutenant Kostya, if he is lagging behind Captain Vassya with respect to promotion, is a lot more judicious in his choice of war booty. He has sent a parcel from Vienna to his lifelong pal Kola, with men's clothes and six pairs of women's high-heeled, pointy-toed shoes. Dressed, thanks to him, in a suit miraculously "made in England," which is rather worn but of impeccable cut, I have to bow before the evidence that the loot taken from the liberated countries is improving our standard of living. Kola, who is good at math, has come up with a complex equation to prove to me that since the influx of war booty, our incomes have increased on the average to two thousand rubles a month. That seems to be stretching things a little, but my math isn't good enough to demonstrate his mistake to him. As for Klava, she can't get used to the pointy-toed shoes; she only wears them to go to the theater, and even there she discreetly removes them under the seat.

At the beginning of March, by a marvelous coincidence, Kostya arrives from Austria at the same time that Vassya and Volodya get back from Germany, and the Musketeers of Myechotka are reunited. Churik and Zeus will also come to the party, as will our wives, and the girlfriends of those on leave—lightning "conquests" opportunely

made in Rostov before the evening out. With fourteen of us in all,
however, we can't possibly squeeze into our apartment. No problem;
our Russian officer friends, the rubles hanging out of their pockets,
invite us all to the Don Restaurant. We are to have the best tables and
food, and also a guitarist to accompany our singing after dessert.
Something tells me that Vassya, the main organizer of the party, is
taking things rather far, and that it will end up badly. "Rostov isn't
Yerevan, and times have changed," he replies with all his captain's
authority. Very well, then, whatever happens, I already have one foot
aboard the convoy bound for Poland.

It's true, we are not in Yerevan, it's quite obvious as soon as we
enter the dining hall. There are no foreigners; officers' uniforms in the
different colors of all the branches of the armed forces predominate.
You would almost say it was a soldiers' party, but of a dignity befitting
victory, around tables covered by white tablecloths. There is laughter, singing, and dancing all around us, so that we can scarcely hear
each other, but we eat extremely well: red caviar, beef Stroganoff. It
isn't the canteen; this little spread will cost our friends a cool twenty
thousand rubles. No, much more than that; after the beef Stroganoff,
Vassya orders *chachliki* to crown our treat. The guitarist will have to
be patient: It is too early, we will only sing after the stewed fruit that
we have ordered for dessert.

The diners at the other tables, however, are already breaking into
song here and there, with songs from the new repertoire of the Russian army expressing the nostalgia of homecoming: "Bulgaria is beautiful, but Russia is the best of all. Where are you, my sweet, with the
chestnut eyes? Where are you, my beloved country?" And another:
"Broken-winged, we fly around in the mists, but we shall find you,
our native land, once again." I am moved. These Russian officers
really seem fed up with uniforms and foreign countries; they want to
go back home and to be with their wives once again. Nothing could be
more reassuring for the future.

"Incidentally, how are you getting on with the German women?"
someone teases Vassya (I think it is Galia's voice). But before he can
answer, there is shouting from the other end of the room. The revelers

have graduated from singing to boxing, naval officers versus those of the artillery. The punches are flying, women are screaming or crying, tables are pushed over like dominoes. Vassya calls for calm, there is no need for panic. He wants to try to separate the combatants, but he hasn't taken two steps in the direction of the trouble when suddenly, upon hearing the whistling sound of the first shots, he orders us, "Get down on the floor!"

It is the Wild West all over again, Russian-style—or Cossack, rather. While plunging to the floor, someone has tugged on the table-cloth and I can feel the stewed fruit flow down my face and over my handsome new suit. But I must protect Klava, and believing that I can recognize her dress, I pull her to me. But velvet dresses all look alike, and from beneath my protective arm emerges Kathinka's blond head, not at all frightened by the gunfire, saying, "My joke has put ideas into your head, admit it, you rascal! But I am not about to make love beneath the table, in front of everyone." And she sticks out her tongue at me before bursting into laughter.

"You will have to explain to them what we are like in reality," Klava says to me as we leave the cinema after having seen *The Star of the North,* an American film on the war in Russia. It has already been shown in 1944, and the audience howled with laughter then just as on this occasion. But I find it interesting because of its stars, Erich von Stroheim and Dana Andrews, and also because two of its protagonists are a student named Klava and a pilot named Kola. They really know how to choose charming names in Hollywood. Admittedly, the plot is improbable and mawkish; it tells the story of the recapture of the village "Star of the North" by Soviet partisans in the earliest phase of the war. Interestingly, it reveals one of the essential elements of the German drive to the East: On this front the Wehrmacht committed atrocities from the beginning of the occupation, and the Russians responded with a fight to the death.

It isn't the description that the Americans give of our partisans' exploits that makes the Rostov audience laugh, but rather the Holly-wood vision of daily life in the USSR. In the village, the people dress in silk and invariably have a balalaika at hand, ready to dance at any appropriate—or inappropriate—moment. They are cared for instantly in a modern hospital, managed by a "great consultant" who is so famous that even the German major (played by Erich von Stroheim) defers to him. At the end, the great Russian doctor will kill the German major, who reveres medical science but has no respect for Russian children. (He steals their blood for wounded Wehrmacht soldiers, and the poor kids die as a result.)

I tentatively defend *The Star of the North*, reminding Klava that Soviet films are not noted for their realism. Hasn't a film been released recently whose hero is a *woman* government minister? "Ah, but that's a projection toward the future. I might one day become a minister myself, while with the Americans it is a matter of crass ignorance of our present reality," Klava insists. To her, I am already thinking like a foreigner.

Like all our friends, she is annoyed when Soviet citizens are depicted as prosperous and rather frivolous people with their balalaikas; neither does she like the idea that foreigners should see their poverty or their sadness. When a delegation from the West came to visit her institute she saw nothing wrong in the fact that the most poorly dressed students were requested to absent themselves. "Poverty is not a fault, certainly, but there is nothing in it to boast about." Nor does she expect me to tell that in a Rostov whose population is half-starving, bacon and eggs were served to all wounded and sick patients in a city hospital when Lady Churchill arrived on an official tour. What must I tell them, then, in that world on the other side of the River Don that shows us so little understanding? "Tell them that we have suffered a great deal and that we would be happy to improve our living standards, extend our education, broaden our culture, and live in peace. That's the truth, and you know it better than anyone." She is half playful, half serious. "You are my personal ambassador abroad, and when I become an engineer, I will join you and build our private embassy. It will have at least fifty-six square meters of habitable space and two sinks—no, one will do—but we will have a separate kitchen and a shower with hot water." I agree with her, let's dream together, the war hasn't left me with much time to dream either.

The period of waiting for my convoy offers Klava the opportunity to fulfill a wish that she had first expressed at the time of our courtship. One evening, in the foyer of the Theater of Musical Comedy, during the intermission, I spot Oleg, the roommate who denounced me to the NKVD in Yerevan. Klava promptly disappears, asking me to excuse her. The next thing I know, Oleg is collapsing in a heap on the floor; those standing by rush to his aid; confusion reigns. It is impossible to say at a distance what has happened. Klava comes back with a perky air and announces, "We have squared accounts with him. Let's go to our seats."

I learn from some people beside me, before the curtain rises, that a man has just been stabbed in the genitals. A tall tale: A shoe, even a pointed one, is not a dagger. Always this Russian habit of exaggerating! I could have told them that this man would recover from the blow he had received a lot quicker than I would from my time in prison and in the camps. Once at home, however, I reproach Klava. Why take such risks in striking this informer? There was no risk, she maintains. He didn't even see her face because she was so quick. If all the Olegs in Russia received from time to time a few kicks in the balls, life would be better all around. It is a distinctively Cossack style of reasoning, not in the least dialectical. As for me, despite my criticism, I am not unhappy about it at all.

On the eve of my departure, fixed for March 15, Klava and I have our marriage annulled at the city hall. The clerk who deals with us doesn't take long to deal with Klava's papers: A long and narrow stamp saying *annulirovano* is placed over the stamp that, in July 1944, "registered" our marriage. Klava says nothing, but her face droops. She would never have believed that such things could be disposed of so easily, without a single question, without the least inquiry. She doesn't close her passport and continues to stare at the canceled page as if to draw the clerk's attention to the fact that the new stamp doesn't entirely cover the previous one, which is much larger and contains all my civilian details.

Next, the clerk tries to exchange my passport for a slip of paper certifying that my passport has been added to the dossier of our marriage annulment. Now this won't do at all, for at the first identity check I will end up in jail. The Soviet militia does not accept any old slip of paper, they require passports. The clerk goes off to consult with the office manager, who brings my passport back to me in person. "We will get it off you before you leave," he says, about as friendly as a prison guard.

In the street, the clerk runs after us. The poor woman has forgotten to stamp my passport and is filled with panic. A grave error: I am a husband without a wife! For the city hall administration, it is a disaster. This little incident revives our spirits. Klava begins to laugh at the frightened expression of the clerk, and makes fun of me too: "So, you thought you could get away without a stamp, did you? Well, you were mistaken, my boy! She has given you two of them, one more than I have!" Two days later, upon learning from *Molot* that on the same day, the title "People's Commissariat" was eliminated—they are now rebaptized "ministries"—she sees all the comedy of the situation: "It was definitely a day for stamps. They must have put an *annulirovano* on all of their passports as well."

My convoy doesn't set out on time, and I feel like someone who is outstaying his friends' invitation after having already said good-bye a thousand times. The railway authorities still haven't found a railroad car for about twenty or so people awaiting repatriation from South Russia. The people from PUR have already gone back to Moscow, but we are still waiting.

I have said very little about these three Polish "purists"—two men and one woman—because it would have taken too long to describe the misunderstandings that arose with them. From our first meeting, Klava took an instant dislike to them and, trusting to her Cossack instincts, announced that they were members of the NKVD, and uncultured to boot. My impression, however, was that they had spent years in Siberia or in Central Asia and had nothing to do with the NKVD. It was true they made mistakes in Russian and knew neither Pushkin nor Alexander Blok very well, but they had simply received a different education from ours. Klava, though, is stubborn. The result was that this trio never set foot inside our twenty-eight square meters, nor did we even find good seats for them, through Fira, to attend any light operas. In the name of hospitality I walked them around Rostov a little, describing to them our large, tank-shaped theater, which had been destroyed by bombing, but they showed no great interest in Soviet architecture. The first misunderstanding arose from Klava's insinuations. I didn't dare speak openly to them, or ask them to which part of Siberia they had been deported. No direct question was possible. They addressed me as *pan komsomolec*, which clearly showed that they were familiar with my NKVD dossier, where I was still classified as a Komsomol member. In reality, since returning to Rostov in 1944, I had had nothing to do with this organization. In short, we were delighted to speak Polish together, but our discussions were distorted by a reciprocal mistrust, based on the suspicion of each other's ultradogmatism. This didn't prevent us from joking about the incongruous aspects of Russian life, because any group of Poles gathered together would never deny themselves this pleasure. With regard to essential questions, though, I never knew what they really thought about the USSR or how they reconciled their experience on Soviet soil with their adherence to the Polish Workers' Party, which opportunistically shunned the word *communist* while remaining unconditionally pro-Soviet.

The second misunderstanding arose from Klava's impression that these people were putting pressure on me to return rapidly to Poland, when in truth they wished for nothing of the kind. Indeed, our conversations had the effect of reducing my *Reisefieber* (in the East, to express the idea of "the fever to be off," one always uses the German expression). Though they were clearly well informed through their access to official channels, their description of life in Poland did not correspond even remotely to the way I remembered it. Poland had been ruined by the war—it had lost one inhabitant out of five—and yet, despite this frightening carnage, certain basic determinants of its political life had remained unaltered. The shift to the left that was very clear in Western Europe had not occurred in Poland, and the new regime, supported by the protective power of the Soviet army, devoted itself to outdoing the nationalists with protestations of patriotism. The keystone of the new ideology was to be the dramatic emphasis put on the value to Poland of her "recovered territories," taken back from Germany (though in fact not claimed for centuries), while alliance with the USSR was justified by the need to defend these new borders. For the "purists," "reasons of state" and our "historic rights" counted above everything, and they proudly showed me certain publications of their party that quoted from *Rota*, an anti-German right-wing hymn. It was a psychological mistake, because I have never been patriotic and I will neither sing the *Rota* in Poland nor Pan-Slavic hymns in Russia.

In Poland, geography and history distort all debate. Even before thinking of how to rebuild their home, the country's inhabitants wanted to know whether they were going to be invaded from the west (by the Germans) or from the east (by the Russians), or by both at once; the memory of the Hitler-Stalin pact still rankles in everyone's mind. Using a few German provinces as fodder to reassure those who most mistrust the Russians (this includes the majority of socialists) would not do the trick. The latter demanded secure frontiers to the east and never, despite the advice of Churchill, Roosevelt, and de Gaulle, did they accept giving up their pre-1939 territories to the east, inhabited mainly by Ukrainians and Byelorussians, which had once again become Soviet after Yalta. During the German occupation, the Communists were banished from the Polish underground, not because of their revolutionary aims, but because they sided with the USSR—and in fact with all the leaders of the Grand Alliance—in this frontier dispute. It was also one of the major reasons for popular mistrust of the new government.

Frankly, my dear Klava is completely mistaken in believing that my meetings with the "purists" could hasten my departure. No one hurries to return to a country that is on the verge of civil war unless he identifies with one side or the other. In fact, without its being clear in my mind, I have a premonition that I will not remain in Poland. Although hostile to the nationalists and to their Catholic-patriotic culture, I don't trust the new regime, either. And it isn't my Gulag experience that prompts my doubts. The mistrust I feel toward the USSR is nourished by my everyday experience in the rather favorable circumstances of my life in Rostov. Let us speak the truth: Stalin writes letters of thanks in honeyed tones to the peasants for their donations, knowing full well that their savings have been extorted from them, in the same way that the state extorts from us our "voluntary" subscriptions for a state loan. And the rigged elections? And our seven voting slips, which failed to be included in the count? And the lies about salaries and prices? What good does it do to add to the examples? For seven years the leaders of this country have done their best to convince me, at every opportunity, that they don't give a damn about their own people. After all that, I cannot honestly stand in Poland as guarantor of their good faith, and ask my compatriots to trust Soviet promises not to interfere in Poland's internal affairs.

The "purists" hope that, thanks to the wealth of the recovered territories, there will be a rapid reconstruction of the country, which will give birth to a Polish government that will enjoy genuinely popular support, and that will also be a loyal but independent ally of the USSR. This seems to me to be a fragile hope, but I decide to keep an open mind until I get there and see for myself. I would be the first to rejoice at such a happy ending; Klava could then come and join me and construct "our embassy." (Nothing went according to this optimistic scenario, however, and, three years later, I left Poland, which had been brought to heel and integrated into the socialist bloc in spite of all the preceding promises.)

When you're kept waiting for your train for a whole month, you seek diversion gladly. Klava and I went out very often—mainly to the movies, despite my dissatisfaction with this aspect of Soviet cultural life.

Because film is considered the most important of all the modern arts by the Communist Party, each movie theater seeks to change its program at least once a week. But Soviet studios would have had to produce at least 210 films during the four war years to enable this to be done. In fact they produced only about thirty, and so the programming of our movie theaters is a carousel on which each film turns around and comes back at least seven times. It is said that this was because no feature film could be released without Stalin's personal approval, and in wartime he was too busy to view films.

These movies, from *Zoya* to *Rainbow*, remind us that we have come a long way after a great deal of suffering, but they no longer correspond to reality. It's an old problem in the Soviet film industry. In Kislovodsk in 1942, when half of Russia was already occupied by the Germans, I was still showing films to my squadron suggesting that no enemy could ever cross Soviet frontiers. The public became used to thinking, "Oh yes, that is what we were supposed to think yesterday."

Just before Soviet troops entered Germany, *Pravda* had given Ilya Ehrenburg a friendly reprimand for his simplistic anti-German judgments, and since then we have been advised to make a distinction between "good" and "evil" Germans just as we do with other peoples. But the "good" Germans in our old movies are conspicuously absent. It isn't very serious, however, since we have become adept at viewing these old films in their original context, and we wait patiently for new ones, realizing the slowness of the Mosfilm studios and the fact that Stalin doesn't have the time to give them distribution permits. Only once, at the beginning of April 1946, did a new full-length feature so completely perplex us that we had to call upon Churik and Galia's superior analytical powers to grasp its significance.

The movie opens with the parade of German POWs in Moscow on June 22, 1944; they have been brought there directly from the front to permit Muscovites, on this third anniversary of the Nazi invasion, to see the vanquished master race close up. But two kindly Russian women notice, in the column of ragged prisoners, a soldier wearing glasses, apparently an elderly intellectual, and they take pity on him: "That fellow there is surely not an evil sort," one says. "You're right," the other replies, "he's probably a decent man who was drafted."

The rest of the film, in flashback, shows the real personality of this intellectual who likes to read Goethe in his splendid library and listens to *lieder* sung by his wife, an overfed Valkyrie—before torturing, like any good, sadistic Nazi, Russian women prisoners. His cruelty is limitless and you need a strong stomach to watch the sequences in which he goes to work on his victims. Klava, who is usually self-possessed, couldn't stop sobbing. But it is the film's moral that intrigues us, for it tends to suggest that there are no "good" Germans, as though the old political line had been resurrected.

Churik makes some rapid calculations to establish that between July 1944 and January 1945—the date of the *Pravda* article "Comrade Ehrenburg Simplifies"—Mosfilm has had the time to release this final contribution to the "Kill them!" genre. Not content, though, with a single hypothesis, Churik puts forward a second that takes into account Stalin's disappointment—and ours as well—at the absence of any popular resistance movement in Germany at the end of the war. With this in mind, and in order to avoid massacres, Stalin gave the order to moderate the anti-German propaganda at the moment that Soviet troops were entering Germany, but he also authorized the release of this film so as to invite us not to trust appearances, to be ready to expose the German beasts, who were notoriously capable of assuming new disguises.

That seemed plausible enough, if rather depressing. In Kislovodsk, when we awoke the inhabitants at seven o'clock in the morning singing that we were fighting for the "world of enlightenment" and the Nazis for the "kingdom of darkness," the situation was simple and clear. Each step forward by our side was supposed to roll back the "infernal night" brought on by the adversary, and in this triumph of good over evil, there was room for anti-Nazi Germans on the side of the good. In practice, however, neither our victories nor those of our allies allowed the Germans to emerge by themselves from the "kingdom of darkness."

Klava listens to us, extremely distraught. This film about a sadistic intellectual seems to have been made deliberately to undermine her confidence in the role of culture for moral progress and the improvement of humanity. In it we were shown a German couple whose library had more books in it than all the Cossacks had ever possessed, and who were nevertheless more monstrous than the worst of them. Klava worships Schiller and puts his works above those of

Tolstoy, and she has always found it hard to understand that the people that gave birth to Marx and Schiller, to Engels and Heine, to Hegel and Thomas Mann, had not possessed sufficient cultural antibodies to ward off "the brown plague." What remedy, she would now like to know, can help cleanse it of its chauvinistic and racist poison?

No one is in a hurry to reply to her. Churik repeats yet again that after the defeat, the German proletarians will carry forward once more the "torch of the class struggle" against those who are responsible for their misfortune, and once again I side with him. Both of us are aware, however, that in this matter there is something that eludes our understanding and that doesn't fit at all with the facts of our century as we know them. Further, if, according to Stalin, the Treaty of Versailles facilitated Hitler's rise to power in 1933, isn't it illusory to want to cure the German illness by amputating territories much vaster than those seized after the First World War?

In Kislovodsk, militarily speaking, we were in the shit, but our morale was better, the situation more promising. Now everything seems to be foundering in a confusion without principles. In February, after the elections to the Supreme Soviet, Stalin was quoted in an interview as saying that capitalism remains based on the struggle for markets and that this will inevitably produce new wars. Churchill evidently deduced from this that Russia covets the markets of the capitalists, and replied with a speech at Fulton, Missouri, of which our only knowledge is that it prompted a run on the food stores in Rostov. All of this is worrisome. We sense that the Grand Alliance is in the process of coming apart even before the question of the Germans is settled, let alone that of the Japanese, who have just had the unique privilege of seeing two of their cities obliterated by atomic bombs, the first ever to be dropped in wartime.

During my crossing of the frozen Bug, I had imagined an altogether different return to Poland. I had hoped to find my family again, spared by the tragedy, and a country that had shed its outdated ideas. Things worked out differently, but for Klava's sake I prefer to appear relaxed, and she is calm too. She is a strong woman who regrets nothing and is afraid of nothing; she wants only to accompany me to the station alone—with Kola, perhaps, but without our other friends.

It is a beautiful late afternoon in April and the passengers of my *tyeplushka* are settling themselves down on their straw mattresses, under the supervision of a young woman in military uniform, surely a Chekist, a member of the NKVD, who takes their passports and assigns a place to each of them. Almost all of them are Jews, four families with grandparents and grandchildren. They know each other from having shared these years of exile together, and they speak Yiddish much better than Russian. As for me, I stay with Klava and Kola on the platform. We quietly promise to write to each other every day or at least three times a week during exam times. Klava is wearing her white linen shirt, because it is too warm for her velvet dress, and, as on the eve of our marriage, she is rehearsing a story for her parents who still haven't understood that I am leaving for a long time. Suddenly, Klava throws herself in my arms, crying, and Kola can no longer contain himself either; both of them have noticed that the train is about to leave. We have promised each other not to cry, because we are going to see each other again. The war is over, it is neither 1939 nor 1941; we have won, we are going to be happy, and we shall only be apart a short time. "You're right, it won't be long," Klava says, and starts to cry.

My neighbor to the left has a limp, and almost no baggage. He is a disabled veteran of the Spanish Civil War, but apart from that fact, I will learn nothing about him. Of a taciturn or mistrustful nature, he will not talk with anyone, particularly not with my neighbor to the right, our blond-haired military escort. She is not very talkative, either, during the early part of our journey, but she has placed her mattress very close to mine, even though our *tyeplushka* is neither full nor short of space.

Until nightfall I talk with the heads of the four Jewish families, who seem to take me for some sort of authority and ask me a great deal of questions about our destination. Natives of a frontier region in Galicia that is no longer Polish, they have heard that they will automatically be brought to the territories taken from the Germans, and that they will no longer have the right to change their place of residence. But they have no wish to live in houses belonging to the Germans, for there is every chance that one day the Germans will come back again.

I do my best to assure them that Poland is now a free country and people can move about as they like. If they choose to set themselves up in the provinces recaptured from Germany, they have nothing to fear from the Germans, for the world has changed and the *Drang nach Osten* will never be repeated; Nazism is dead forever. In short, I serve up to them four-fifths of the theories of the "purists"; I fail only to dwell on Stalin's support for the safeguarding of Polish frontiers, because I suspect that they won't find it particularly reassuring.

They listen attentively to everything, but being early-to-bed types, they don't prolong the conversation. To get to my mattress, I brush lightly against that of my fair-haired neighbor, who doesn't even give me time to excuse myself for it. Her mouth is already pressed on mine, her arms draw me toward her warm body. In all my life I have never experienced such a passionate embrace from a woman whose name I don't even know, and without my having shown the slightest gesture of interest in her direction. Admittedly, this strange circumstance is not disagreeable, but what lends the situation special spiciness is the fact that this woman is a Chekist. Vassya's theory on "love revenge" springs immediately to mind, and I tell myself that I have been presented with a golden opportunity to take my revenge on Captains Strel and Abak, on the mustachioed colonel of the Volgalag, on the entire NKVD. It is nature that has determined it so. The Chekist is underneath me, in rapture, and it is I who am the master.

Nevertheless, I disengage myself from the embrace of the ardent blonde. Let's talk first about her functions, her rank within the evil NKVD. She recovers her breath, but doesn't understand. "Is it because of the girl who was crying at the station?" she asks.

"And I suppose you sleep with every available man?"

A clumsy question. Insulted by it, she pushes away and launches into a long catalogue of complaints arising from her experiences as a military woman bundled about in a man's world like a small boat, anchorless in the storm. So much for my revenge. There are tears on this woman's face. She doesn't know what men want. They run after her, then they reject her; some have humiliated her or even raped her, others have merely taken advantage of her; all of them have abandoned her to her infinite solitude. She flatly denies being a Chekist; she is only a nurse, and escorts those who are being repatriated on behalf of the Soviet army medical services.

"Why don't you go back home?" I ask. "The war is over, you will soon find yourself a husband."

"Where is home? Everything was destroyed and my family was killed or else died of hunger. In the army, at least, you get enough to eat."

Were we a privileged group in Rostov, then, young people with hopes and dreams for the future, who had come through the war suffering less than the rest? But can you believe a girl who gives herself to you without even saying a word?

"What's your name?" I ask.

"Kathia," she says, as if it were quite natural. Just think of that, now. Has destiny arranged things so that I should be unfaithful to Klava with a Kathinka?

"Good night," I say, and turn my back on her.

"Are you going to sleep?" she asks, astonished, as though it were the very last thing to do in the middle of the night in a *tyeplushka* full of people.

Too bad. No doubt she will make out a report to her bosses in the NKVD, to the effect that I am impotent; one falsehood more in their dossier on me. The uniformed blonde ends up going to sleep too, but she gets up before me, and when I awaken, she presents me with some tea, and hot water for a shave. Taking advantage of her familiarity with the stations, she regularly goes off somewhere at each of our stops to fetch me something that will make my journey more comfortable. On her small alcohol stove she even makes me an omelet. A mistress, or even a wife, would probably not have shown such devotion while receiving nothing in return. All the passengers in the *tyeplushka* imagine they are witnessing an affair, but nothing happens between the blonde and me; even our conversations are platonic. Why, then, all this display of kindness? If it had been in order to write a report, she would have questioned me about Klava, my friends, the other Kathinka, but she simply smiles at me like a contented lover. Is it in order to convince me, then, that she isn't a Chekist and that she has told me the truth about her job and her life?

In Przemysl, a frontier town, our *tyeplushka* is detached from the Soviet train, and its destination no longer interests me because I am going to leave directly on my own for Lodz. Kathia meets up with me once again in the station, and asks me a simple favor: "Don't think badly of me, and don't forget me."

And it's true, I still remember her! With time, this episode has taken on an even greater significance than it had for me in the course of that forty-eight-hour journey between Rostov and Przemysl. It reminds me that, in the end, I was lucky in Russia; having arrived there at the age of fifteen and a half, I left it seven years later, enriched by an experience that would serve me for the rest of my life. Thanks to my Russian friends, I am among those who, as Klava put it, "know the truth"—*their* truth—sorrows endured and hopes disappointed. The blond-haired Kathia on the train was a messenger sent to me to make sure I understood, one last time, how much her country had suffered—and, just as important, that I shouldn't forget.

ABOUT THE AUTHOR

K. S. KAROL was born in Poland in 1924. After the partitioning of that country in 1939, he spent seven years in the Soviet Union, where he studied political science at the University of Rostov and fought in the Red Army on the Caucasian front. Like many of his countrymen, he suffered Soviet jails and camps. Karol left Russia after the war and has since lived in Paris, writing for the *New Statesman*, and currently for *Le Nouvel Observateur*. He is the author of numerous books, including *Visa for Poland, China: The Other Communism,* and *Guerrillas in Power: The Course of the Cuban Revolution.*